W9-BWJ-260

Gandhi and Beyond

Gandhi and Beyond

Nonviolence for an Age of Terrorism

David Cortright

Paradigm Publishers
Boulder•London

All rights reserved. No part of this publication may be transmitted or reproduced in any media or form, including electronic, mechanical, photocopy, recording, or informational storage and retrieval systems, without the express written consent of the publisher.

Copyright © 2006 by Paradigm Publishers.

Published in the United States by Paradigm Publishers, 3360 Mitchell Lane Suite E, Boulder, CO 80301 USA.

Paradigm Publishers is the trade name of Birkenkamp & Company, LLC, Dean Birkenkamp, President and Publisher.

Library of Congress Cataloging-in-Publication Data

Cortright, David, 1946-
    Gandhi and beyond : nonviolence for an age of terrorism / David Cortright
        p. cm.
    Includes bibliographical references and index.
    ISBN 1–59451–265–5 (hardcover : alk. paper) — ISBN 1–59451–266–3 (pbk. : alk. paper)
    1. Nonviolence. I. Title.
    HM1281.C6715 2006
    303.6'1—dc22

    ISBN (hc) 10-digit 1–59451–265–5   13-digit 978–1–59451–265–0
    ISBN (pbk) 10-digit 1–59451–266–3   13-digit 978–1–59451–266–7

                                                                2005036550
Printed and bound in the United States of America on acid-free paper that meets the standards of the American National Standard for Permanence of Paper for Printed Library Materials.

Designed and typeset by Straight Creek Bookmakers.

09 08 07 06 3 4 5

Contents

List of Photographs   ix

Introduction   1

1. Grasping Gandhi   9
   Hindu Roots   11
   Christian Influences   12
   Truth Is God   14
   Means and Ends   17
   Action for Truth   18
   Learning from the Suffragists   20
   Politics and Sainthood   21
   An Aversion to Coercion   25
   Sacrifice and Strength   28
   Courage   30
   Highlights of Gandhi's Life   35

2. Gandhi USA   37
   Early Impressions   37
   Cross-fertilizations   41
   A Tool for Social Justice   44
   The Struggle for Peace   47

3. Martin Luther King Jr.: An American Gandhi   53
   Gandhi's Example   53
   Christian Roots   55
   Toward a "Realistic Pacifism"   59
   The Power of Love   60

Divine Inspiration   62
Sacrifice   65
Learning by Doing   66
Applied Gandhianism   69

4. Gandhi in the Fields   73
    Origins   74
    Learning Gandhi   76
    La Huelga   79
    Boycotting Grapes and Lettuce   81
    The Boycott: A Powerful Instrument   85
    Fasting   91

5. Dorothy Day: A Mission of Love   97
    Conversion   98
    The *Catholic Worker*   102
    A Gandhian Faith   104
    A Peace Devotion   107

6. The Power of Nonviolence   111
    Challenges to Nonviolence   115
    Barbara Deming and Revolutionary Nonviolence   116
    Coercion   121
    Property Damage   123
    The Two Hands   126
    Creative Energy   128
    The Third-Party Effect   130
    The "Great Chain of Nonviolence"   134

7. Learning Lessons   137
    A Tale of Two Cities   137
    Project "C"   140
    The Success of the Unruly?   144
    Nonviolence and the Global Justice Movement   146
    Polite Rebels   152
    Toward the Mainstream   153
    Winning While Losing   156
    Iraq: The Continuing Struggle   159

8. Gender Matters   163
    Of Love and Lust   166
    Elevating Women   168
    Less Than Equal   170
    The Nature of Women   173
    Battling Sexuality   174

The "Sacrifice"   176
"Fleshly Faults"   180
Overcoming Sexism   183
Nonviolence and Feminism   186

9. Principles of Action   191
Understanding Power   191
Organizational Strength   193
Internet Organizing   195
Clarifying Goals   196
Financing Change   199
The Power of the Media   201
Evaluating Tactics   204
Alinsky's Rules   207
Nonviolence: The Constructive Alternative
    to Terrorism   211
Means of Change   215
What Is Success?   217
The Long Haul   219

Notes   223
Index   253
About the Author   265

Photographs

Gandhi walking at Sevagram Ashram in India	16
Gandhi sharing a joke with Jwaharlal Nehru	24
Vietnam-era soldiers listen to speakers at an antiwar protest	31
Martin Luther King Jr. at a Southern Christian Leadership Conference staff meeting	58
Civil rights leaders during the march from Selma to Montgomery, Alabama	64
Dorothy Day being arrested	78
Cesar Chavez with Senator Robert F. Kennedy	92
Dorothy Day as correspondent for the *New York Call*	99
Dorothy Day in front of her Staten Island bungalow	103
Barbara Deming at a peace rally in 1968	117
Civil rights demonstrators brace themselves against fire hose spray	143
Crowd at the Rally to Halt the Arms Race, 1982	152
Candlelight vigil on the Washington Mall, 2003	157
Cindy Sheehan at "Camp Casey"	160
Mahatma Gandhi and Margaret Sanger	165
Gandhi and his wife, Kasturba	172
Gandhi at Birla-House (Delhi) with his grandniece Abha and his granddaughter Manu	177
Moratorium Day peace rally, 1969	209

Introduction

My commitment to peace began, ironically, when I was drafted into the U.S. Army during the Vietnam War. I came from a conservative, Catholic, working-class family, which meant no lawyers or doctors to finagle a deferment. As I learned about war and militarism firsthand, I experienced what theologian John Howard Yoder later told me was a crisis of conscience. I was overwhelmed with doubt and disillusionment and came to see the war as unjust and evil. It was a shattering experience that turned my world upside down. I began to speak out publicly against the war and became part of the GI peace movement, openly opposing the war while on active duty. Thus began a lifelong dedication to peace that included ten years as executive director of SANE during the height of the nuclear freeze movement; that prompted my opposition to the war in Iraq and leadership in the Win Without War coalition; and that led to my present position as a professor of peace studies and president of the Fourth Freedom Forum.

This volume began as an attempt to answer the persistent and often troubling questions of students. Nonviolence is nice in theory, but is it really practical? Are the beliefs and principles of Mohandas Gandhi and Martin Luther King Jr. still relevant? Is nonviolence possible in a world gripped by the fear of terrorism? Will nonviolence work against adversaries without conscience, who deny every form of legal redress? What about Malcolm X's

claim that nonviolence is too weak? Are more forceful methods of protest, such as sabotage and street trashing, justified
in the struggle against corporate globalization? In attempting
to respond to these challenges I found a deeper meaning to
nonviolence. I began to see nonviolence as more than a method
of social action. It is a philosophy of life, a radically different
way of being and doing. Nonviolence is not merely a tactic but
a strategy. It is not only a pragmatic option but a philosophical
choice, a concept of profound importance to the future progress
and survival of humankind. An inquiry into nonviolent social
change turned into a quest for truth and the meaning of life.

The search for deeper meaning does not negate the importance
of effectiveness, however. There is no contradiction between
acting out of deeply held belief and striving to achieve concrete
results. Nonviolent social movements are sometimes successful, and it is important to know why. This is especially vital for
young people, who in their energy and idealism often want quick
results. I share their impatience, and have spent too many years
working for practical change to discard the notion of effectiveness. I constantly search for the methods and strategies that are
most likely to achieve success.

There is another reason for focusing on effectiveness—to
overcome the powerful pull of cynicism. Perhaps the greatest
obstacle to social progress is the debilitating belief that nothing can be done. Most of us know that social conditions must
change. We recoil at the evils of racism, social injustice, sexism,
war, and environmental ruin. We can see that rational solutions
exist for many of our social ills. Yet, we do not act. We feel helpless, paralyzed before the immense power of governments, global
corporations, and giant institutions. Because we doubt that our
actions can make a difference, we retreat into our private lives,
in the process ceding further power to the forces that control
and oppress us. We come out of our shells occasionally, perhaps
to protest a particularly outrageous abuse such as the U.S. invasion of Iraq, but we are always haunted by that nagging sense
of doubt. Is it worth it?

We can never fully overcome doubt. Nor do we need to. As the
philosopher Søren Kierkegaard observed, faith and doubt are
intimately intertwined, the uncertainty of knowledge providing
the necessity for belief. There is no sure path to social progress. I have studied social movements and been an activist for

more than thirty years, yet I grapple every day with doubt. The nonviolent method can be extraordinarily successful, as in the "velvet" revolutions of Central and Eastern Europe in 1989 and afterward, the people power movement that helped bring down the dictatorship of Ferdinand Marcos in the Philippines in 1986, and the student-led resistance that toppled the Milošević regime in Serbia in 2000. The Orange Revolution of Ukraine also followed the nonviolent action model to achieve democratic reform in 2004. But nonviolent protest sometimes fails spectacularly, as in the brutal suppression of the Tiananmen Square uprising in 1989 and the intransigence of Burmese generals against the democracy movement of Aung San Suu Kyi.

The movement against war in Iraq was unprecedented in its scale and sophistication. The worldwide antiwar rallies of 15 February 2003—in which nearly ten million people demonstrated in hundreds of cities across the globe, more than a million in London alone—represented the largest single-day outpouring of antiwar sentiment in human history. Virtually the entire world stood united in opposition to U.S. policy. Yet this vast movement was unable to prevent the Bush administration from unleashing its unnecessary and ill-advised military attack. Assurances of success are impossible. But we know that certain strategies and tactics are more likely to succeed than others and that the study of strategic effectiveness matters.

This book examines the ingredients of social movement success, and it attempts to forge a synthesis among a wide range of sometimes-diverse thinkers and doers in the field of social change. It is an interpretation of past movements and a response to present events. I combine within one analytic framework the ideas of Gandhi, King, Cesar Chavez, Dorothy Day, Barbara Deming, Gene Sharp, Saul Alinsky, and many others. Towering over all is the giant figure of Gandhi, rightly revered as one of history's greatest prophets of nonviolence. I extol Gandhi's many important contributions but also probe his limitations, especially on gender issues. Next in stature is King. He modernized the Gandhian method and applied it to American conditions but had his own problems relating to women. By selecting the key insights of Gandhi, King, and other historical figures, I hope to bring new coherence and critical insight to the understanding of nonviolent social change. I also explore practical questions of strategy and tactics, drawing historical lessons from the U.S. civil rights movement and the struggles in which I have been involved—the Vietnam antiwar movement, the nuclear weapons freeze campaign, and the Iraq antiwar movement. From these I hope to glean insights that can be useful for future social action campaigns.

A Nonviolent Response to Terrorism

In the aftermath of the terrorist attacks of September 11, 2001, nonviolence seemed to become less relevant. What good is nonviolence against the likes of Osama bin Laden? The indiscriminate killing of nearly three thousand people aroused intense feelings of anger and generated a political backlash of war and militarism. The Gandhian concept of nonretaliation seemed to have few takers. Yet even in those difficult circumstances, the philosophy of nonviolence offered important insights for how to respond.

The day after the 9/11 attacks I was asked to address an all-school convocation at Goshen College, a small liberal arts college in Indiana owned by the Mennonite Church. I felt uneasy speaking so soon after the tragedy, with the fires still burning at the World Trade Center. Emotions were running high, and I worried that my comments might be misconstrued. I decided to accept, though, because I wanted to explore how advocates of nonviolence might respond to such acts of extreme violence. I began by emphasizing the criminal nature of the attacks, and the need for vigorous law enforcement efforts to bring the perpetrators to justice. Nothing can justify such heinous acts of mass murder, and no effort should be spared in tracking down those responsible. The International Criminal Court, I suggested, would be an ideal vehicle for mobilizing worldwide legal action. I acknowledged the temptation for revenge but cautioned against unilateral military actions that could make matters worse. The terrorists have given us a stark vision of their kind of world, I said. "We must deny them the victory they seek. We must resist the fears ... that would have us respond with more violence."[1] The United States should seek instead to understand the causes of terrorism and cooperate with other nations in developing a strategy to prevent such attacks in the future.

Since 9/11 there has been a growing recognition around the world that the strategy against terrorism must emphasize cooperative law enforcement rather than unilateral military force.

The strategy must also seek to undermine the social base of terrorism by driving a wedge between militants and their potential sympathizers. Differentiating between person and social role, Gandhi argued, puts the focus where it belongs: on the social evil, not the person who carries it out. In overcoming terrorism, it is vital to differentiate between hard-core militants and those who support them. The goal should be to separate militants from their support base by resolving the political injustices that terrorist groups exploit. "Terrorism is essentially a political act," concluded the UN Working Group on Terrorism in 2002. "To overcome the problem of terrorism it is necessary to understand its political nature as well as its basic criminality and psychology."[2] Coercive measures against potential sympathizers can be counterproductive and may drive third parties toward militancy. The aim instead must be to isolate hard-core elements. This requires a political approach that addresses deeply felt grievances, promotes good governance, and supports sustainable economic development.

In December 2004 the UN High-level Panel urged "a global strategy of fighting terrorism that addresses root causes and strengthens the rule of law and fundamental human rights."[3] Among the approaches recommended by the UN panel were promoting democracy and representative government, addressing political grievances, ending military occupations, reducing poverty and unemployment, and halting state collapse. This strategy, combined with cooperative law enforcement and coercive pressure against the militants, can erode the operational capacity of terrorist groups and dry up the sources of political, social, and economic support that sustain them.

The Bush administration's war against Iraq has made the terrorist danger worse. Many of us who tried to prevent the war cautioned against the chaos and violence that would result from unprovoked military aggression and the collapse of the Iraqi state. We argued that UN inspections, diplomatic containment, and targeted sanctions could isolate Saddam Hussein and assure Iraq's disarmament without war. We warned that military invasion would create more innocent victims, arouse greater anti-American hatred, and provoke armed resistance. War would cause more terrorism, not less. Unfortunately our predictions proved correct in the war's horrific aftermath. As Gandhi often said, "an eye for an eye leaves the whole world blind." Better to keep our eyes open as we search for more effective means of achieving justice while countering the cycle of violence. At the international level as in intersocial relations, nonviolence provides answers to many of our most pressing questions.

The Plan of This Volume

The book is divided into three parts. Chapters 1 through 3 explain the basic concepts and social action techniques of Gandhi, his influence in the United States, and the development and application of the Gandhian method by Martin Luther King Jr. The second section examines the further evolution of the principles of nonviolent action through the actions and words of Cesar Chavez, Dorothy Day, and Barbara Deming. Chapters 4 and 6 explore the ways in which boycotts and other forms of mass noncooperation exert effective political power to undermine oppressive authority and win political support for social justice. The last three chapters explore critical challenges for the future. Chapter 7 draws lessons from civil rights, global justice, nuclear disarmament, and antiwar movements. Chapter 8 addresses gender-related issues and offers a feminist critique of Gandhi and King. The last chapter summarizes some of the most important practical considerations for effective nonviolent action.

The purpose of this volume is both theoretical and practical. It is born of scholarship and activism. It is inspired by and primarily intended for students, who ask those persistent questions about the meaning and relevance of nonviolence. It is dedicated to all who seek creative ways of challenging injustice and violence. There is also much here to interest academic scholars and veterans in the field. I address some of the key scholarly controversies: the role of sacrifice and morality, pragmatic versus principled nonviolence, the importance of disruption, communications strategies and framing, the significance of third parties, and the contributions of feminism. I draw from social movement analysis and political theory and view history from the bottom up. The book examines how ordinary people sometimes shape their own destiny and become the subjects of history rather than its objects. It identifies the most important principles underlying effective social action. I offer these observations not as dogma but as the humble reflection of one person's experience and research. I intend this work as a small contribution to an already-rich literature on nonviolence and social change, but also as a guide to more effective action. This book is not for armchair strategists but for those who seek to act on their beliefs. As a great philosopher once said, the point is not merely to understand the world but to change it. Precisely, Dr. Marx, except that our commitment is to change it nonviolently.

Chapter 1

Grasping Gandhi

Despite a lifelong commitment to peace and nonviolence, I did not study Gandhi until late in life. My attempts to comprehend his message were impeded by the man himself. Every time I tried to approach Gandhi, I found myself intimidated and overwhelmed—not only by the enormity of his accomplishments but also by the austerity and eccentricities of his personality. Gandhi seemed almost inconceivable. How could one so spiritual and detached from the material world achieve so much in altering the course of history? He commanded no army and held no government position, yet he and the movement he led shook the foundations of the British empire, entirely through the power of disciplined nonviolence. He was revered in his homeland and around the world, and was once called the greatest man in history. All this from a frail-looking, toothless man dressed in a loincloth—a "half-naked fakir," as Winston Churchill derisively labeled him. A religious ascetic who renounced physical needs and material wants, whose earthly possessions at the time of death—glasses, writing utensils, sandals, hand-woven garment—fit easily into a small box.

I found Gandhi's asceticism too extreme, his views on sexuality and women bizarre and offensive. When I attempted to read his autobiography, *My Experiments in Truth,* I recoiled at his puritanical preachments and guilt-ridden battles against sexual "temptation." His prudish beliefs reminded me too much of the Catholic indoctrination I had rebelled against as a young man. Gandhi practiced celibacy, I knew, but he seemed to want everyone else to do the same. I wanted to know more about Gandhi's theories of nonviolence and social change, but I couldn't get past his views on women and sexuality.

Only when I read *Gandhi's Truth* by psychologist Erik Erikson did I finally come to grips with these issues. Erikson's moving "Personal Word," written as a letter to Gandhi and placed unexpectedly at the center of his narrative on Gandhi's emergence as a national leader, gently but firmly challenged the contradictory and even violent elements in his beliefs and practices. By separating Gandhi's views on sexuality from his larger and more valuable contributions to nonviolence, Erikson made Gandhi more human and accessible. The Gandhian method, he wrote, "must not remain restricted to ascetic men and women who believe that they can overcome violence only by sexual self-disarmament."[1] Erikson showed that accepting Gandhi's truth has nothing to do with sexual abstinence or misguided views about women. These and other Gandhian beliefs and practices can be dismissed as the peculiar products of his particular time and life experience.

Erikson's analysis removed the impediments to understanding and set me on a path of exploration to better understand Gandhi's enormous contributions to the struggle for truth and justice. The results of that search are presented in this chapter and those that follow. In the present chapter I draw from the writings of Stanley Wolpert, Judith Brown, Joan Bondurant, Louis Fischer, and others to examine the religious roots and core concepts of Gandhi's philosophy of nonviolence and the central role of sacrifice in his method of social action. I explore the tension between nonviolence and coercion—between pressure and persuasion—and review Gandhi's sometimes-confused thinking on these matters. I assess his strengths and limitations as a political leader, while attempting to show the enduring relevance and necessity of his political method. By offering a critical evaluation and refinement of Gandhi's message, I hope to lay the foundation for a renewed and deepened dedication to nonviolence as a path to social progress.

Hindu Roots

The basic concepts of nonviolence were instilled in Gandhi at an early age. His beliefs were shaped by Jainism, a pacifist branch of Hinduism influential in the Gujarat region of western India where he was raised. The Jain belief system is similar to Buddhism in embracing selflessness and asceticism.[2] Jainists believe in noninjury to all other living beings and practice strict vegetarianism and pacifism. They tend to be traders since this allows them to avoid harming animals and other life forms. Indeed, the Gandhi family name means *grocer*. Jainist monks go to extreme lengths in their nonviolent zeal. They wear white masks to avoid inhaling microbes or insects and even sweep the ground where they walk so as not to stomp ants, worms, or other living creatures.

Gandhi did not go to these lengths and was never a formal practitioner of Jainism—or of any other religion, for that matter, since he embraced all faiths. He was most strongly influenced by Hinduism, of course, but he was strongly attracted to other faiths as well. In the movie *Gandhi,* director Richard Attenborough has the Mahatma saying, "I am a Muslim, and a Hindu, and a Christian."[3] Gandhi considered the separate religions of the world "different roads converging to the same point."[4] His belief in the essential unity of all life reflected the deepest currents in Eastern religious thought and provided the foundation for his commitment to nonviolence and respect for others. He did not believe that all people are alike, but rather that different cultures and faiths could find common understanding and work together harmoniously.

One of the most sacred Hindu texts is the *Bhagavad Gita,* written several centuries before Christ and described by Fischer as the "brightest gem" of Hindu scripture.[5] The *Gita* has had a powerful influence on many Western thinkers, among them J. Robert Oppenheimer, director of the World War II Manhattan Project, whose apocalyptic comment upon the first atomic explosion, "I have become death the destroyer of worlds," came from the sacred Indian verse. Gandhi loved the *Gita.* He referred to its teachings constantly and, according to his disciple and secretary, Mahadev Desai, tried to live its message every moment of his life.[6] Gandhi translated the *Gita* from Sanskrit to his native Gujarati with commentary. He believed the central teaching of the *Gita* to be selflessness and detachment. Love and sacrifice should be offered unconditionally without thought of reward. In the *Gita*, Krishna, the divine incarnation, teaches to "be not moved by the fruits of works." The one who "casts off all desires ... comes unto peace."[7] The highest form of spirituality comes with nonattachment to the fruits of labor. The truly spiritual person does not "brood over results," said Gandhi, but is detached from the fruits of action. Equanimity in the face of pleasure or pain, success or failure, is the surest path to wisdom and spiritual attainment. Complete selflessness means "freedom from pride and pretentiousness; nonviolence, forgiveness, uprightness, service." These sacred ideals guided Gandhi's life.

One of the important influences of the Jain and Buddhist faiths on Hinduism is the principle of *ahimsa*, or nonharm.[8] One must strive at all times to avoid hurting other living creatures. It is better to suffer than to cause suffering to another. Ahimsa is not just a passive concept, though. It implies a positive recognition of the right of every living being to strive for fulfillment and an obligation to uphold and protect that right. Ahimsa must go beyond mere noninjury, believed Gandhi, to include "action based on the refusal to do harm."[9] Ahimsa is positive love, the commitment to resist evil and do good to all unconditionally, even to the wrongdoer. "Hate the sin and not the sinner," Gandhi often said. Active nonviolence commands us to resist injustice even as we refuse to harm those who perpetrate it.[10]

Christian Influences

Although of Hindu origin, Gandhi was once described as "one of the most Christlike men in history."[11] This observation reflects not only his extraordinary service to others but his genuine interest in the teachings of Christ, especially the Sermon on the Mount, which he considered of sublime beauty and importance. He kept a picture of Christ in his office in South Africa and on the wall of his ashram in India, and he often read passages from the Gospels before encounters with his Christian adversaries.[12] He considered Christ the "sower of the seed" of nonviolent philosophy.

Few Christians understand or appreciate fully the depth of Christ's message of love and nonviolence. Pastors and religious teachers tend to rush past the Gospel passages where Jesus consoles the poor and challenges the rich, or commands us to love everyone, even our enemies: "Love your enemies; do good to those who hate you. Bless those who curse you and pray for those who treat you badly. To the one who strikes you on the cheek, turn the other cheek; to the one who takes your coat, give also your shirt" (Matthew 5:39). As Bible professor Walter Wink has written, nonviolence is "the essence of the Gospel."[13] Nonviolence is not a peripheral concern but the very heart of Christ's message. Love and nonviolence are core commitments in all the great religious traditions—Buddhism, Taoism, Hinduism, Islam, Judaism, and Christianity. The problem, as Gandhi said, is that civilization largely ignores this religious message of nonviolence. The Sermon on the Mount is a great teaching, Gandhi said; too bad so few Christians follow it.

Part of the problem for Christians is interpreting what Christ meant when he said to turn the other cheek. Are we merely to accept oppression and evil, to turn our backs when someone we love is attacked, to go meekly like lambs to the slaughter? Wink argues that Christ's teachings are not orders to submit but illustrations of how the oppressed can defy and resist the powerful while maintaining human dignity and the spirit of love.[14] Christ did not say that we should accept blows without response. His meaning was more subtle and creative. His instructions to turn the other cheek, give the other garment, or walk the extra mile are not meant to be taken literally, according to Wink, but are "examples to spark an infinite variety of creative responses." Turning the other cheek is a way of denying the oppressor the power to humiliate.[15] "Try again," it says, "your first blow didn't work. You have not demeaned me." Such a response morally disarms the one who strikes the blow. If the victim refuses to be humiliated, the blow has served no purpose. The tables have turned. Christ taught his followers to challenge injustice without breaking the covenant of God's love.[16] Gandhi found the same meaning in the Gospel, without the benefit of theological exegesis. He instinctively understood the transformative power of returning love for hatred, good for evil, and he set out in his public life to harness this force for social change.

Gandhi's attraction to Christian nonviolence was reinforced by the teachings of Leo Tolstoy, the great Russian novelist. Late in life Tolstoy renounced material possessions and embraced absolute pacifism. He urged resistance to state authority and became an advocate of civil disobedience. This former czarist military officer advised soldiers to reject military service. He called on recruits to renounce "the shameful and ungodly calling of a soldier." To be truly Christian, he wrote, a soldier should fight "not with external foes ... but with his own commanders who deceive him ... not with fists or teeth, but with humble reasonableness and readiness to bear all suffering."[17] That excerpt from Tolstoy's "Notes for Soldiers" caught the attention of some of us who served in the U.S. Army during the Vietnam War. It was very popular among those who opposed the war and participated in the GI movement. Many Vietnam-era GIs did indeed give up the military calling by either deserting or filing for conscientious objector status.[18] I stayed in the army to "fight my commanders" by pursuing a federal court case and organizing antiwar protests.

Gandhi interpreted Tolstoy's call to resistance as an invitation to collective action. He was particularly impressed by Tolstoy's 1909 "Letter to a Hindoo," originally published in *Free Hindustan* and later reprinted with commentary in Gandhi's own journal, *Indian Opinion*. In the letter Tolstoy wrote that the Hindu people were responsible for their own oppression because they allowed colonial domination to continue. Gandhi wrote, "The English have not taken India; we have given it to them."[19] He summarized Tolstoy's message as "slavery consists in submitting."[20] Freedom requires disobedience and the rejection of colonial authority. Through collective resistance the people of India could free themselves of their foreign masters.

Truth Is God

Gandhi's emphasis on the active element in nonviolence was motivated not only by his search for an effective method of political struggle but by his search for deeper spiritual meaning. The refusal to do harm and the commitment to tolerance and love are necessary elements of the quest for truth. Because there are strict limits to human knowledge, said Gandhi, it is impossible to know moral truth absolutely. The search for truth requires humility. Only God is omniscient; we humans can glimpse only a small part of ultimate reality. The apostle Paul wrote in the

Gandhi walking at Sevagram Ashram in India (photo: Vithalbhai Jhaveri, courtesy of the GandhiServe Foundation).

first epistle to the Corinthians that we mortals "see through a glass darkly" and can only "know in part" God's ultimate truth.[21] Human understanding is always conditional and relative. There is no ultimate answer, only the continuous search for truth. The search is the ultimate answer, the highest pursuit of life.

The search for truth excludes the use of violence, said Gandhi, "because man is not capable of knowing the absolute truth and therefore not competent to punish."[22] Once we recognize that our conception of truth is incomplete, we are forced to be humble rather than self-righteous. We can never have the level of certainty about a perceived truth that would entitle us to commit violence on its behalf. Because of the impossibility of absolute knowledge, we have no right to impose our version of truth on another by physical force. When we are confronted with a different interpretation of truth, we must be prepared to reexamine our own position and consider the merits in the other's position. If we disagree we must attempt to convince the other with persuasion and gentleness, not violence. The search for knowledge requires humility and an open mind, a willingness to accept and listen to other opinions. This attitude of openness is antithetical to sectarianism or dogmatism. It precludes the use of violence, which is an attempt to impose one's opinions on another by force.

The search for enlightenment requires strict adherence to nonviolence. "Without *ahimsa* it is not possible to seek and find Truth," Gandhi said. "*Ahimsa* and Truth are so intertwined that it is practically impossible to disentangle and separate them."[23] As Joan Bondurant observes, "if there is dogma in the Gandhian philosophy, it centers here: that the only test of truth is action based on the refusal to do harm."[24]

Reinforcement for this Gandhian metaphysics, if we dare call it that, can be found in the etymology of the Hindu word for truth, *satya.* Satya is derived from *sat,* which means "being." Truth is thus derived from being. Truth is being-ness. It is the realization of being, the foundation and purpose of existence. If we define God as Absolute Being, then God is also Absolute Truth. God is Truth, goes the familiar saying, but Gandhi gave the statement an unusual twist. He argued that it is more correct to say "Truth is God" than the traditional "God is Truth."[25] The difference between the two is easily overlooked. Gandhi admitted that God and truth are convertible terms, but he insisted that the distinction between the two statements is significant. Truth is not merely an attribute of God; it *is* God. "The more truthful we are, the nearer we are to God."[26] The way to God is through the commitment to truth.

This Gandhian insight can be profoundly liberating, especially for those of us who are skeptical about conventional anthropocentric conceptions of God. When pastors or religion teachers assert "God is Truth," we stumble over the meaning of the first part of the sentence. "Who or what is God?" Reversing the order of the sentence makes all the difference. Truth we can try to understand. God is unfathomable. Focusing on the search for the former offers a way of reaching toward the latter, of grasping the imponderable.

In the movie *Sleeper,* Woody Allen's character is asked whether he believes in God. "I believe there is intelligence in the universe," he quips, "except for certain parts of New Jersey." An ultimate intelligence seems to guide the universe, despite the glaring irrationalities of daily life. But this higher intelligence is unknowable to our limited human understanding. We can gain only a small glimpse of the divine through the search for truth. It is in this striving toward truth that we come closer to God.

God is not only infinite truth but infinite love. The commandment to love is at the heart of the Judeo-Christian tradition and of other major religions. Gandhi believed that a commitment to service and compassion for others is the path to divine truth. "I know that God is found most often in the lowliest," he said. "Hence my passion for the service of the suppressed classes."[27] Compassion is the act of entering into another's condition, the crossing of boundaries to help those who suffer or are less fortunate. Christ ministered to the lame and the poor, to sinners and outcasts. The call to help the needy is a core message of the Bible. Take out the biblical passages on the needs of the poor, and the Bible is a tattered, incomplete shell.[28] All faith traditions have a similar commitment to helping the downtrodden. Gandhi embraced these universal religious concepts—truth, love, and justice—and turned them into pathways of revolutionary social change. He had what Wolpert describes as an "undying, passionate faith in the powers of love and its other divine side, truth."[29]

Means and Ends

As Gandhi contemplated the limits of human knowledge and the essential link between truth and God, he saw the inseparable connection between ends and means. The compatibility of ends and means is an essential principle of Gandhian philosophy. Ends and means are not distinct categories of analysis but complementary components of the same reality. Conventional philosophy attempts to analyze ends and means separately, but Gandhi reconciled the two.[30] To say that truth is the end and nonviolence the means is to link the two in a continuous process of striving toward truth and higher being. Ends and means partake of a common search for truth through the reconciliation of opposites.[31]

As Gandhi examined these questions, he came to focus increasingly on means rather than ends. The commitment to nonviolent means became more specific and urgent, while the realization of particular ends seemed increasingly indeterminate.[32] If ultimate truths are unknowable, he concluded, ultimate ends are also uncertain. The ends of human action may be unpredictable, but the means employed are concrete and certain. Political philosopher Hannah Arendt makes a similar observation: means may have more impact on the future than the declared ends. "Since the end of human action ... can never be reliably predicted, the means used to achieve political goals are more often than not of greater relevance to the future world than the intended goals."[33] The use of moral means ensures a moral end. As activist A. J. Muste phrases it, there is no way to peace, peace is the way. According to Gandhi, "if one takes care of the means, the end will take care of itself."[34] Indeed, the means are the end. Gandhi's system is end creating rather than end serving, said Bondurant.[35] Gandhian theorist Robert Burrowes describes it as "goal-revealing."[36] Where Marxism and other systems of thought focus on the pursuit of ends, often justifying even the most extreme means in the service of utopian ideals, Gandhianism emphasizes the primacy of means and the necessity of nonviolent methods. A strict adherence to nonviolent methods is essential to finding truth and assuring a just outcome.

The Gandhian approach has similarities to the Hegelian concept of the dialectic.[37] The German philosopher Georg Hegel believed that progress toward ultimate truth is achieved through the interaction of contending forces, thesis and antithesis leading to synthesis. In the Marxian adaptation, these contending forces are social classes, and the synthesis is achieved through violent revolution. Gandhi applied the dialectic method but rejected the violent components of the Marxian interpretation. He believed that the search for truth involves the interplay of contending interpretations of reality and that a synthesis of these competing forces can reveal a higher truth. Knowledge is forged in the crucible of social contention and the consideration of alternative interpretations. In the Gandhian method, contending forces are synthesized through the medium of love into a new reality and higher order of truth.[38]

Action for Truth

Uncovering the core concepts of Gandhi's philosophy is not an easy task. He cared little for grand theorizing and never attempted to organize his thoughts into a coherent philosophical whole.[39] The ideas outlined here are gleaned from diverse and often disjointed comments scattered throughout his ninety-eight volumes of writings. Gandhi was more a doer than a thinker. As he wrote, "I am not built for academic writings. Action is my domain."[40] He allowed his actions to speak for his beliefs. Indeed action was his philosophy. As he often said, "My life is my message."

Gandhi's greatest contribution was the method of nonviolent social action, which he defined as *satyagraha. Satyagraha* is a difficult word for Westerners to understand. Gandhi coined the term in 1906 during the campaign against racist registration laws in South Africa, when thousands of Asians refused to register or comply with onerous new government restrictions. Gandhi was dissatisfied with the term *passive resistance* then commonly used. He sought one that would more accurately reflect the active elements of the noncooperation campaign, while also embodying the philosophical search for truth. He issued a call from his Phoenix ashram near Durban for the development of a new term to describe the method of active nonviolent resistance and mass noncooperation. The resulting word combined the twin themes of truth and firmness. *Satya,* as noted, means "truth"; *agraha* means "forcefulness or grasping." Satyagraha is thus persistence for truth, firmly holding onto or striving for truth. At times Gandhi defined satyagraha as "pure soul-force or truth-force."[41] Perhaps this latter phrase, "truth-force," is the closest to a simple definition in English. It means forceful but nonviolent social action to realize and uphold truth.

Writer George Orwell was no great admirer of Gandhi, and he reviled pacifism, but he recognized the unique strength and importance of Gandhi's new method. "Gandhi's attitude was not that of most Western pacifists," he wrote. "Satyagraha ... was a sort of nonviolent warfare, a way of defeating the enemy without hurting him and without feeling or arousing hatred."[42] Gandhi would have corrected Orwell to say that the goal is not defeating the adversary but achieving understanding and political accommodation, but otherwise he would have agreed with Orwell's description. The Gandhian method introduced a revolutionary new form of political struggle into human history. It provided a way of fighting against injustice without resorting to violence and without stirring the intense passions of hatred and revenge that usually accompany armed conflict. It combined the quest for religious truth with the struggle for social justice.

Satyagraha is a dynamic concept, involving constant action and a willingness to change and accept new understandings of truth. It goes far beyond mere pressure tactics or civil disobedience. Western activists who equate the Gandhian method with getting arrested at a demonstration fail to appreciate the depth of the satyagraha concept. Satyagraha is the ethical search for truth through nonviolent action.[43] It is a method of testing truth and transforming conflict through the power of love. It encompasses a broad range of actions designed to find truth through the interaction of contending social forces.[44] At times mass disobedience may be necessary to dramatize an injustice, but for Gandhi this action came only after a rigorous investigation of the facts and attempts at negotiation and dialogue with the adversary. Only an unjust law should be disobeyed, Gandhi insisted, and if we are to break a law, it must be with voluntary (Gandhi would say even cheerful) acceptance of the penalty.

Learning from the Suffragists

During his years of struggle for the rights of Asian immigrants in South Africa, Gandhi twice traveled to London to lobby British officials. On his visits in 1906 and 1909, Gandhi inevitably absorbed the contemporary currents of British society. One of the most powerful of these was the women's suffrage movement. Women in England had been campaigning for the right to vote for more than forty years, but with the turn of the century, the movement expanded and adopted more assertive methods. Frustrated by the unwillingness of male political leaders to heed their reasoned arguments, women began to resort to mass petitions, public demonstrations, and, beginning in 1905, disruptive action. Suffragists began to heckle political speakers, organize mass marches, and engage in civil disobedience. The press notoriety and political uproar that resulted from these actions convinced many that assertive tactics were a powerful new weapon in the struggle for the vote. The women activists developed a conscious strategy of provoking police reprisals as a way to embarrass male politicians and attract sympathy and support for their cause.[45]

This new method of disruptive action was just emerging when Gandhi visited London in 1906 and 1909. Gandhi was greatly impressed by the courage and determination of the suffragists.[46] He referred to the suffrage movement several times in *Indian Opinion.*[47] He believed that the men of Asia could learn lessons from the women of England. In a 1907 article, "When Women Are Manly, Will Men Be Effeminate?" Gandhi attached great importance to the assertiveness and courage of the women demonstrators. Referring to a march of eight hundred women on Parliament, he wrote, "We believe these women have behaved in a manly way."[48] If women forcefully demanded the franchise, he wrote, "it could not but be granted." The lesson was obvious: "justice is often not to be had without some show of strength.... Our bondage in India can cease this day, if all the people unite ... and are ready to suffer any hardships that may befall them."[49] If the men of India were as determined and courageous as the women of England, their demands would be met.

The example of the suffragists strengthened Gandhi's belief in direct action and mass noncooperation as essential means of social change. Of course, the women's movement was not the only influence on Gandhi. By the time of his visits to London, he had been organizing for social change for more than a decade and had already sponsored mass action campaigns. Many influences and insights contributed to his satyagraha method. But the militancy and tenacity of the suffrage movement corroborated his commitment to the emerging approach that would come to be known as Gandhian.[50] Writes Wolpert, "The remaining forty years of his life would be spent in explaining, in reiterating, and in implementing this passionate, inspired prescription for winning freedom."[51]

Politics and Sainthood

Jim Wallis, the Christian leader for social change, has termed the Gandhian method a form of spiritual politics.[52] It is an apt description. Gandhi attempted to reconcile the often coarse demands of political struggle with higher principles of religious and moral belief.[53] "Men say I am a saint losing myself in politics," Gandhi said. "The fact is that I am a politician trying my hardest to be a saint."[54] This spiritual form of politics was essential to Gandhi's method, according to activist Dave Dellinger: "The genius of Gandhi and the basis for his remarkable success lay in his insistence that religion and politics could not be separated."[55] Gandhi's conception of politics was very different from that of his colleagues in the Indian independence movement or of conventional politicians today. The goal of political struggle, Gandhi believed, is to reach agreement for the sake of social betterment. Political power is not an end in itself but a means of enabling people to better their condition. He engaged in political struggle because he wanted to end oppression and serve the needy. "I cannot render this service," he said, "without entering politics."[56] The notion of obtaining political power for personal gain was completely alien to him. He viewed politics as a form of religious commitment that transcends narrow self-interest and embraces the common good through a willingness to sacrifice.[57]

Gandhi's political method emerged from his concept of politics as an expression of religious commitment, as a way of seeking truth. He applied the principles of nonviolence to develop unique and highly effective forms of political struggle. Orwell wrote that "inside the saint, or near-saint, there was a very shrewd" political leader.[58] In Gandhi's political campaigns there were three stages of activity—persuasion, sacrifice, and noncooperation. Before engaging in direct action, the activist attempts to persuade the adversary through the presentation of facts and rational argument. Gandhi showed what Brown calls "a meticulous concern for the collection of properly documented evidence."[59] When factual argument fails to persuade, as is often the case, the activist proceeds to the next stage, resorting to dramatic acts of self-sacrifice. Through disciplined nonviolent action and a willingness to suffer arrest or physical harm, the activist attempts to reach the conscience of the adversary. After dramatizing the issues and arousing moral concern, the activist then moves to the final stage, mass noncooperation. Through boycotts and other forms of direct action, the movement pressures the adversary to change policy by withdrawing consent and undermining the exercise of abusive power. Martin Luther King Jr. developed a similar typology of social action steps to guide his nonviolent movement. I will have more to say in subsequent chapters about the stages of nonviolent action, and the strategies and tactics that flow from each.

Gandhi's political concerns went beyond matters of government policy. He espoused a multidimensional struggle that included a broad range of demands. He told his colleagues in the Indian freedom struggle that the objective was not only political independence but a moral revolution within India. He was as concerned with social and spiritual transformation as he was with political liberation. He wanted to free the people of India from the prejudices and outmoded practices that held them in bondage as tightly as British colonialism. Muslim-Hindu unity, an end to untouchability, and the empowerment of women were as important to him as political independence. He considered these social reforms necessary for people to govern themselves responsibly. He fought particularly hard in his final years to prevent the partition of India and stem political extremism among both Muslims and Hindus. Political freedom without communal unity and a revolution of values, he feared, would bring tragedy. Sadly, the history of conflict between India and Pakistan has confirmed Gandhi's gloomy prognosis. The people of India ultimately gained independence, but they did not achieve the spiritual enlightenment needed to enjoy the fruits of political freedom. Shackled by ethnic animosity and religious hatred, the subcontinent remained mired in communal conflict, its resources and energies squandered on military and even nuclear competition, with hundreds of millions suffering abysmal poverty.

Gandhi was criticized at times for his inadequacies as a political leader, a charge he did not deny. He admitted, for example, that his decision to call off the massive noncooperation campaign of 1920–1922, because of a single incident of violence by his followers in Chauri-Chaura, was "politically ... unwise," although he claimed it was "religiously sound."[60] His followers were "bewildered and indignant" at this precipitous cancellation of the resistance movement just as it was reaching a climax.[61] Gandhi was also criticized for ending the great salt satyagraha campaign of 1930–1931, on the paltry promise of a roundtable conference with British leaders in London.[62] In the midst of a "rising tide of popular enthusiasm," as Gandhi scholar B. R. Nanda termed it, with some sixty thousand resisters in jail and British textile imports devastated by an effective boycott, Gandhi prematurely ended the campaign in exchange for the release of some prisoners and the opening of roundtable negotiations.[63]

Gandhi, sharing a joke with Jawaharlal Nehru, 1946 (photo: Vithalbhai Jhaveri, courtesy of the GandhiServe Foundation).

It was a meager bargain, one that troubled Jawaharlal Nehru and other Indian nationalist leaders. Gandhi genuinely believed in the prospect of meaningful dialogue with the British leader in India, Viceroy Lord Irwin, although by his own admission he returned from the 1931 London roundtable "empty-handed." In 1908 Gandhi was betrayed by South African political leader Jan Smuts on the issue of forced registration for Asians. When Smuts promised to revoke compulsory measures, Gandhi convinced his fellow Indians to register voluntarily. He risked the wrath of his compatriots and was physically attacked for agreeing to such a compromise, only to see Smuts back out of the agreement. When Smuts ruled that unregistered Asians would be subject to enforced measures, Gandhi and his colleagues shifted back to a strategy of resistance, and thousands of Indians burned their registration cards. Wolpert described Gandhi as an "agitator-negotiator."[64] In his social action campaigns as in his earlier law practice, he preferred bargaining to battling. Gandhi's colleagues considered him naive for relying on the promises of British leaders. They thought him too ready to negotiate, too eager to reach agreement. Gandhi defended his readiness to bargain. Better to err on the side of compromise, he believed, than confrontation.

Nonviolence scholars Peter Ackerman and Christopher Kruegler have argued that Gandhi's leadership was at times "a mixed blessing" and that his "personal foibles burdened the movement."[65] Wolpert speaks of Gandhi's "oft-repeated retreat from the brink of victory."[66] While Gandhi was often brilliant in developing resistance tactics and inspiring the masses to action, he sought reconciliation prematurely, especially during the great salt satyagraha campaign. According to Ackerman and Kruegler, "It can be argued that Gandhi's preference for compromise over coercion, as well as his underestimation of Congress' power, made the ultimate objective in [the salt satyagraha] campaign impossible to achieve."[67] Persistence is a vital principle of strategy. Social change requires a long-term commitment of continuous political pressure. When the resistance movement is at its peak and the adversary is reeling under the pressure, as was the case in 1931, it is a mistake to bargain away the sacrifices of millions of devoted followers for a few meager crumbs from the negotiating table. At times it is right to seek compromise, but at other times continuing the struggle is crucial, and maintaining pressure is necessary to achieve concrete results. Gandhi sometimes misjudged this crucial calculation and sold the movement short of what it could have achieved. The challenge of wise leadership is deciding when to negotiate and when to apply pressure, and how to mix the two. There is little doubt that in the 1920–1922 noncooperation campaign and in the great resistance struggle of 1930–1931, Gandhi's emphasis on spiritual purity, his misplaced trust in British officials, and his preference for negotiation over confrontation all combined to sap the movement's potential.

An Aversion to Coercion

Gandhi's accommodating style of political leadership derived in part from his ambiguity toward the use of coercion. He considered satyagraha more a means of moral persuasion than a form of political pressure. Gandhi believed that humans are capable of spiritual and moral perfection, and that they can be persuaded through reason to do the right thing. This hope sustained him, but as Brown observes, it also imprisoned him.[68] He was at times overly trusting in the power of reason and moral argument. He did not want to admit that satyagraha might be coercive in some ways, for this view would have diminished its religious character, which he considered of paramount importance. But Gandhi could not avoid coercion. The concept of forcefulness was built into his method from the very outset. The word *agraha*, part of *satyagraha*, means "firmness or forcefully grasping." However much he may have wanted to deny it, Gandhi's campaigns often employed coercive elements. His boycotts and mass noncooperation campaigns were a means of achieving political change through the force of social action.

Theologian Reinhold Niebuhr describes Gandhi's attempts to deny the coercive elements of satyagraha a "pardonable confusion in the soul of a man who is trying to harmonize the insights of a saint with the necessities of statecraft."[69] He is critical of Gandhi's attempts to straddle the fence and his view of satyagraha as a form of pure spiritualism. Elements of coercion are unavoidable, Niebuhr argues. "The selfishness of human communities must be regarded as an inevitability. Where it is inordinate it can be checked only by competing assertions of interest; and these can be effective only if coercive methods are added to moral and rational persuasion."[70] Pure pacifism or "nonresistance" is not an adequate response to social oppression and institutionalized tyranny, Niebuhr believes. Coercion becomes necessary when purely moral or rational pleas fall on deaf ears, as they so often do. Injustice cannot be willed away or removed solely through persuasion. It must be resisted by every moral means available, which may require the use of nonviolent compulsion.

Wink helps explain the role of coercion by distinguishing between force and violence. The application of force does not necessarily require violent means. Force can also mean "a legitimate, socially authorized, and morally defensible use of restraint to prevent harm being done." Violence, on the other hand, is "the morally illegitimate or excessive use of force."[71] As long as forcefulness avoids causing physical harm, it fits within the definition of nonviolence.

Niebuhr believes that Gandhi came to recognize the necessity of some degree of physical coercion as "political realism qualified religious idealism."[72] Louis Fischer, however, argues that Gandhi in his latter years became more absolute in his commitment to pacifism. Gandhi refused to countenance an armed response by Jews, Czechs, or other subjugated peoples to the horrors of Hitlerism in Europe, and he was unwilling to consider armed resistance even as Japanese armies occupied Burma and seemed poised to invade India.[73] Perhaps both interpretations of Gandhi's thinking are correct. He became more accepting of the coercive elements within satyagraha, while simultaneously becoming more sickened by and unwilling to accept the barbarism of war and armed conflict. He became more of an absolute pacifist, but he also became a more determined nonviolent resister.

Nonviolent action is not free of ambiguity. It can exert real pressure and harm the adversary. Boycotts and strikes may lower incomes or reduce property values. Mass civil disobedience may interrupt vital services, prevent the implementation of policy, or stop business as usual. Nor does nonviolent action necessarily distinguish well between the guilty and the innocent. The boycott against British textiles during the Indian independence movement was directed at policymakers in London, but the cotton spinners of Lancashire were the ones who suffered most (although they greeted Gandhi warmly when he visited in 1931). The sit-down strikes of the 1930s in the United States were aimed at factory owners who refused to accept collective bargaining, but the entire community, including workers' families, suffered from the resulting economic disruption. In the civil rights struggle of the 1960s, movement leaders tended to boycott only selected downtown merchants, but their efforts inevitably had impacts in the black community as well.

The line between violence and nonviolence is not always clear. An action is nonviolent if it avoids imposing physical harm and if it does not deprive people of necessities or lower living standards below subsistence. Mass noncooperation can be considered nonviolent, even if it causes serious economic hardship, so long as it eschews physical force and avoids actions that threaten life. This is not a definition that would satisfy Gandhi's aspirations to religious purity, but it is realistic and, I would argue, morally justifiable.

Sacrifice and Strength

The Gandhian method, whether as pressure or persuasion, requires a willingness to suffer. "The purer the suffering," Gandhi believed, "the greater the progress."[74] The readiness to sacrifice is a key feature of satyagraha and accounts for its political impact. Wolpert describes Gandhi's life as a "pageant of his conscious courting of suffering."[75] The specter of innocent people facing arrest or unprovoked violence can be a powerful means of dramatizing injustice and overcoming moral indifference. The sacrifice of nonviolent resisters may spark a sympathetic response from bystanders, altering the political dynamics of a conflict. The willingness to suffer may also be a spiritual expression of love and selflessness. One of Gandhi's great insights was his understanding that change does not occur solely or even primarily through logical argument or reason. He wrote, "Things of fundamental importance to the people are not secured through reason alone but have to be purchased with their suffering. . . . If you want something really important to be done you must not merely satisfy the reason, you must move the heart also."[76]

The role of suffering in the Gandhian method has been the subject of considerable debate. Some scholars, such as sociologist Kurt Schock, argue that "suffering is not an essential part of nonviolent resistance."[77] Others, such as peace studies expert Michael Nagler, believe that personal sacrifice is integral to the very definition of nonviolent action. One cannot properly speak of nonviolence without it.[78] Scholar Gene Sharp emphasizes that nonviolent resisters may suffer hardships during the political struggle and must be willing to face the repression that usually results from challenges to established authority. The point is not to incur suffering, however, but to accept and withstand repression and continue struggling until mass noncooperation undermines the adversary's power. If the resisters persist, mass noncooperation has the potential to overcome the adversary and achieve political success.[79] Sharp thus acknowledges the importance of suffering but does not give "the pageantry of suffering" a central role in the process of political transformation. He recognizes, though, that suffering can be a means of overcoming indifference and rationalization to convert or win over the adversary.[80] He also notes that the brutalities of repression against nonviolent resisters may arouse a sympathetic response among third parties, which can split the ranks of the adversary and win political support for the nonviolent challengers from previously uncommitted constituencies.[81] (We shall have more to say about the importance of the third party effect later, especially in chapter 6.)

The importance of sacrifice in the Gandhian method highlights the spiritual dimensions of nonviolent action. While it is true, as Sharp and others emphasize, that religious belief is not a requirement for nonviolent action and that many practitioners of the method are nonbelievers, striking parallels are evident between Gandhian nonviolence and traditions of religious sacrifice. The redemptive power of unmerited suffering is a central element of Christianity and other religious traditions. Christ saved humankind from sin through his suffering and death on the cross. The prophets and religious teachers of the Judeo-Christian tradition suffered to atone for the sins of their oppressors. In the process they inspired others to make similar sacrifices for justice. As civil rights leader John Lewis notes, "the purity of unearned suffering is a holy and *affective* thing [emphasis in original]. It affects not only ourselves, it touches and changes those around us as well. It opens us and those around us to a force beyond ourselves, a force that is right and moral, the force of righteous truth that is at the basis of human conscience. Suffering puts us and those around us in touch with our consciences. It opens and touches our hearts. It makes us feel compassion where we need to and guilt if we must."[82] Gandhi also saw suffering as a path to self-realization and spiritual fulfillment.[83] He appropriated this religious dimension of suffering and transformed it into a method of social action.

Self-suffering is directed primarily at moral persuasion. A willingness to suffer personal hardship can cut through an adversary's rationalizations and defenses. It can act as a kind of shock therapy to open the adversary's heart and allow the consideration of alternative viewpoints. Suffering can also be a dramatization of the evil being challenged, as Martin Luther King Jr. and his colleagues demonstrated in the civil rights movement. Their submission to police violence dramatized the everyday brutality of the segregationist system and brought to light the oppression that was often hidden from view or that observers chose to overlook. The acceptance of suffering does not always succeed in dislodging deeply ingrained prejudice or fear, writes Dave Dellinger, but "its general effect is always to work in that direction."[84]

Action based on refusal to harm often requires accepting the opponent's violence on oneself. This suffering is another way in which truth is tested, for both the practitioner and the opponent. The ultimate test of love is a willingness to accept the consequences of an opponent's violence. The seeker of truth must be prepared to pay a price to achieve higher awareness, said Gandhi. "We should learn to dare danger and death, mortify the flesh, and acquire the capacity to endure all manner of hardships," he wrote.[85] Christian philosophers have also emphasized the importance of sacrifice. Thomas Merton, a Catholic monk, writes, "The key to nonviolence is the willingness of the nonviolent resister to suffer a certain amount of accidental evil in order to bring about a change of mind in the oppressor and awaken him to personal openness and to dialogue."[86]

In Hinduism and other religions, self-suffering is aimed at purification. It promotes nonattachment to physical, bodily wants. It emphasizes the superiority of spirit over matter. In social action, too, suffering can have a purifying role. It is intended to promote nonattachment to material interests and prevent the narrow pursuit of power. It allows us to focus on the spiritual dimension of satyagraha and the search for truth, to rise above self-interest or the corruptions of power. It has a cathartic effect and helps achieve the moral enrichment that is essential to the power of nonviolence.

Courage

Gandhi repeatedly emphasized that his method is for the strong, not the weak. It takes courage not to fight. It takes strength to suffer for a cause and not to respond with violence. This approach is the opposite of what our culture teaches. When some of us resisted the Vietnam War, we were called cowards. Critics said we were unwilling to fight for our country, that we were seeking the easy way out. The critics didn't understand that we had to make sacrifices, that we faced harassment and punishment for speaking out. It was not easy to refuse the draft or oppose the war from inside the army. Those of us who resisted knew that we were taking risks and might have to suffer, but we felt we had

Vietnam-era soldiers listen to speakers at an antiwar protest (photo: David Cortright collection).

no choice. We could not participate in such an unjust war and were willing to pay a price to help bring it to an end.

In an oft-quoted but frequently misunderstood statement, Gandhi asserted that if there is only a choice between coward-ice and violence, it is better to be violent.[87] He did not mean to excuse violence but to emphasize the cardinal importance of courage. If I choose nonviolence because I am afraid or because I am unwilling to suffer, I am not truly following the Gandhian way. Only if I am prepared to accept suffering can I fully appre-ciate and express the power of nonviolence. Gandhi insisted on the highest standards of personal bravery. He believed that satyagraha is at its most effective when those practicing it are in a position to use physical force but consciously choose not to do so. Nonviolent sacrifice is never demoralizing, he said, while cowardice always is.[88] "Courage, endurance, fearlessness and above all self-sacrifice are the qualities required for our leaders," he wrote.[89]

According to Wink, Gandhi wanted his followers to have a "fury at injustice" and a motivation to fight for freedom, but he also wanted them to have the strength to struggle nonviolently.

Wink argues that it is necessary to pass through the stage of righteous indignation and the desire to fight before advancing to the higher plane of assertive nonviolence.[90] Barbara Deming also describes the cathartic role of anger. It is natural to be outraged at injustice and oppression. Anger can be healthy if it is based on hope rather than fear, if it is translated into a "determination to bring about change."[91] Gandhi often emphasized the need for courage and a readiness to sacrifice. Only by overcoming the fear of retaliation can we be free of the power of oppression. The ability to shed fear is the key to gaining freedom.

The ultimate sacrifice is one's life. Gandhi said he was willing to die for the cause of truth but never to kill for it. On numerous occasions he reminded his followers of the heavy price they might have to pay. He did not mince words. During his address at the assembly to protest anti-Asiatic measures in Johannesburg in 1906, he told his colleagues of the potential consequences of signing the pledge not to register. "Every one must be true to his pledge even unto death."[92] He offered similar entreaties to his followers before other major campaigns. It is better to die, he insisted, than to resort to violence. He himself was brutalized on a number of occasions, almost fatally in 1908, and ultimately fell to an assassin's bullets in 1948. Gandhi never flinched in the face of danger and urged his followers to similar feats of bravery. He genuinely believed that death in the pursuit of truth ennobles the struggle for justice and is the highest form of religious sacrifice. Nonviolence is "a spiritual challenge of epic proportions," writes Wink. "It calls upon the soul's authentic longing for heroism, for risking one's life for an infinite stake, for self-transcendence in giving oneself to others."[93]

This is the ultimate test of our commitment: Are we truly willing to die for what we believe, to die but not to kill? Our militarized culture extols the virtue of dying in battle, but little prepares us for the more demanding challenge of being ready to die in the cause of nonviolent struggle. The martyrdom of Gandhi, King, Salvadorean archbishop Oscar Romero, and many others reminds us that this ultimate burden is a very real possibility. The civil rights memorial in Montgomery, Alabama, which commemorates the fifty-five Americans who died in that nonviolent struggle, provides an enduring reminder of the heavy price that some have had to pay for justice.

Many of us in the comfort and security of middle-class life never expect to face personal injury or death because of social activism, but for others the threat is very real. In numerous cases all over the world, resisters have faced jail, physical abuse, or death in the struggle for freedom. Some of the most spectacular historical examples of nonviolent struggle have featured extraordinary acts of personal heroism and sacrifice—Catholic nuns kneeling before Philippine army tanks in 1986, residents of South African townships braving police brutality to protest apartheid, a Chinese student standing before a tank near Tiananmen Square in 1989, Aung San Suu Kyi standing up to military authorities in Burma. These and countless other examples illustrate the courage and willingness to sacrifice that are at the heart of the method of revolutionary nonviolence Gandhi pioneered.

Mustering the courage to resist authority is extremely difficult, perhaps as much in a tolerant democracy as in a repressive dictatorship. In North America or Europe, the chains that bind are looser but no less effective than those employed in a police state. Here the mechanisms of control are internalized. We fear the loss of job security or position; we worry how family, friends, and employers will view us. We are so entangled in the comforts of society that we find it difficult to take risks, even for causes we hold dear. Yet Gandhi taught that we must be prepared to sacrifice. We may not actually suffer harm in a particular campaign, but we must be prepared morally and materially to do so. This is the ultimate test of our faith, the hard but unavoidable test of personal commitment.

In these reflections, my purpose is not to bury Gandhi but to deconstruct him, to register overwhelming approval of his core philosophy of nonviolence while noting some points of disagreement. Peace scholar Johan Galtung observes, "We can always learn enormously much from Gandhi, but not if we accept him uncritically."[94] Gandhi said that he himself was not a Gandhian, by which he meant that he was constantly revising and updating his views as he learned more and interacted with his adversaries.

As Brown writes, "Gandhi was no plastic saint." He was caught in the inevitable compromises and contradictions of political life. But he asked "the profoundest questions that face humankind," and even if he didn't always have answers, he courageously sought truth in every setting.[95] He selflessly served the poor and devoted himself to helping the downtrodden, constantly striving, in Wolpert's words, "to liberate humankind from the shackles of prejudice, fear, and hatred."[96] Gandhi's flaws were many, but they were overshadowed by his towering achievements and by his unflagging commitment to all that it is noble and good in the human spirit. He uncovered a bold new method of political change, one with profound meaning for the future of humankind. He revolutionized the very concept of revolution and developed new means of peaceful political transformation.[97] He challenged hierarchies of caste, religion, and imperialism. He preached the value of social harmony against the pressures of national and ethnic division. Most significantly, he raised the concept of nonviolence to that of ultimate principle, illuminating its role as both personal and social salvation. For all his eccentricities, Gandhi was thoroughly modern, even postmodern. His message has enduring relevance for the ages.

Highlights of Gandhi's Life

1869   Born in Porbunder, Gujarat

1888   Leaves for London to study law

1891   Passes law examination, enrolls at High Court, and returns to India

1893   Leaves India for legal work among Asian immigrant merchants in Durban, South Africa; encounters race prejudice (thrown off train at Pietermaritzberg) and begins organizing petitions for redress

1894   Founds Natal Indian Congress

1903   Launches first newspaper, *Indian Opinion*

1904   Creates Phoenix ashram near Durban

1906   Launches first satyagraha campaign against the Asiatic Ordinance Bill requiring registration of all Asians in South Africa; thousands of Indians burn their registration cards

1910   Creates Tolstoy Farm near Johannesburg

1913   Launches campaign against new Asiatic Immigration Bill; organizes illegal march of striking Indian miners across Transvaal border

1914   Negotiates agreement with General Smuts for partial lifting of restrictions on Asians

1915   Arrives back in India

1917   Engages in first local campaign, on behalf of tenant indigo growers in Champaran, Bihar

1918   Supports two additional local struggles, among mill workers in Ahmedabad and peasants in Kheda near Bombay

1919   Founds *Young India* journal

1920–21 Launches first all-India satyagraha mass noncooperation campaign

1925   Creates All-India Spinning Association

1928   Supports tenant farmers in nonpayment of land taxes in Bardoli, Gujarat

1930   Leads historic march to sea to launch "great salt satyagraha"

1931   Negotiates with viceroy in India and attends roundtable conference in England

1934   Leads new All-India Village Industries Association

1940   Begins campaign of individual civil disobedience against British war policy

1942   Launches "quit India" campaign

1946–47 Visits Noakhali and other parts of Bengal to soothe Hindu-Muslim tensions

1948   Assassinated in New Delhi

Chapter 2

Gandhi USA

Gandhi never traveled to the United States, but his impact on American life has been substantial. Through his influence on generations of activists for peace and civil rights, Gandhi's spirit lives on as part of the American experience. Images of the Mahatma are commonplace not only among peace groups but in the larger society as well. Statues of Gandhi grace the Embarcadero in San Francisco, Union Square in New York, and Embassy Row in Washington, D.C. Even Madison Avenue has appropriated Gandhi's greatness. Apple Computer used Gandhi in its "Think Different" advertising campaign, displaying his billboard image in cities all over the United States. Richard Nixon was a most un-Gandhian character, but even he invoked Gandhi's name. In the final days of his presidency, as he ruminated over the possibility of jail for his Watergate crimes, Nixon remarked that like Gandhi, he might have time for writing.[1]

Early Impressions

Americans have been intensely interested in Gandhi since news of his early achievements in South Africa first arrived in the years before World War I. Gandhi exerted profound influence on the

African American community in particular, especially on Martin Luther King Jr., who became the principal vehicle through whom Gandhi's ideas reached millions of Americans. Gandhi appealed to American reformers in part because a tradition of nonviolent resistance was already well established in the United States, through the efforts of the Religious Society of Friends (Quakers), the abolitionists, suffragists, and others. As activists and historians Staughton and Alice Lynd note, the United States has a "distinctive tradition of nonviolence" dating back to colonial times.[2] Gandhi himself was influenced by Americans, especially the New England transcendentalists, who had established contact with Indian counterparts in the nineteenth century. Gandhi knew of the work of abolitionists Adin Ballou, William Lloyd Garrison, and the New England Non-Resistance Society, which as early as 1838 advocated nonviolent action methods against slavery. Gandhi also read Henry David Thoreau's classic *On Civil Disobedience,* which left a "deep impression" on him and from which he published lengthy extracts in his journal *Indian Opinion.*[3]

One of the first Americans to take notice of Gandhi was Reverend John Haynes Holmes, who helped found the American Anti-enlistment League in 1915. A seminal figure in the peace and civil liberties movements of the early twentieth century, Holmes was a founder of the War Resisters League and a leader of both the American Civil Liberties Union and the Fellowship of Reconciliation. Holmes extolled Gandhi's method of mass noncooperation as a way of effectively resisting war and tyranny while remaining true to the principles of nonviolence. He called Gandhi "the greatest man since Jesus Christ." After 1917, Holmes frequently referred to Gandhi in sermons and his many articles and was one of the first to popularize the concept of nonviolence as a practical alternative to war.[4] From 1926 to 1929, Holmes published Gandhi's autobiography, *My Experiments in Truth,* in installments in the Unitarian journal *Unity.* This was twenty years before the book was officially published in the United States.[5]

Another American influenced by Gandhi was the great African American intellectual, W. E. B. Du Bois, a founder of the National Association for the Advancement of Colored People (NAACP) and a giant figure in American letters for more than half a century. Du Bois promoted the theme of international

racial solidarity and strongly supported decolonization movements at the end of World War I, giving special emphasis to
the freedom struggle in India. He wrote an article in the March
1922 issue of the NAACP's official journal, *The Crisis*, which
praised Gandhi and the 1920–1922 noncooperation campaign
in India. Du Bois felt that Gandhi had discovered a marvelous
new method of nonviolent struggle that could be used to liberate black Americans.[6] In 1929, on its twentieth anniversary,
The Crisis featured a front-page message from Gandhi to "the
12 million Negroes," with a comment from Du Bois. "Agitation,
nonviolence, and refusal to cooperate [are] leading all India to
freedom," Du Bois proclaimed.[7] Other African American publications and newspapers also praised Gandhi. In December 1921,
the *Chicago Defender*, one of the largest and most influential
black newspapers in the United States, called Gandhi the "greatest man in the world today."[8]

The most significant mass leader of the African American
community during and immediately after World War I was
Marcus Garvey, president of the Universal Negro Improvement
Association (UNIA), which was established in Jamaica in 1914
and in Harlem in 1917. Garvey's "back to Africa" movement
advocated the liberation of Africa from Western colonialism and
the creation of a free nation in Africa where blacks from all con-
tinents could develop their potential without racial restrictions.
Garvey claimed a UNIA constituency of one million members.[9]
He spoke often to large mass meetings in New York and other
cities, instilling a sense of collective pride and cultural identity
among African Americans. Garvey also promoted international
solidarity and frequently referred to the freedom struggles of
Egypt and India. His journal, *The Negro World*, reported extensively on the Indian independence movement and extolled
Gandhi's leadership. In a 1922 speech reprinted in *The Negro
World*, Garvey called Gandhi "one of the noblest characters of
the day."[10]

The African American press was particularly interested in the
1930–1931 great salt satyagraha and devoted extensive coverage to the Gandhian movement. Gandhi appealed to African
Americans in part because he was a colored person struggling
against white oppressors. His stand against untouchability also
struck a responsive chord among those suffering the abuses
of segregation. One could sense an almost palpable longing in

the African American community for a Gandhi-like solution to the problem of racial oppression in America.[11] The *Chicago Defender* asked in a 1932 editorial, "Will a Gandhi Arise?" and offered the opinion that "what we need in America is a Gandhi who will fight for the cause of the oppressed in this country."[12]

Knowledge about Gandhi spread rapidly in the United States after the 1930–1931 campaign. He was mentioned often in press reports and even won a place in popular culture, in the lyric of Cole Porter's hit song, "You're the Top" ("You're the top, you're Mahatma Gandhi"). During his stay in London for the round-table conference, Gandhi met Charlie Chaplin, George Bernard Shaw, and other cultural and literary figures. Gandhi was widely admired among progressive intellectuals on both sides of the Atlantic, and his ideas made a great impression in universities and theological schools.

One of the first theologians to give serious notice was Rein-hold Niebuhr. Niebuhr was critical of Gandhi in some respects, but he saw the Gandhian method as a new approach to the problem of conflict and injustice that transcended the limits of traditional Christian pacifism. In his early career, Niebuhr had been a leader of the Fellowship of Reconciliation, but he rejected absolute pacifism and challenged the traditional concept of nonresistance as an inadequate response to oppression and the realities of social evil. Niebuhr saw the Gandhian method as the best option for reconciling the struggle against evil with the moral commitment to nonviolence. Niebuhr described Gandhi's method as a "strategic instrument for confronting oppression." Speaking of the race problem in America, Niebuhr observed presciently, "The emancipation of the Negro race in America probably waits upon the adequate development of this kind of social and political strategy."[13] He added that "the technique of nonviolence ... if persisted in with the same patience and dis-cipline attained by Mr. Gandhi and his followers [will] achieve a degree of justice which neither pure moral suasion nor violence could gain."[14]

Another important event in spreading Gandhi's influence was the 1934 publication of Richard Gregg's book *The Power of Nonviolence.* A lawyer specializing in industrial relations, Gregg was keenly interested in the problem of conflict and went to India in 1925 to learn about Gandhi's methods. Gregg became a personal friend of Gandhi, living at his Sabarmati ashram for seven months and remaining in India for nearly four years.[15] Gregg viewed Gandhi's method of nonviolent struggle as a necessary antidote to the traditional pacifist tendency to avoid conflict. He was one of the first to provide a systematic analysis of nonviolence, as we shall examine in chapter 4, focusing on the psychological dynamics of nonviolent action as a creative and effective means of confronting oppression. Gregg's work was later republished in several editions and was influential in the civil rights movement. Martin Luther King Jr. read Gregg's book while at Crozer Theological Seminary and wrote a foreword for the second revised edition in 1959.

Cross-fertilizations

A number of Gandhi's colleagues from India helped bring his message to the United States, devoting special attention to the African American community. C. F. Andrews, the British missionary who became a close friend of Gandhi, was especially influential and considered Gandhi's voice to the West.[16] During his visit to the United States in 1929, Andrews met Du Bois. In February 1930, he spent ten days at Washington's Tuskegee Institute in Alabama. While there he completed the manuscript for his book *Gandhi's Ideas,* dedicating the volume to the institute's staff.

Madeline Slade, the British disciple and coworker of Gandhi, came to the United States in 1934. She gave a series of lectures on satyagraha and the Indian independence movement at Howard University. Her visit was well covered in the African American press.

Krishnalal Shridharani, one of those who accompanied Gandhi in the great salt march of 1931, entered graduate school at Columbia University in 1934. His dissertation on Gandhian nonviolence became the influential book *War without Violence: A Study of Gandhi's Method and Its Accomplishments.* Issued in 1939, Shridharani's book was essential reading for a generation of civil rights and peace activists. The Fellowship of Reconciliation published an abridged version in its journal *Fellowship.* Shridharani worked directly on several civil rights initiatives in the United States, including the early activities of the Congress of Race Equality (CORE).

The exchange between African American leaders and the Gandhian movement also went in the other direction, as several prominent African Americans went to visit Gandhi in India. The first group was a delegation that included Howard Thurman, dean of Rankin Chapel at Howard University, and his wife, Sue Bailey Thurman, a social historian and editor. The group had a three-hour meeting with Gandhi at his camp near Bardoli in February 1936. It was during this meeting that Gandhi uttered his prophetic comment: "It may be through the Negroes that the unadulterated message of nonviolence will be delivered to the world."[17] Upon their return, the Thurmans kept an active schedule of lectures and meetings to report on their encounter with Gandhi, delivering presentations in Chicago, Atlanta, Philadelphia, and other cities. Another delegation made the sojourn to India a few months later. It included Channing Tobias, a secretary of the YMCA and later chair of the board of directors of the NAACP, and Benjamin Mays, president of Morehouse College in Atlanta where King later studied as an undergraduate. Mays was a major influence on King's life and education. Upon his return, Mays wrote a series of articles for the *Norfolk Journal and Guide* and lectured widely on Gandhi's philosophy and method.

Another proponent of Gandhi's philosophy and method was Mordecai Johnson, longtime president of Howard University and one of the most prominent African American educators of his time. Mays called Johnson "one of the great prophets of the twentieth century."[18] Johnson encouraged the students at Howard University to study Gandhi as an alternative to communism. In a 1930 speech, he declared, "Gandhi is conducting the most significant religious movement in the world, in his attempt to inject religion into questions of economics and politics."[19] Johnson visited India in 1949, on a study tour to interview Gandhi's followers and examine his methods.

Howard University also connected to Gandhi through William Stuart Nelson, dean and vice president of the university. Nelson was a senior member of an American Friends Service Committee delegation that accompanied Gandhi on his arduous trek through Noakhali in northeast India in 1947 to quell Muslim-Hindu hatred. Nelson had the benefit of several "intimate and searching" conversations with Gandhi and thoroughly absorbed the principles of Gandhi's method.[20] He later published several works on Gandhi and lectured widely on nonviolent action. He introduced a course at Howard University on the philosophy and methods of nonviolence, one of the first of its kind in the United States. My own course, "The Strategy and Tactics of Nonviolent Social Change," follows Nelson's tradition. Nelson was a supporter of the civil rights movement and accompanied King on the march from Selma to Montgomery in 1965.

Another disciple of Gandhi was James Farmer, who studied Gandhi as a student at Howard University (under the guidance of Howard Thurman) and later helped found CORE. CORE was the first explicit civil rights organization in the United States. It was created by Farmer and other members of a biracial Gandhi study group in Chicago.[21] Farmer described it as "a coordinated movement of mass noncooperation as with Gandhi."[22] The charter of CORE specifically committed the organization to Gandhian principles, vowing to confront racial prejudice in the United States without fear, hatred, or violence. CORE pioneered the application of Gandhian techniques to the American problem of racial segregation. The group launched the first experiments with the sit-in method in Chicago during World War II. In 1947, it sponsored the first freedom ride, then called the Journey of Reconciliation. These early efforts did not attract the mass following of the later sit-ins and freedom rides of the civil rights movement, but they were important steps in the development of the Gandhian method in the United States.

Among the founders of CORE was Bayard Rustin, who later played an essential role in both the civil rights and the Vietnam antiwar movements. Rustin was the youth secretary of the Fellowship of Reconciliation for twelve years. During World War II, he protested Japanese internment and refused military service and was imprisoned for more than two years. After his release, he helped organize the Free India Committee and led sit-ins at the British Embassy in Washington, D.C. Rustin was invited to India in 1948 by the Indian National Congress and spent six months studying Gandhi's philosophy and strategy of action. He returned to the United States more determined than ever to spread the message of peace and justice, and to apply Gandhi's method of nonviolent resistance in America. He served for more than ten years as the executive secretary of the War Resisters League, using his position to urge greater linkages between the peace movement and the struggle for civil rights. In 1955, Rustin was invited to Montgomery, Alabama, as the historic bus boycott got under way. He provided crucial training and organizational expertise to King and his colleagues in Montgomery and for the next seven years served as King's special assistant. Rustin played a central role in the founding of the Southern Christian Leadership Conference (SCLC), the principal organization of the civil rights movement. He was the chief organizer of the 1963 march on Washington at which King gave his famous "I Have a Dream" speech. Rustin pioneered the adaptation of Gandhian methods to the cultural and social traditions of the United States. His contributions to the peace and civil rights movements were substantial, notwithstanding a controversial shift to the political right in his final years.

A Tool for Social Justice

The unique approach of Gandhi was his emphasis on mass action. Civil disobedience and other forms of nonviolent protest were known in the United States long before Gandhi's time, but they were usually the efforts of solitary intellectuals. The nonviolence of Garrison emphasized the individual's moral obligation to disobey the laws of slavery. Much of the civil disobedience that emerged during World War I was also on an individual basis. It was Gandhi who discovered in South Africa and India that masses of people could engage in organized nonviolence. By demonstrating the power of collective disobedience as a force for political change, he turned mass noncooperation into an instrument of political struggle against oppression.[23]

Reports of Gandhi's campaigns in the 1930s had an especially important impact on the generation of young activists who came to maturity during the Great Depression. This was the generation that confronted mass impoverishment in the United States and the rising threat of tyranny and militarism in Europe and Asia. The political left in America experienced tremendous growth during these years, as support for peace and social justice multiplied. Many activists were attracted to the Communist movement, but others objected to its methods. The skeptics admired the Communist Party's commitment to organizing workers and aiding the poor, including African Americans, but they could not accept its rejection of spirituality and its willingness to employ violent methods. For these activists Gandhi's theory and practice of nonviolent resistance offered a welcome alternative. They saw the Gandhian approach as a morally superior means of struggling for justice and resisting evil, far preferable to the manipulative methods of communism.

One of those who was attracted to Gandhi in the 1930s was radical activist David Dellinger. Then an undergraduate at Yale University, Dellinger saw the Gandhian method as a forceful and effective technique for confronting social evil without recourse to violence. In 1939, Dellinger joined with others to form the Newark Commune, also known as the Newark Ashram, a self-styled Gandhian community in the heart of the Newark ghetto that served the urban poor and sponsored campaigns for social justice.[24] This was the beginning of Dellinger's long career in nonviolent activism for peace and justice. Dellinger later went on to become one of the most influential figures in the U.S. peace movement, where he had a significant influence on me and others of the Vietnam generation. Dellinger was the editor of *Liberation* magazine, a leader of the Vietnam Mobilization Committee, one of the Chicago Eight defendants, and an active supporter of Mobilization for Survival and the Central America solidarity movement of the 1980s.

The Gandhian method appealed as well to A. J. Muste, another important peace leader of the twentieth century. Muste was ordained a minister in the Dutch Reformed Church of America in 1909 and in World War I became a pacifist, joining the Fellowship of Reconciliation. In 1919, Muste supported the great textile strike in Lawrence, Massachusetts, and for the next twenty years was a leading labor organizer and educator, helping develop the sit-down strike method that gave birth to industrial unionism in the United States. In the 1930s, Muste embraced Marxism-Leninism and founded the American Workers Party, which allied with the Trotskyists. By 1936, Muste became disillusioned with Trotskyism and rejected the Marxist approach. He returned to his original religious pacifist convictions and resumed his involvement with the Fellowship of Reconciliation. Gandhi's example helped Muste make the transition from Marxism-Leninism back to nonviolence. "The main thing Gandhi did for me was ... in giving me inspiration through his successful application of nonviolent action in a large-scale political situation."[25] Inspired by the example of Gandhi and the Indian independence movement, Muste saw radical nonviolence as a politically powerful, morally superior alternative to Marxism: "I knew by 1936 that I could no longer apply the techniques of Lenin and Trotsky because they violated my personal convictions. Watching Gandhi achieve political ends in a way with which I could agree was enormously encouraging. . . . It was Gandhi who confronted Lenin in this era."[26]

Shridharani's *War without Violence* was crucial in awakening Muste to the importance of Gandhianism: "I wrote and talked about [the book] and was influential in getting other pacifists to read it. . . . His book was a sociological and political study of Gandhi's movement, not just an inspirational tract. It was in line with my own long-term conviction that pacifism had to be related to social and political realities."[27]

Muste became the executive secretary of the Fellowship of Reconciliation in 1940, and from that position he tirelessly spread the message of Gandhian nonviolence within the American peace community and beyond.[28] In 1949, he visited India for the first time and became even more convinced that Gandhian techniques could be applied on a mass basis to prevent war.[29] He led many peace campaigns and encouraged the use of civil disobedience, conscientious objection, and war tax resistance. At the end of his life in 1967, he was a leading force in the growing Vietnam antiwar movement.

Gandhi's influence also extended to A. Philip Randolph, president of the most influential African American labor union, the Brotherhood of Sleeping Car Porters. Randolph was a major leader of the U.S. labor movement and of the African American community for nearly half a century. In many respects, Randolph was an unlikely Gandhian. He was no pacifist and did not share Gandhi's religious and spiritual principles. He seemed at the time more Marxist than Gandhian. Yet he, too, adopted nonviolent methods as the most practical and potentially effective strategy for achieving social and racial justice.[30]

In the 1940s, Randolph launched the March on Washington movement to demand jobs for African Americans and the desegregation of the armed forces. He proposed a mass march on Washington and a campaign of civil disobedience to pressure the federal government into permitting African Americans to contribute to the war effort on an equal footing. In speeches before mass rallies in Chicago and other cities, Randolph referred to the Indian independence movement and promoted Gandhi's method of mass noncooperation. In a 1943 series of articles in the *Chicago Defender,* he explicitly linked his movement to Gandhi and spelled out how nonviolent action and mass civil disobedience could be used to overcome economic and racial injustice in the United States. He thoroughly integrated the core principles of Gandhianism into his March on Washington movement.[31] For various reasons, Randolph never carried through on the plan for a march on Washington during World War II. Twenty years later, however, he was one of the principal organizers and supporters of King's March on Washington.

The Struggle for Peace

Gandhi's influence has also been substantial within the religious pacifist community: the Quakers, Mennonites, and Brethren. These pacifist churches have a tradition of refusing military service and have assumed a large role in U.S. peace campaigns, notwithstanding the small size of their congregations. The Quakers have been particularly influential and through the American Friends Service Committee (AFSC) have been at the heart of every major peace movement in modern American history—the Ban the Bomb movement, the Vietnam antiwar movement, the Nuclear Weapons Freeze campaign of the 1980s, and the movements for peace in Central America and the Middle East. AFSC national secretary Clarence Pickett was a founder of the Committee for a SANE Nuclear Policy (SANE) in 1957, and AFSC staffers Pam Solo and Terry Provance helped create the Nuclear Weapons Freeze campaign in 1981.[32] The American Friends Service Committee has been a leading voice for nonviolence in the United States for more than seventy-five years.

The Friends were naturally attracted to Gandhi and his use of nonviolence as a means of social change for justice. The British Quaker leader Horace Alexander was a longtime friend and frequent correspondent of Gandhi, and author of *Gandhi through Western Eyes.*[33] The founder of the AFSC, Rufus Jones, also acknowledged "my debt to this wonderful man" and wrote that Gandhi "had a profound influence on my own philosophy of life and on my actual *way* of life [emphasis in original]."[34] Jones visited Gandhi at his ashram in Ahmedabad in 1926.

There he not only learned the methods of satyagraha but had the opportunity to deepen the Mahatma's knowledge of Christian pacifism. Jones introduced Gandhi to St. Francis of Assisi and also recounted for him the life and deeds of John Woolman, the outstanding American Quaker of the eighteenth century who practiced nonviolent resistance against British persecution. Gandhi reportedly told Jones that it was a Quaker in South Africa, Michael Coates, who introduced him to the Sermon on the Mount and gave him an intimate understanding of Jesus' Gospel of love.[35]

Unlike other pacifists, Quakers do not shy away from confronting social evil. They have a tradition of "speaking truth to power" rather than withdrawing from the affairs of state and society. William Penn, the Quaker founder of Pennsylvania, said that "true godliness" does not turn men out of the world but "excites their endeavors to mend it."[36] Gandhi's open disobedience of British colonial laws echoed a tradition of Quaker resistance to unjust authority dating back to the community's founding in seventeenth-century England and its early struggles for freedom in America. Gandhi's abhorrence of war and his use of nonviolent methods were completely compatible with Quaker beliefs and methods.[37] One author claims that the idea of nonviolent resistance "began with the Quakers ... and was finally put into action by Mahatma Gandhi. To complete the cycle, present-day Quakers have taken up its study and practice."[38]

One of those who studied Gandhianism was AFSC staffer James Bristol, who spent two years in India in the 1950s working with Gandhi's followers. Bristol was an escort for Martin Luther King Jr. during his visit to India in 1959. Many other Quakers studied Gandhi's method and sought to apply it to the political issues and social conditions of the United States.

Gandhi's ideas also exerted influence among Mennonites, an Anabaptist community that first emigrated to North America from Switzerland and Germany in the sixteenth century. In recent decades, Mennonites have played an active role in activist campaigns for peace and justice. This was not always the case, however. The traditional Mennonite approach was to avoid conflict. The central concept was nonresistance. Following from the Gospel injunction to "resist not evil," Mennonites and other pacifists tended to withdraw from violence and evil. They preferred to live a quiet existence as farmers in isolated rural communities and to register as conscientious objectors to military service.

This approach was reflected in Guy F. Hershberger's classic, *War, Peace, and Nonresistance,* published in 1944. A leading Mennonite religious teacher, Hershberger argued that the Gospel is "entirely nonpolitical" and even claimed that the victims of Nazi oppression in Europe must "suffer in subjection rather than to violate the principle of nonresistance." Hershberger saw the Gandhian method as distinct from Christian pacifism. Disobedience to the state should not include "pressure methods to force the government's hands," he asserted.[39] Because Gandhi's method was coercive and applied pressure on wrongdoers rather than withdrawing from evil, Hershberger considered it beyond the pale.

In recent decades, however, Mennonites have become increasingly uncomfortable with the limitations of traditional nonresistance. Many are unwilling to stand by in the face of war and tyranny. After World War II, these feelings became especially acute. The usual approach of simply opting out of military service through conscientious objection became less acceptable. Many felt if not guilt at least a sense of inadequacy in standing aside from the great social struggles against racism, oppression, and war. They yearned for an approach that would permit resistance to evil while remaining true to the principles of nonviolence. For many of these Mennonite and Brethren believers, Gandhi's ideas and method provided a welcome solution to the contradictions of pure pacifism. Gandhi offered a means of forcefully confronting social evil while adhering to nonviolence. His ideas stood as a shining beacon, lighting the way through the darkness, promising a new tradition of active nonviolent engagement against war and oppression.

Gandhi's influence has also been substantial among Catholic pacifists, who are important members of the peace community in the United States and elsewhere. Today's Catholic peace movement owes much to Dorothy Day and the founders of the Catholic Worker, who in turn were influenced by Gandhi and his commitment to nonviolence. Combining a radical commitment to social justice with a deep dedication to pacifism, the Catholic Worker movement emerged during the Great Depression to minister to the needs of the unemployed, while simultaneously challenging the structural causes of poverty. Gandhi's pacifism, his personal poverty, and his struggles on behalf of "the least of these" matched perfectly the Catholic Worker ethos. So did his religiously based motivation. Catholics well understood the virtue of suffering, made familiar by the practice of penance to redeem sin. Perhaps most significant were the successes Gandhi enjoyed, which demonstrated that nonviolent methods could achieve results.[40] Activists in the 1930s intensely debated whether to use violent or nonviolent methods. This became a voting issue within the Socialist Party and the Fellowship of Reconciliation. Gandhi's proof that nonviolence could be a powerful tool of social change helped attract support to the Catholic Worker cause and gave legitimacy to nonviolent methods generally.[41]

The integration of Gandhianism into the Catholic peace movement has had enduring consequences. The modern antinuclear peace movement emerged in the 1950s from protests against compulsory civil defense training led by Day.[42] These early actions raised public awareness of the insanity of the nuclear arms race and helped spark the emergence of a broader disarmament movement. SANE, Women's Strike for Peace, and the Council for a Livable World were founded at this time.[43] When the United States waged war on Vietnam, Day and the Catholic peace movement were actively involved in the earliest antiwar protests. The example of Day and her colleagues inspired the founding of Pax Christi, the Catholic pacifist organization. Day continued to speak out against war and injustice right up to her last days in 1980, constantly espousing her unique blend of radical Christianity and Gandhianism. Her legacy of nonviolent resistance to militarism was inherited, according to activist priest Daniel Berrigan, "from Gandhi, King, and, above all, Jesus."[44]

Pax Christi played a crucial behind-the-scenes role in molding the peace pastoral letter of the U.S. Catholic bishops in 1983.[45] The bishops' pastoral *The Challenge of Peace* condemned nuclear weapons and critiqued the assumptions underlying the Reagan arms buildup. The bishops based their case against nuclear weapons primarily on just war criteria, but they also acknowledged the merits of nonviolence. In their discussion of the "value of nonviolence," the bishops' letter credited "the non-Christian witness of Mahatma Gandhi and its worldwide impact."[46]

The bishops' pastoral gave a significant boost to the nuclear freeze movement. For those of us who were active in the disarmament campaigns of the 1980s, this intervention from the Catholic bishops, with help from Pax Christi, seemed like manna from heaven—almost literally. The bishops cast a mantle of respectability over the nuclear freeze movement. No one could question the anticommunist credentials of the Catholic bishops. Their letter spread the message of disarmament far beyond the usual peace community. The bishops concluded their pastoral letter by repeating words from Pope John Paul II that Gandhi would have approved: "The whole world must summon the moral courage and technical means to say 'no' to nuclear conflict; 'no' to weapons of mass destruction; 'no' to an arms race which robs the poor and the vulnerable; and 'no' to the moral danger of a nuclear age which places before humankind indefensible choices of constant terror or surrender. Peacemaking is not an optional commitment. It is a requirement of our faith."[47]

Chapter 3

Martin Luther King Jr.: An American Gandhi

Martin Luther King Jr. was one of the greatest prophets of nonviolence in U.S. history and the most significant interpreter of Gandhianism for many Americans. It was through King that many of us came to understand the power of the nonviolent method and its relevance to the contemporary problems of American society, especially the dilemma of race. King successfully adapted the Gandhian method to the U.S. civil rights movement and changed the course of history.

Gandhi's Example

King's interest in Gandhi was initially academic. His adviser and favorite professor at Crozer Seminary was George W. Davis, a pacifist and ardent admirer of Gandhi who encouraged King's study. King knew of Gandhi and, like many African Americans, was greatly impressed by his accomplishments, but he was skeptical of pacifism and doubted that love alone could be a force for social change.[1] The success of the Indian independence movement helped overcome that skepticism and seemed to show that Gandhian nonviolent resistance could be a potent political tool. The victory of the Indian independence movement reinforced the deep respect for Gandhi that already existed, especially in the African American community, and together with his assassination brought new attention to the meaning of his life. As Andrew Young, King's longtime assistant, phrased it, "Gandhi's monsoon, the independence of India, was stirring up tornadoes in America."[2]

King's interest in Gandhi was piqued in 1950, when he attended a lecture in Philadelphia by the president of Howard University, Mordecai Johnson, who had just returned from a visit to India. Johnson provided an in-depth account of the Mahatma's teachings and his methods of nonviolent action. King described Johnson's lecture as "profound and electrifying" and said that he went out and bought a "half-dozen" books on Gandhi's life and message.[3] Thus began an intensive interest in Gandhi that carried through his graduate studies and continued during his years of activism for civil rights.

King's reading of Gandhi was essential to his intellectual formation and the development of his thinking on nonviolent action. Ironically, Gandhi helped restore his belief in the power of Christian love. Like so many others, King saw Christ's message of love as pertaining primarily to interpersonal relationships. He doubted that it could have political implications or be taken as a solution to problems of social injustice. How could one turn the cheek in the face of Nazi oppression or when confronted with racial brutality in his native South? During his academic studies, King read the work of philosopher Friedrich Nietzsche and was "temporarily shaken" by his critique of Christian morality as weak and impotent.[4] The meekness of the lamb, Nietzsche argued, is an invitation to slaughter. King sought to transcend this challenge by combining the Christian commitment to love with determined resistance to racial injustice. His study of Gandhi helped him reach that synthesis. He realized that the expression of love in nonviolent action, far from being a sign of weakness, was a potent force for social change.[5] As King wrote, "Gandhi was probably the first person in history to lift the love ethic of Jesus above mere interaction between individuals to a powerful and effective social force on a large scale. Love for Gandhi was a potent instrument for social and collective transformation. It was in this Gandhian emphasis on love and nonviolence that I discovered the method for social reform that I had been seeking for so many months."[6] When the Montgomery bus boycott began in 1955, King wrote, "I was driven back to the Sermon on the Mount with its sublime teachings on love, and to the Gandhian method of nonviolent resistance."[7]

King not only derived from Gandhi his philosophical commitment to nonviolence but many of the specific methods of nonviolent action he and his colleagues employed in the civil rights movement. He considered the Gandhian method of nonviolence "one of the most potent weapons available to an oppressed people in their struggle for freedom."[8] Nietzsche's view was too limited, he realized. There is no inherent contradiction between Christian love and the will to power.

What impressed King about the Gandhian method was not only its success in winning independence but its ability to achieve victory without stirring the rancor and bitterness that often result from revolutionary change. Gandhi had once predicted that the British would some day simply pack up and go home without anger or violence, and that is exactly what happened. The peaceful and even amicable way in which the British handed over power in 1947 was in some respects as significant as the winning of independence itself. This double victory of Gandhi reinforced King's belief that the nonviolent method could reconcile the twin requirements of love and resistance to evil. King appropriated the method and many of the core principles of Gandhianism in his struggle for racial justice in the United States. He was indeed "the American Gandhi" of which African American journalists had written. He was the person who more than any other brought to life Gandhi's ideas and methods and developed nonviolent action as an effective instrument of political change.[9]

Christian Roots

While King was influenced by Gandhi, the fundamental inspiration for his commitment to nonviolence came from the Gospel. As the son, grandson, and great-grandson of Baptist preachers, King was inevitably steeped in the Christian tradition. He saw nonviolence and the commandment to love as the essential core of Christ's teaching. Indeed, his attraction to the Gandhian method was strengthened by its embrace of these principles. As King said, "I went to Gandhi through Jesus."[10]

A major influence on King's thinking was the philosophy of personalism. King went to Boston University for his doctorate to study with Edgar S. Brightman and L. Harold DeWolf, leading proponents of this school of thought. Personalism espouses the concept of a personal God and emphasizes the centrality of the person in the divine creation. King described personalism as "the theory that the clue to the meaning of ultimate reality is found in personality."[11] Our encounter with God, King believed, comes not from metaphysical abstraction but from personal experience. The most fundamental fact of existence is the person, the thinking self. This is also how to conceptualize God: as ultimate personhood, as the mind and source of order in the universe. The concept of personalism is difficult to understand for some of us, for it seems to imply that God has specific human characteristics. But if we view personalism as more of an intellectual construct than an exact representation of reality, it becomes clearer and more meaningful. Personalism is a way of translating the impenetrably abstract concept of an all-powerful creator into terms that can be grasped by the human mind. The concept of personality is the closest approximation we have to understanding the divine presence at the center of the universe and at the core of our being.

If ultimate reality is characterized by personality, then the human person takes on ultimate significance. A person is the reflection of the image of God, with inherent worth and goodness. This belief is reflected in philosopher Immanuel Kant's famous ethical imperative, that a person must be treated "always as an end, never merely as a means."[12]

Philosopher Martin Buber deepened this Kantian ethic, defining it in existential terms. In an I-Thou relationship we encounter the other authentically, as a full, complete person. In the relationship of I and Thou a sacred interconnectedness is affirmed.[13] In an I-It relationship, on the other hand, we view the other as object. This is the stance of the racist, who views the other as "It," never as "Thou."[14] To encounter another authentically, Buber wrote, is to forego all designs and instrumental purposes. It is to give of self in order to understand and appreciate the other.[15] This stance precludes the use or exploitation of another. It elevates personhood to supreme importance, placing the human being in all her or his particularity at the center of the universe.[16] It makes the well-being of another person the ultimate end of human endeavor, surpassing all other purposes or ideologies. This personalist philosophy gave King a theological basis for his belief in the dignity and value of each person. It also strengthened the case for a social order that treats all people fairly and that provides opportunity for each person to achieve her or his God-given potential.[17]

As King came to understand the social implications of Christ's teachings, he placed increased emphasis on the obligation to care for the oppressed and overcome injustice. In this he was following the tradition of the social gospel movement, which holds that Christ's message has a social as well as an individual dimension.[18] The writings of Walter Rauschenbusch left an "indelible imprint" on King's thinking.[19] Rauschenbusch was a pastor and theologian whose ministry among the poor in New York's Hell's Kitchen area in the late nineteenth century led him to found the social gospel movement, which emphasized the Christian duty to promote social justice. Religion must be concerned not only with personal morality, Rauschenbusch taught, but with social and economic justice. Rauschenbusch gave King a theological basis for the social concerns he had acquired growing up as a sensitive African American confronting racial abuse. It is not enough merely to struggle against evil in our personal lives. Our faith also calls us to eliminate social evil. Jesus identified with "the least of these" and frequently spoke to the needs of the downtrodden. In his first sermon at Nazareth, Jesus announced his ministry as bringing "good news to the poor." As Jim Wallis emphasizes, the primary message of the Bible is deliverance for the poor and the oppressed.[20]

Christ sought to bring justice and the spirit of love into a broken world.[21] The church, as the embodiment of Christ, has an obligation to carry on this mission, said Rauschenbusch. The church should be "bravest to speak against every wrong, and strongest to rally the moral forces of the community."[22] These teachings strengthened King's conviction that his vocation as a minister of the church was to commit himself to the struggle for social justice. A church that fails to address social conditions, King believed, is "spiritually moribund," lacking in meaning and purpose. As he wrote, "a religion that ends with the individual, ends."[23] Christianity is not merely about piety and the hereafter but about love and social justice here on Earth.

Martin Luther King Jr. at a Southern Christian Leadership Conference staff meeting, April 1964 (photo: Flip Schulke/CORBIS).

Too often, King believed, the church fails in its mission to society. It is too timid in the face of injustice. King's "Letter from a Birmingham Jail" was written to Alabama clergymen who had appealed for moderation and opposed "extreme" actions. In response to their plea for patience, King recounted the indignities of segregation that had persisted for nearly a century and the barbarities of slavery before that. He decried those who stand aside in the face of great injustices, "merely mouth[ing] pious irrelevancies and sanctimonious trivialities."[24] While he was disappointed at the complacency and timidity of the established church, King acknowledged the many people "from the ranks of organized religion" who broke loose from "the paralyzing chains of conformity" and joined the freedom movement. Many clergy and lay workers participated in marches, freedom rides, and other actions. Some faced real danger, and others were rebuked by their church. King called their witness "the spiritual salt that has preserved the true meaning of the Gospel."[25]

Toward a "Realistic Pacifism"

The personalists and Rauschenbusch were firmly in the camp of Christian idealism. They saw human nature as divinely ordered and perfectible. King was greatly influenced by this view, but he could never accept the "superficial optimism" about human nature that sometimes characterized these philosophies.[26] When he read Reinhold Niebuhr, he was strengthened in his skepticism. King described Niebuhr as a "prime influence" on his thinking, and he spent much of his time in graduate school studying Niebuhr and the implications of his philosophy.[27] King scholar Taylor Branch contends that Niebuhr affected King more deeply than any other figure, including Gandhi.[28]

King agreed with Niebuhr's emphasis on the reality of evil.[29] He was especially conscious of social evil, which he described as "stark, grim and colossally real."[30] As an African American suffering the degrading abuses of racial segregation, King was all too aware of the human capacity for evil. His personal experiences and his reading of Niebuhr and the Bible led him to adopt a more nuanced approach to nonviolence. The teachings of Jesus and the Hebrew prophets reinforced King's understanding of the problem of human sinfulness and the power of God's love to bring healing. The Gospel commands us to be nonviolent, King agreed, but it also calls us to resist evil and injustice. From these influences, King adopted what he called a "realistic pacifism." He retained a strong commitment to nonviolence, but this was tempered by a realization of the limitations of human nature.[31]

King also came to recognize that ethical appeals alone could not guarantee justice and that coercive pressure may be necessary to achieve social change. As Niebuhr observed, human reasoning is constrained by self-interest. "Even the most rational men are never quite rational when their own interests are at stake."[32] It is not reason but power that determines politics, Niebuhr taught. Power "continues to exploit weakness until it is challenged by countervailing power."[33] These insights helped King recognize that social power would have to be added to moral reasoning if political change is to occur. It is utopian to believe that ethical appeals alone will bring justice. "This does not mean that ethical appeals should not be made," King wrote. "It simply means that those appeals must be undergirded by some form of constructive power."[34] The quest to build this "constructive" power through nonviolent social action became a central purpose of his life.

The Power of Love

Christ's injunction to "love your enemies" is the most difficult of Christ's commands, King believed, but it is also the most important. Through the power to love even our enemies, we appeal to that divine spark of goodness that exists in every person and that is necessary to overcome the forces of evil. Although King was a Niebuhrian realist, he was not completely pessimistic about human nature. King shared Gandhi's view that "no human being is so bad as to be beyond redemption."[35] He believed that even the most ardent segregationist had a potential for goodness and could be reached through the power of love. Like the force of magnetism, love has a unique power to attract. In some instances, it can draw the adversary to our side. Even when it does not affect the adversary, it attracts the support of bystanders and third parties and helps win support for the nonviolent cause. Love is the strongest form of human energy and has transformative power both personally and socially.

The love that King emphasized was not aesthetic or filial love but the deeper, selfless love of *agape*, that "overflowing love which is purely spontaneous, unmotivated, groundless, and creative."[36] It is a "disinterested love," he wrote. Love for the sake of love, the unrestrained giving of self. Agape is similar to the Hindu concept of nonattachment, which played such a central role in Gandhi's thinking. In the Eastern tradition, spiritual fulfillment comes through complete selflessness and detachment from the fruits of labor. Love and sacrifice are offered entirely for their own sake, without thought of reward. Agape is equally demanding. King considered agape the love of God working in the human heart, the capacity to love others not because of what they may do for or against me but because they are children of God. Agape is the means through which we seek to mold the human community in God's image. It enables us to love the person who commits evil even as we resist the evil being committed. Said King, "At this level we love the person who does an evil deed, although we hate the deed that he does."[37]

Like Gandhi, King conceived of this selfless love as proactive. Agape is not passive but active, an affirmative commitment. The command to love, King wrote, is also a command to act, to resist evil and work for justice.[38] Just as Gandhi believed that the Hindu principle of ahimsa requires active opposition to evil, so King believed that the Christian concept of agape includes an obligation to work for social justice. "My study of Gandhi convinced me that true pacifism is not nonresistance to evil, but nonviolent resistance to evil. Between the two positions there is a world of difference. Gandhi resisted evil with as much vigor and power as the violent resister, but he resisted with love instead of hate."[39] In the Gandhian method King found a positive means of overcoming injustice through the power of love, a method "passive physically but strongly active spiritually."[40] It was the key to his realistic pacifism, a means of resisting social evil through assertive yet nonviolent means.

Gandhi also reinforced King's belief in the essential compatibility of ends and means. "Nonviolence demands that the means we use must be as pure as the ends we seek," King wrote.[41] One cannot achieve a just result with unjust means, a peaceful result with violent means. This belief was the basis of King's rejection of communism. While King was attracted to Marxism's concern for economic justice—"its protest against the hardships of the underprivileged"—he condemned the ethical relativism of communism. The notion that the end justifies the means, that an equitable society could be achieved by immoral or violent means, was utterly repulsive to King. "In the long run," he asserted, "destructive means cannot bring about constructive ends because the end is preexistent in the means."[42]

King believed that nonviolence could turn adversaries into allies. The goal is not to defeat but to convert the adversary, to forge unity out of division. In *Stride toward Freedom* he wrote, nonviolence "does not seek to defeat or humiliate the opponent, but to win his friendship and understanding.... The end is redemption and reconciliation."[43] King recognized that blacks and whites would have to continue living together in the same communities when the civil rights movement was over. It was essential to wage the struggle in a way that would preserve the prospects for cooperation and harmony in the future. As Dave Dellinger wrote at the time, the strategy of nonviolence "must flow from an understanding of the underlying unity of all human beings.... Real nonviolence requires an understanding that white oppressors and black victims are mutually entrapped in a set of relationships that violate the submerged best instincts of everyone."[44] The nonviolent method provides a way of freeing both sides. It helped win freedom for blacks while also liberating whites from the burdens of participating in an unjust system of racism.

Divine Inspiration

Underlying King's commitment to nonviolent social change was a conviction that the struggle for justice is God's work, that it helps fulfill the divine plan for the universe. In many of his speeches and sermons King proclaimed that "the arc of the moral universe is long, but it bends toward justice." He believed that God works through and in history. The struggle against the forces of evil not only reveals God's purpose but is made possible by God's infinite power to actualize the good.[45] King found support for this concept in Old Testament teachings that emphasize the duty of humans to work in partnership with God to vanquish injustice.[46] God has a plan for the universe, he believed, and it is our duty as humans to help fulfill this purpose and speed the coming of a more just and loving social order. John Lewis termed this concept the "spirit of history." According to Lewis, there is a "moral force of the universe" that is "on the side of what is ... right and just."[47] This spirit acts through human beings who are prepared to surrender themselves to the inexorable power of this larger moral force.

This idea of human beings working to fulfill God's will was embodied in the concept of "the Beloved Community," which King defined as a society where "brotherhood is a reality," a community of love and justice.[48] Lewis defined the Beloved Community as "the kingdom of God on earth," the belief that human existence inexorably strives toward a community of greater love and cooperation.[49] According to religion professors Kenneth Smith and Ira Zepp (Smith taught King at Crozer Seminary), the vision of the Beloved Community was "the organizing principle of all of King's thought and activity."[50]

It connected his commitment to social justice here on Earth with his belief in a divinely ordained order in the universe.

The concept of the Beloved Community was not just a millennial hope, however. It was the goal of the struggle for justice in the here and now. As King wrote, "Many have attempted to say that the ideal of a better world will be worked out in the next world. But Jesus taught men to say 'Thy will be done on earth as it is in heaven.'"[51] According to Lewis, believers in the Beloved Community insist that it is the "moral responsibility of men and women with soul force ... to struggle nonviolently against the forces that stand between a society and the harmony it naturally seeks."[52]

King was strongly influenced in these beliefs by Abraham Joshua Heschel, one of the most important Jewish thinkers of the twentieth century. In his seminal book, *God in Search of Man*, Heschel argued that God is intimately involved in human affairs and is in search of humans to serve the divine purpose. Heschel developed a theology of "divine pathos" in which God is concerned with and acts through human history.[53] Human beings serve God through the search for truth and the quest for a more compassionate and just society. When the divine spirit tugs at our conscience, it is our moral duty to follow, to give ourselves selflessly to others. The commitment to social justice was, in Heschel's view, an act of worship. He practiced what he preached and was an active opponent of the Vietnam War and supporter of the civil rights movement. One of the most famous photos of the civil rights era shows Heschel, arm in arm with King, marching in the famous pilgrimage from Selma to Montgomery in March 1965. For Heschel that experience of marching with King had spiritual meaning: "I felt as though my legs were praying."[54]

While King believed that God is immanent in history, he was careful to distinguish between the perfection of the divine and the imperfection of the human. He was too deeply schooled in Niebuhrian pessimism to ignore human sinfulness. Our moral pilgrimage may not reach its destination, King wrote, and the kingdom of God will remain "not yet."[55] King thus transcended both the facile optimism of the pacifists and the excessive pessimism of Niebuhr to fashion a creative synthesis. He combined a belief in the divine guidance of history with an insistence on the necessary commitment of human beings to help bring about this divine purpose.

Civil rights leaders Ralph Abernathy, Martin Luther King Jr., former UN ambassador Ralph Bunche, and Rabbi Abraham Joshua Heschel (left to right) during the march from Selma to Montgomery, Alabama, March 1965 (photo: Bettmann/CORBIS).

A belief in divine purpose does not mean that the Beloved Community will evolve on its own. There is no certainty that communities of love will emerge naturally in the course of time. King warned against what he called "the myth of time"—the belief that progress unfolds inevitably in history. White moderates in Birmingham condemned the assertive actions of the civil rights movement, arguing that the time was not right, that African Americans should wait. It's only a matter of time, they claimed, until segregation collapses. King sharply rejected such views. "This 'wait' has almost always meant 'never,'" he objected. Negroes have endured hundreds of years of abuse and humiliation, he wrote, and still find themselves "harried by day and haunted by night." When the "cup of endurance runs over," he pleaded, there is "legitimate and unavoidable impatience."[56] With Rauschenbusch, King believed that God calls us to the kingdom but that human effort must bring it into being.[57] "Justice never rolls in on the wheels of inevitability," he wrote. It comes about through the tireless efforts of men and women "willing to be co-workers with God."[58] King agreed with the former slave and abolitionist leader Frederick Douglass, who famously proclaimed in 1857:

> The whole history of the progress of human liberty shows that all concessions ... have been born of earnest struggle.... If there is no struggle, there is no progress; those who profess to favor freedom and yet deprecate agitation are men who want crops without ploughing the ground; they want rain without thunder and lightning. They want the ocean without the awful roar of its many waters.... Power concedes nothing without a demand. It never did and it never will.[59]

Sacrifice

Like Gandhi, King believed that the nonviolent activist must be prepared to sacrifice and suffer for the cause of justice. As he wrote in *Stride toward Freedom*, "the nonviolent resister is willing to accept violence if necessary, but never to inflict it."[60] King frequently emphasized that "unearned suffering is redemptive." He found theological foundation for this belief in Christ's suffering and death on the cross, which was meant to redeem the sins of the world. As children of God, he believed, we also must bear a cross of suffering. Our individual and collective human suffering has redemptive power and can partially atone for social evil. A willingness to sacrifice is crucial to the moral power of the nonviolent method. This moral power is exerted not only on the adversary but on those who are bystanders in a dispute and who might be motivated to support the nonviolent cause because of the courageous suffering of the activists. According to Lewis, the sufferer must have "a graceful heart" and hold no malice toward those who inflict suffering.[61]

Sacrifice requires courage, King emphasized. Like Gandhi, he believed that overcoming fear is the essential requirement for nonviolent action. King recognized the importance of courage both in practical terms and in a deeper theological sense. His doctoral dissertation focused in part on the thinking of theologian Paul Tillich, whose masterful *The Courage to Be* emphasizes the necessity of affirming ourselves ontologically despite our finitude and the certainty of death.[62] King faced death threats constantly in his public ministry and was gunned down by an assassin at the age of thirty-nine. He frequently evoked the possibility of death, both in public (his "I've been to the mountain top" speech) and in meetings with his closest aides. He always reminded his colleagues of the necessity of sacrifice. The nonviolent method is not for cowards, he emphasized. He agreed with Gandhi that if the choice is only cowardice or violence, it would be better to choose violence. "As much as I deplore violence," King said, "there is one evil that is worse than violence, and that's cowardice."[63] Courage and sacrifice are key to successful nonviolent action, the means to redemption and reconciliation. King captured this idea magnificently in the following response to segregationist violence from the Birmingham "Letter":

> We shall match your capacity to inflict suffering with our capacity to endure suffering. We shall meet your physical force with soul force. Do to us what you will, and we shall continue to love you.... Throw us in jail, and we shall still love you. Bomb our homes and threaten our children, and we shall still love you. Send your hooded perpetrators of violence into our community at the midnight hour and beat us and leave us half-dead, and we shall still love you. But be assured that we will wear you down by our capacity to suffer. One day we shall win freedom, but not only for ourselves. We shall so appeal to your heart and conscience that we shall win you in the process, and our victory will be a double victory.[64]

Learning by Doing

King's scholarly training prepared him well for the embrace of nonviolent action, but it was the actual experience of the civil rights movement that sealed his commitment to Gandhi's philosophy and method. King learned by doing and in the process became the world's most important proponent of nonviolent resistance. The civil rights movement became the first successful mass application of the Gandhian method in the United States and a beacon of hope to advocates of nonviolent change throughout the world. According to Andrew Young, the civil rights movement created "a new togetherness, a new communion.... No more was there the feeling that lonely, individual, uncoordinated, modest protest actions or voter registration drives in out-of-the-way towns would only bring reprisals or violence to no greater end. Now ... these individuals were part of a larger whole that was moving—thus the deeper connotation of the word 'movement.'"[65]

When the Montgomery bus boycott began in 1955, King wrote, the guiding philosophy of the movement was Christian love as articulated in the Sermon on the Mount.[66] Gandhian doctrines of nonviolence and mass noncooperation were not mentioned. But references to Gandhi soon began to appear. A letter to the *Montgomery Advertiser* compared the bus boycott to the Gandhian movement in India. A growing number of observers saw a direct comparison between King's methods and those of Gandhi, drawing parallels between the civil rights movement and the Indian independence struggle.[67] By the end of the boycott, according to King, the name of Gandhi was well-known in Montgomery, and the leaders of the movement were consciously applying Gandhian methods to the struggle against racial oppression.[68]

The Montgomery boycott attracted widespread support. Two who traveled to Alabama and helped enlarge King's understanding of the Gandhian method were Bayard Rustin and Glen Smiley. Rustin arrived in Montgomery a couple of months after the beginning of the boycott and became a valued adviser and assistant to King during the campaign and afterward. During several long conversations with King in which he drew on his own experiences and travel to India, Rustin explained the principles and methods of Gandhian nonviolence. Smiley, a minister who also worked with the Fellowship of Reconciliation, came to Montgomery at approximately the same time and had similar opportunities to discuss Gandhianism and the theory of nonviolence with King. When he first asked King about his familiarity with Gandhi, King confided that he knew "very little" about him.[69] Smiley supplied additional books and pamphlets and guided King toward a deeper understanding of and commitment to the Gandhian method.

As King's appreciation of Gandhi intensified, he became interested in going to India and learning firsthand about the Mahatma's accomplishments. Rustin and others encouraged King to make such a trip. Prime Minister Jawaharlal Nehru traveled to the United States on a state visit in 1956, just as the

Montgomery boycott was gaining international recognition, and publicly expressed the wish that King would visit India. Chester Bowles, former U.S. ambassador to India, wrote King to encourage the trip. Another who supported the idea and helped make it possible was Harris Wofford, who later served in the White House during the Kennedy administration and for a time was a U.S. senator from Pennsylvania. The hope of Rustin, Wofford, and others was that King would absorb Gandhianism more fully and use the trip to build on the experience of Montgomery in creating a stronger, more vibrant civil rights movement in the United States.

After several delays, the trip finally came in February 1959. Said King, "To other countries I may go as a tourist, but to India I come as a pilgrim."[70] The American Friends Service Committee helped make the visit possible, through a grant from the Christopher Reynolds Foundation. King was accompanied by his wife, Coretta Scott King, and by Lawrence Reddick, who had written a biography of King, *Crusader without Violence.* The trip began inauspiciously, however, as the trio missed a plane connection in Europe because of fog and arrived in India two days late.[71] The delay stranded an awaiting crowd at the New Delhi airport and forced Prime Minister Nehru to cancel a state dinner he had prepared in King's honor. When the King party finally arrived, Nehru graciously rescheduled the dinner, after which he and King reportedly spent long hours discussing Gandhi and the problems of the world.[72] The rest of the trip went smoothly, and the King party was greeted warmly and enthusiastically. King was hailed as the hero of the Montgomery bus boycott and the pioneer of Gandhian nonviolence in the United States. He met with Gandhi's son and grandsons, spoke with many of the Mahatma's colleagues and disciples, and visited his ashrams and the many memorials to his life and accomplishments.

King's visit to India widened his social vision and deepened his commitment to nonviolence. As he wrote, "I left India more convinced than ever before that nonviolent resistance is the most potent weapon available to oppressed people in the struggle for freedom."[73] He acquired a more sophisticated understanding of the power of disciplined nonviolence to bring about social and political change.[74] He longed for the creation of a dedicated cadre of activists who could apply Gandhi's ideas in the United States. He wanted to encourage a long-term commitment to social change. "We shall have to have people tied together in a long-term relationship," he said, "instead of the evanescent enthusiasts who lose their experience, spirit and unity because they have no mechanism that directs them to new tasks."[75] He was much taken by the concept of the *shanti sena,* what Gandhi called the army of nonviolence, and hoped that such a force could be created in the United States to overcome the scourge of racial segregation.

Applied Gandhianism

After returning from India, King established the Institute for Nonviolent Resistance to Segregation to provide more serious study of the Gandhian method and to train activists for the nonviolent campaigns he and his colleagues planned for the future. King spoke of organizing an "American salt march."[76] The first instructors for the nonviolent institute included Bayard Rustin, Richard Gregg, and Reverend James Lawson. Lawson provided a direct connection between the teachings of Gandhi and the emerging civil rights movement.[77] He had been a conscientious objector during the Korean War and went to India as a Methodist minister on alternative service. He spent three years there studying Gandhi's ideas and methods, becoming an expert in Gandhian philosophy. When he read about the Montgomery bus boycott in the *Nagpur Times,* Lawson was overjoyed. He returned home immediately, determined to apply the principles of Gandhianism in the civil rights and peace movements.

At King's invitation, Lawson created the Nashville Workshops on Nonviolence, which became a central training ground for the students who led the 1960s sit-in movement and who sustained the 1961 freedom rides. The students trained in Lawson's Gandhian workshops became the nonviolent shock troops for the civil rights movement. They are portrayed in David Halberstam's *The Children.* In the dark days of the freedom rides, when several riders had been bloodied and buses were burned and attacked, these dedicated young activists—the "new Gandhians," they were called—put their bodies on the line and drove through the night to Alabama to continue the freedom rides.[78] Nashville students Diane Nash, James Bevel, John Lewis, and others suffered indignities and physical abuse "for the cause of human freedom," as Lewis put it.[79] All of these students were trained in the Gandhian method. "We discussed and debated every aspect of Gandhi's principles," said Lewis.[80] When Bevel heard Lawson speak about Gandhi, for example, he went to the library and checked out every book he could find on the Mahatma.[81] Bevel was an activist gadfly within the civil rights movement who constantly challenged King and others toward more assertive action. He especially appreciated Gandhi's commitment to action and encouraged his fellow students in Nashville to read and follow Gandhi's example.

Gandhian principles were also taught in the citizenship schools set up by the SCLC in 1961. The idea of the citizenship schools was to recruit and train activists from local communities across the South where voter registration campaigns were being organized. The activists were brought to Dorchester, Georgia, for an intensive week-long curriculum of study and training that included an introduction to the philosophy of nonviolence and the ideas and methods of Gandhi. As Andrew Young recounted, "In the citizenship schools we meticulously taught Gandhi's method."[82] Hundreds of local leaders returned from these sessions to spread the ideas of Gandhian nonviolence in their communities and to launch local campaigns for desegregation and voting rights.

Through the citizenship schools, the Nashville workshops, and the Institute for Nonviolent Resistance, King and his colleagues in the civil rights movement recruited a core of activists and developed an effective action strategy for confronting racial segregation and overcoming the barriers to political participation. The years that followed saw countless marches, noncooperation campaigns, sit-ins, and boycotts employing and in some cases elaborating the methods of nonviolent action developed by Gandhi. Many thousands of Americans displayed extraordinary courage and bravery in countless actions and demonstrations throughout the South during the civil rights movement. In Albany, Birmingham, Selma, and many other cities, African Americans and their white allies stood up to the fury of segregationist violence and willingly accepted economic deprivation, physical blows, and even death in the cause of freedom.

The moral power of their sacrifice had a transforming impact on U.S. politics and culture. The specter of disciplined masses nonviolently suffering police brutality had a catalytic effect, attracting sympathy and political support for the nonviolent cause. Police dogs and fire hoses in Birmingham led to passage of the Civil Rights Act in 1964. The attack with mounted police and tear gas in Selma led to passage of the Voting Rights Act in 1965. Gandhian mass action helped end legal segregation in American society, and history turned on a hinge.

Chapter 4

Gandhi in the Fields

Cesar Chavez stands next to Martin Luther King Jr. as one of the greatest nonviolent leaders in U.S. history. Through the United Farmworkers movement, which he founded and led for more than thirty years, Chavez successfully applied Gandhian principles to the farm fields of America. He combined the nonviolent strategies of Gandhi, Catholic social teaching, and the organizing methods of Saul Alinsky in a unique blend that was part labor union, part social movement, and part religious crusade. He and his colleagues improved the lives of hundreds of thousands of America's poorest and most oppressed workers. He was, said Robert F. Kennedy, "one of the heroic figures of our time."[1]

When Chavez launched *la causa* in 1962, farmworkers were paid as little as a dollar an hour.[2] The Mexican and Filipino families who picked America's agricultural bounty lived a miserable existence of backbreaking labor, continuously moving from one squalid camp to another, facing job insecurity, abusive labor contractors, and dehumanizing conditions. They had no right to organize, no health insurance, no pensions or paid vacations. Many did not even have access to toilets or fresh drinking water. Fewer than half had tap water in their homes. Educational opportunities were bleak, and many children, including Chavez himself, did not finish high school.[3]

All of this changed because of the United Farmworkers movement. Through strikes and picketing, and especially through the pioneering use of boycotts, Chavez and his partners won important victories. Wages increased sharply. For the first time migrant workers gained medical insurance, pension benefits, and the right to bargain collectively. These and other improvements resulted from the nonviolent struggle founded and led by Cesar Chavez.

Origins

Chavez achieved his remarkable influence in a humble, self-effacing manner. His family had been forced off their small farm in Arizona during the Depression, and he spent much of his childhood and early adult life stooped over in the fields. Like Gandhi, he was deeply religious and vegetarian. Even after he became an organizer and union leader, he remained ascetic in his personal lifestyle. He eschewed wealth and luxuries and dressed simply in worker clothes. The meager union salary he paid himself ($5 a week) amounted to a virtual vow of poverty.

Chavez was short and unassuming as a person, and he was not a compelling public speaker. I remember being surprised by his low-key manner when he spoke at a Nuclear Weapons Freeze national committee meeting in Atlanta in the early 1980s. I had expected fiery oratory from one of such historic stature. But he offered no rhetorical flourishes and delivered few applause lines. His style was unassuming and conversational. His message was strong, however, and his gentle manner and genuine passion for justice were magnetic. He had an extraordinary ability to inspire trust and confidence, and to motivate others to join the struggle.

There was little in Chavez's heritage, or in that of the Chicano and Filipino workers who followed him, to suggest a readiness for nonviolent action.[4] Mexican American culture is deeply imbued with the traditions of machismo. Violence is widely accepted and sometimes even glorified as a natural response to attack on one's honor or family. Among the photo images on the walls of Chavez's United Farmworkers office was that of Emiliano Zapata, the bandolier-laden revolutionary who has inspired Mexicans for generations and who is the namesake for the recent rebellion and liberation movement in Chiapas. Chavez saw no contradiction in admiring Zapata. He reinterpreted Mexico's revolutionary traditions and turned the concept of machismo on its head.[5] The true spirit of Zapata, he believed, was not in armed rebellion but in disciplined nonviolent resistance. "The truest act of courage, the strongest act of manliness," he told his supporters, "is to sacrifice ourselves in a totally nonviolent struggle for justice."[6]

The intellectual and spiritual influences on Chavez were many. First was the devout Catholicism he learned from his mother and the priests and nuns he encountered growing up in the church. As an altar boy, Chavez was even more steeped in Catholic traditions than his family and friends. Later, when he became leader of the union, he incorporated Catholic symbols and rituals into the movement, appropriating the virgin of Guadalupe as matriarch of the farmworkers' struggle. (In Poland, Catholic activists in the Solidarity movement similarly used church symbols in their struggle against communism.) Father Donald McDonnell, a neighborhood priest he met as a young man, introduced Chavez to the traditions of Catholic social teaching.[7] McDonnell read to him from papal encyclicals extolling social justice and the rights of labor. This experience must have been exhilarating for Chavez, as it was for me when I learned the same subjects. It was a revelation to discover that the Catholic Church, which otherwise espouses personal piety and conservative values, also promotes a vision of dignity for the poor. This gave Chavez a spiritual foundation for his struggle to achieve economic justice.

Chavez's introduction to political organizing came when he met Fred Ross, an organizer for Saul Alinsky's Community Service Organization (CSO). Ross visited Chavez's San José barrio in 1952 to recruit local activists for a voter rights campaign. Ross's persistence and sensitivity to the Chicano community broke through the barriers of language and culture and soon won the confidence of Chavez and many of his neighbors. Thus began a lifelong friendship and partnership between Chavez and Ross. Chavez was soon working for CSO and in 1959 became its executive director in Los Angeles. From Ross and Alinsky (whom he met in person in 1958), Chavez learned the organizing methods that had helped build industrial unionism in the United States in the 1930s and 1940s and that became the foundation of many successful community organizations in subsequent decades.

Learning Gandhi

Chavez made a life project of reading and learning about Gandhi. He was greatly impressed as a boy after viewing a movie newsreel on Gandhi, and he began to read as much as he could about "this little half-naked man without a gun" who had triumphed over the British empire.[8] Chavez read slowly but methodically, and he quickly absorbed the principal elements of Gandhi's thinking and method. He kept a photo of Gandhi in his United Farmworkers office, alongside the pictures of Zapata and the virgin of Guadalupe.[9] Chavez found many things to admire in Gandhi: his great success in winning Indian independence, his uncompromising commitment to nonviolence, his use of the boycott, and his fasting. He found similarities between his own efforts to overcome racial prejudice and poverty and Gandhi's attempts to end untouchability and empower the downtrodden. Gandhi's inventive methods of protest fascinated Chavez throughout his life.[10] He was viscerally attracted to the humble brown man in a loincloth who challenged British imperialism. Chavez once reflected on his initial exposure to Gandhi:

> I've been greatly influenced by Gandhi's philosophy and have read a great deal about what he said and did. But in those days I knew very little about him except what I read in the papers and saw in the newsreels. There was one scene I never forgot. Gandhi was going to a meeting with a high British official in India. There were throngs of people as he walked all but naked out of his little hut. Then he was filmed in his loincloth, sandals, and shawl walking up the steps of the palace.[11]

In Gandhi Chavez found a leader who could inspire poor people to challenge the rich and powerful, a formula of obvious relevance to oppressed migrant workers facing wealthy growers. He found in Gandhi someone who led by example, who never asked his supporters to do what he himself would not do.

The practical-minded Chavez was especially impressed by Gandhi's record of success. Through the use of nonviolent methods, particularly the boycott, Gandhi and his colleagues had wrested independence from London. As Chavez learned of Gandhi's campaigns in South Africa and India, he realized the immense political power that disciplined nonviolence could exert. His enthusiasm for nonviolent methods was reinforced by the achievements of the U.S. civil rights movement. Chavez was thrilled by the example of African Americans standing up to the indignities of segregation. He saw the nonviolent method as an effective tool for achieving social justice.

Chavez's embrace of nonviolence was both principled and pragmatic. Some writers see a distinction between pragmatic and principled nonviolence. The former focuses on the practical advantages of the nonviolent method, the latter emphasizes religious or ethical motivations.[12] Gene Sharp's writings have focused on the pragmatic dimensions of nonviolent action and have tended to downplay the role of religiously inspired leaders.[13] For Chavez, however, as for King and Gandhi, religious principles were extremely important. So were the practical considerations in favor of nonviolent methods. The two were equally important. Chavez believed passionately in the moral superiority of nonviolence, but he also emphasized the pragmatic necessity of avoiding destruction or injury to others. Although he and his colleagues faced frequent assault—from farm foremen, security guards, the police, and the Teamsters union—Chavez insisted on maintaining nonviolent discipline. Like Gandhi, he made his followers take a vow of absolute nonviolence. He repeatedly urged union activists not to inflict physical violence or cause property damage. The use of violence, he cautioned, would be counterproductive. It would alienate the movement's supporters in the religious community and among liberals.[14] Violence would also give the police greater license to assault union picketers. Damaging growers' property would only stiffen their resistance. As he told a crowd on Mexican Independence Day in 1965, "We are engaged in another struggle for the freedom and dignity which poverty denies us. But it must be a nonviolent struggle, even if violence is used against us. Violence can only hurt us and our cause."[15]

As a devout Catholic and apostle of nonviolence, Chavez was naturally attracted to Dorothy Day. Chavez shared Day's emphasis on the rights of labor and the importance of building a workers' movement grounded in religious faith and the sacredness of life. Chavez visited Day at her Catholic Worker community in

Dorothy Day being arrested as she picketed in support of a strike by the United Farm Workers, August 1973 (photo by Bob Fitch).

New York in 1967 and again in 1979, the year before her death. Day reciprocated by visiting him in California several times. Day actively supported the grape and lettuce boycotts and joined farmworker picket lines on several occasions. Her last stay in prison, at the age of seventy-five, came in California in August 1973 when she joined a United Farmworkers picket in violation of a police injunction. The photo of her being carted off to jail, sitting serenely in a chair, is perhaps the best-known and most widely viewed image of Day.[16] Chavez drew encouragement and inspiration from her principled commitment to nonviolence and her selfless dedication to serving the poor and needy.

Through his study of Gandhi, Chavez fully integrated the key concepts of nonviolence into his thinking. He emphasized the inseparability of ends and means. "There is no such thing as means and ends," he told a union audience in 1969. "Everything that we do is an end, in itself, that we can never erase."[17] Nonviolence is not for cowards, Chavez said, echoing Gandhi and King. It is for those who are prepared to sacrifice and apply constant pressure on the adversary. "In some instances," Chavez remarked, "nonviolence requires more militancy than violence."[18] Chavez also incorporated into his approach the Gandhian notion of purification. To practice nonviolence requires nothing less than a spiritual rebirth, he believed.[19] Those who engage in nonviolent struggle must be prepared to endure suffering. They must maintain a spirit of love and reconciliation regardless of the hardships and humiliations they may endure. "Love is the most important ingredient in nonviolent work," he said. "Love the opponent.... If we're full of hatred we can't really do our work. Hatred saps [our] strength and energy."[20]

Chavez instinctively understood and consciously applied the concept of moral jujitsu in his nonviolence campaigns.[21] He recognized, as Gandhi and King demonstrated, that a key strategic objective of nonviolent action is to throw the adversary off balance. The strength of the adversary can sometimes be a liability. When the opponent uses excessive force against a spiritually pure and disciplined nonviolent movement, the political tables may turn to the movement's advantage. By willingly suffering and accepting the opponent's brutality, the movement could gain the sympathy and support of bystanders and thus shift the political balance to its favor. Chavez put it this way: "By some strange chemistry, every time the opposition commits an unjust act against our hopes and aspirations, we get tenfold paid back in benefits."[22]

La Huelga

Chavez and the farmworkers movement burst on the national stage in 1965 with what became known as the great grape strike, or *la huelga*. Initially Chavez and his colleagues had planned, following the Alinsky method, to build their membership and organizational base gradually, refraining from mass actions until they had a sufficiently large base of support. Their organization, the National Farmworkers Association (later the United Farmworkers of America, or UFWA), still had relatively few members and little money. When the grape strike began there were only two hundred dues-paying members.[23] But as so often happens in social change movements, events raced ahead of the planned timetable. The catalyst for action came in September 1965 when a group of Filipino grape workers in California's Coachella Valley went on strike after growers lowered their wages. The workers requested the help of the Farmworkers Association, and Chavez and his colleagues felt they had no choice but to respond. Pickets went up at major farms, and many of the valley's five thousand grape workers walked off the job.

Chavez was greatly aided in building the farmworkers movement by Dolores Huerta. A native of New Mexico and daughter of a migrant laborer and coal miner, Huerta became deeply involved in worker justice issues after graduating from college in Stockton, California. She met Chavez through the Community Service Organization. She founded and became secretary-treasurer of the Agricultural Workers Organizing Committee, a farmworkers support group that merged with Chavez's fledgling organization in the early 1960s to form the National Farm Workers Association. Huerta played a vital role in the union's social action campaigns. She organized strikes, managed picket lines, mobilized support for the grape boycott, negotiated contracts with growers, and later headed the union's political action arm. She was a skilled lobbyist and negotiator. She managed all of this while mothering eleven children and supporting the women's movement and many other social causes. Huerta remained a leader of the farmworkers union into the 1990s. For more than thirty years she was Chavez's most loyal and trusted assistant.

As the grape strike spread in 1965, Chavez traveled and spoke indefatigably to generate public support. He made a special effort to recruit clergy and student activists from the civil rights and free speech movements then stirring social idealism in California and throughout the nation. The strike also attracted crucial support from national unions and the AFL-CIO. Among those who came to union headquarters at Delano to join the picket lines was United Auto Workers union president Walter Reuther, who had also marched with, and provided financial support for, Martin Luther King Jr. Reuther told a crowd of cheering farmworkers in December 1965, "There is no power in the world like the power of free [people] working together in a just cause."[24]

Another noteworthy person who came to support the farmworkers was Senator Robert F. Kennedy. During hearings in

Delano before his Senate subcommittee, Kennedy ridiculed the local sheriff's policy of arresting picketers preventively—placing workers in jail without charging them with a crime. Said Kennedy, to applause, "I suggest that ... in the luncheon period ... the sheriff and the district attorney read the Constitution of the United States."[25] After the hearings, Kennedy visited the union hall and joined farmworkers on the picket line. He and his wife Ethel Kennedy remained loyal supporters of the farmworkers movement throughout their lives.

As the strike dragged on into 1966, Chavez decided to dramatize the continuing struggle with a long march from Delano to the state capitol in Sacramento. Emulating Gandhi's march to the sea and King's march from Selma, Chavez set out with a hundred supporters in what he labeled a *peregrinación,* or pilgrimage. It was the longest protest march in U.S. history up to that time. The peregrinación, begun during the Lenten season, had the theme of "pilgrimage, penitence, and revolution." Chavez said that the peregrinación would prepare workers for the long struggle ahead. "We wanted to be fit not only physically but spiritually, and we wanted to stress nonviolence even more, build confidence, and have more visible nonviolent tactics."[26] By the time the marchers reached Sacramento on Easter Sunday, they numbered in the thousands.

It was at this time that Chavez and his supporters had their first taste of victory. One of the major growers, Schenley, agreed to recognize the Farmworkers Association, signing a contract that raised wages by thirty-five cents an hour. Several other major growers followed suit in subsequent months, and the union won its first representation elections that fall. A long struggle lay ahead, however, since the initial contracts covered only about five thousand workers, only about 2 percent of California's farmworker population.

Boycotting Grapes and Lettuce

As the farmworkers sought ways to convince the major vineyards to negotiate, they turned to more forceful means of applying pressure. The union had launched selective boycotts of individual growers in the early days of the strike. The first boycott action came after the November harvest of 1965, when longshoremen at the docks in Oakland agreed not to load a shipment of grapes from Delano, leaving a thousand ten-ton crates of grapes to rot on the piers.[27] Subsequent boycotts targeted large companies such as Giumarra, but the growers responded by rebranding their grapes under different labels. It became too confusing and difficult for consumers and volunteers to decide which grapes to boycott. It was hard enough to communicate the message of the farmworkers campaign without having to ask consumers to identify a particular brand of grapes to boycott. After much discussion and debate, the union decided to expand the boycott to cover all California table grapes. This was an easier message to convey, and it increased the pressure on the growers.

In January 1968, the Farmworkers Association announced a national boycott of California grapes. The campaign caught on quickly in those activist days and eventually spread across the nation and internationally. The grape campaign was later described as "the most ambitious and successful boycott in American history."[28] The grape campaign and the subsequent lettuce boycott became the signature achievements of the farmworkers movement. They were Chavez's greatest contribution to the development of nonviolent social action. The success of the grape and lettuce campaigns confirmed that boycotts can be an enormously powerful tool of nonviolent social change.

The boycott gradually grew and expanded in 1968 and 1969. UFWA organizers fanned out to cities all over North America, including Detroit, Chicago, Toronto, New York, and Boston. Civil rights organizations, trade unions, student activists, antiwar groups, and religious bodies actively supported the campaign. The grape boycott and the latter campaign against lettuce became part of the radical culture of the 1960s and 1970s, a part of the alternative lifestyle of those challenging war, racism, and economic injustice.

Those of us who were active in the GI peace movement had a special reason for joining the boycott campaign. In 1969, the Department of Defense began buying huge quantities of nonunion grapes and shipping them to the troops in Vietnam. Richard Nixon ordered the Pentagon to quadruple table grape shipments to Vietnam, from 550,000 pounds in 1968 to nearly 2.2 million pounds in 1969.[29] The Pentagon's complicity in attempting to undermine the boycott gave antiwar soldiers a powerful political education in the connections between militarism and economic oppression. It also strengthened our resolve to resist the war and the military's complicity in perpetuating social injustice. The underground newspapers published by soldiers at many U.S. military bases featured articles about Chavez and the grape boycott. "Don't buy scab grapes" graffiti began appearing on military bases, and many of us joined picket lines in support of the boycott. Some sailors on navy ships threw boxes of grapes overboard. Soldiers on kitchen duty "accidentally" let grapes rot in the pantry.

By 1969, the grape boycott was beginning to have a major impact. Millions of Americans and Canadians were refusing to buy grapes. From a public opinion poll taken a few years later, it was estimated that seventeen million Americans stopped buying grapes or Gallo wine because of the boycott.[30] Sales in 1969 were down compared to 1966 (a year of similar yield) by 34 percent in New York, 41 percent in Chicago, and 53 percent in Baltimore—all cities that had active grape boycott committees. Across North America, shipments fell by one-third.[31]

In response to this pressure, major growers in California began to negotiate. In Coachella, California, a group of forty growers began to negotiate with the farmworkers and reached a settlement that raised wages and benefits. Soon the growers in Delano followed suit. When the largest grower in the state, Giumarra, signed a contract in July 1970, all the remaining grape growers quickly fell in line. The union had finally won its long battle for justice in the vineyards. Chavez and his followers had successfully organized a national and even international grape boycott. The combination of an effective boycott, continuous strikes, and constant picketing forced the growers to the bargaining table and brought victory to the farmworkers campaign. *Time* magazine ran a cover story on the farmworkers movement, and Chavez became a nationally known hero of nonviolent struggle.

Before the ink had even dried on the initial grape contracts, however, a new labor dispute broke out in the lettuce fields of the Salinas Valley. In the summer of 1970, nearly every major grower in the valley signed secret labor contracts with the Teamsters union in an attempt to thwart the influence of the United Farmworkers.[32] The lettuce workers were not even consulted on these sweetheart deals. They were forced to accept contracts they had no role in negotiating and a union they didn't know or want. When workers objected, they were fired. Chavez and his colleagues never intended to launch another major campaign so soon after the grape strike, but when faced with such injustices and an obvious attempt to undermine the union, they had no choice but to act. In August 1970, they called a strike, and soon the union's Aztec eagle banners waved over fields for more than a hundred miles in all directions.[33] Thousands of workers walked off the job, paralyzing the world's largest vegetable industry.

The union called for a lettuce boycott, focusing on the biggest grower in the valley, Bud Antle. Once again the union sent out envoys to build support for the boycott, and once again activists from other movements responded with picketing and educational campaigns. All across the country lettuce disappeared from dining tables, just as grapes had vanished two years earlier. Labor, peace, and religious groups responded again to the call of the farmworkers. In our GIs for Peace group at Fort Bliss, Texas, we distributed information about the boycott and urged fellow soldiers and their families not to buy scab lettuce. Some GI groups picketed local food stores and demanded that army mess halls stop buying nonunion lettuce.

The lettuce boycott had an immediate impact, as major growers began to accede to union demands. One of the largest growers, InterHarvest, signed a generous contract with the farmworkers union. Other major growers followed suit, rescinding their sweetheart deals with the Teamsters and negotiating contracts with the farmworkers union. In early 1971, enough progress was made for Chavez to suspend the boycott, pending negotiations with the Teamsters and the growers. No further progress was achieved, however, and the lettuce boycott was resumed a few months later and continued for several years thereafter.

In 1973, the grape boycott was also resumed. This action was taken when major vineyards followed the earlier example of the lettuce growers and signed sweetheart contracts with the Teamsters. The union launched a new boycott, this time against Gallo, the world's largest vintner, which broke its contract with the UFWA to sign with the Teamsters. The union was now boycotting lettuce, grapes, and Gallo wine. The boycotts continued for years, but the halcyon enthusiasm of the initial grape and lettuce boycotts gradually faded. Boycott activity around the country became increasingly desultory, and the tactic lost much of its effectiveness.

In the years after 1980, when the UFWA reached a peak membership of one hundred thousand, the union began to lose membership and support.[34] Although the union remained a vital force in the fields, it never regained its previous level of power and influence. As the organization became more of a conventional labor union and less a social cause, public support and sympathy declined. Economic conditions also worked against the union, as agricultural surpluses, a flood of undocumented workers, and depressed farm prices led to cuts in jobs and union membership rolls. When the union launched a new grape boycott in the mid-1980s to protest pesticide use, the public response was lackluster. Within the union, concerns emerged about Chavez's autocratic leadership style. Some activists urged Chavez to share leadership duties and called for a more decentralized decision-making structure. The combination of these internal and external challenges sapped the movement of its earlier dynamism.

The Boycott: A Powerful Instrument

Many nonviolent action campaigns have used the boycott as an effective tool of social change. Gandhi organized massive boycotts in all of his major political campaigns in India. During the 1920–1922 campaign, Indians refused to participate in British-run schools, government offices, and courts. They boycotted British cotton imports, instead making their own homespun cloth. Gandhi's devotion to the spinning wheel was an expression of the message to boycott foreign cloth and a call for self-reliance. As the boycott spread and the spinning movement grew, imports of British cloth dropped, while imports of yarn for spinning increased. Gandhi and his colleagues organized an even larger boycott of British goods during the 1930–1931 salt satyagraha.[35] The boycott and an accompanying "no-tax" campaign had a significant impact on British revenues. Imports of British cloth, primarily from the Lancashire mills, dropped dramatically, falling from more than one million yards in 1929 to 720,000 yards in 1930. The commercial clothing centers in Amritsar, Bombay, and Delhi came to a virtual standstill.[36] Government revenues from the liquor tax fell 40 percent. The British secretary of state for India reported an overall 25 percent

reduction in trade with India, only one-quarter of which was at-
tributable to the worldwide economic depression.[37] According
to Peter Ackerman and Christopher Kruegler, these efforts to
reduce British revenue were the most effective of all the tactics
employed by the Indian independence movement.[38]

Boycotts were also a key feature of the U.S. civil rights movement. In Montgomery, African Americans refused to ride segregated buses for 381 days. Similar citywide bus boycotts were
organized in Baton Rouge and Tallahassee.[39] The Montgomery
boycott cost the local bus company more than $3,000 a day
and produced financial losses among white-owned downtown
businesses.[40] In combination with a federal court suit against
bus segregation laws, the bus boycott resulted in the civil rights
movement's first major victory.

The Nashville movement featured an effective boycott of
downtown stores. The Nashville boycott was launched just as
the 1960 Easter shopping season was about to begin. Instead of
buying a new dress or suit for Easter, as was the custom, African
Americans stayed at home and made do with what they had.
As a result, the white-owned downtown stores stood virtually
empty. "It was like a ghost town down there," recalled civil rights
organizer Bernard Lafayette.[41] John Lewis said, "It was those
empty stores—and empty cash registers—that brought an offer
from the mayor's committee" to negotiate.[42] The combination of
the boycott and dramatic sit-in demonstrations convinced local
authorities to bargain and led to the successful desegregation
of Nashville's downtown stores.

The historic Birmingham campaign of April–May 1963 also
featured a boycott of downtown stores. Martin Luther King Jr.
and his colleagues carefully planned the Birmingham campaign
and calculated that a consumer boycott would provide crucial
leverage. According to Andrew Young, "while the direct-action
demonstrations and sit-ins were effective primarily in dramatizing our cause outside of Birmingham, the economic boycott
was what finally brought the campaign home to the local seats
of power." The boycott was "almost totally effective" and was
"visibly hurting" the targeted stores. Young estimated that the
boycott reduced the profits of downtown stores by 15 to 20 percent.[43] The boycott combined with other forms of social action
to produce a significant victory for the civil rights movement in
Birmingham.

Boycotts can apply to political participation, education, sports, and even cultural activities. The freedom struggle in South Africa featured the extensive and effective use of various kinds of boycotts. One of the first major actions of the United Democratic Front, the broad coalition of antiapartheid groups founded in 1983, was an Anti-Election Campaign in 1984 to boycott proposed constitutional changes. Although white voters approved the measures, the boycott convinced more than 80 percent of mixed-race and Asian voters to stay away from the polls and thus undermined the legitimacy of the election result.[44] Election boycotts are used frequently in political struggles around the world. Their purpose, as in South Africa, is to deny legitimacy and political authority to reactionary governments and their oppressive policies. Electoral boycotts carry risks, however, and may have the short-term effect of giving reactionary opponents an easy victory—as was the case when democratic reformers in Iran boycotted national elections in 2004 and allowed hard-line Muslim clerics to consolidate their political control. The success of an electoral boycott strategy depends on a broad base of support within the affected population and the ability to build the long-term political legitimacy of the opposition, while continually eroding the authority of the reactionary regime.

In South Africa, the antiapartheid movement was able to achieve success by combining its electoral boycott activities with a wide range of other forms of economic and social noncooperation, and by gaining the support of a global antiapartheid and economic boycott campaign. Within South Africa, the UDF and affiliated groups organized rent boycotts, student strikes, consumer boycotts, and worker "stayaways."[45] The unions within the Congress of South African Trade Unions organized the most successful general strike in South African history in June 1988 to commemorate the Soweto uprising and massacre of 1976. An estimated 70 percent of the workforce participated in the three-day stayaway. A similar mass strike two years later commemorated the killings at Sharpeville in 1960.[46] Rent boycotts were also widespread, involving fifty-four townships and some half a million households by 1986. The rent boycotts cost the state an estimated R187 million in 1987. This undermined state-controlled community councils that depended on rent revenues.[47] In some communities, rent boycotts led to improved housing and urban services.

Consumer boycotts were also prevalent and were used to end racial segregation in stores. They were used strategically to drive a wedge between white business owners and the nationalist government. Local chambers of commerce in some communities were forced to lobby the government to end segregated town council meetings.[48] This was the same strategy used by the civil rights movement in Birmingham, Alabama, where activists boycotted downtown stores as a means of pressuring beleaguered white owners to convince hard-line officials in the city government to negotiate the movement's demands. The UDF and its affiliates found that boycotts were most successful when they were organized in support of specific local initiatives.[49]

The same was true of boycott campaigns in the United States. The short-term, localized boycotts employed by King and his colleagues brought quicker results and were easier to organize and sustain than the long-term, national and international campaigns mounted by Chavez. The more localized the target, the easier it is to inform and mobilize consumer support, and the more concentrated the economic effects are likely to be. Chavez and the farmworkers were shouldering a much weightier burden when they attempted to boycott an entire sector of the food industry and sought sustained consumer support across North America and beyond. The farmworker boycotts had significant impact, but over time their effectiveness faded.

The power of a boycott does not depend solely on its direct economic leverage. Business research has shown that consumer boycotts often have only limited financial impact on the targeted companies.[50] Boycotts are most effective when they are combined with other forms of social action, including demonstrations and civil disobedience. The successful campaigns of Gandhi and King employed all of these elements—boycotts, direct action, and the creative use of the media.

Contemporary boycott campaigns increasingly rely on media communications, as illustrated in the international boycott against the Nestlé Corporation. This boycott was initiated by human rights and religious activists in 1973 to protest the marketing of infant formula in developing countries.[51] The actual financial impact of the boycott was modest, estimated at approximately $60 million in lost revenue,[52] but the damage to the company's public image was considerable. Buoyed by support from United Nations agencies and the backing of U.S.

senators, notably Edward Kennedy, the campaign produced films and sponsored media events charging that the use of formula caused infant deaths. When Nestlé overreacted and filed a lawsuit against the groups, the campaign benefited from the resulting publicity and gained considerable public sympathy and support. In 1984, Nestlé agreed to abide by a World Health Organization code on the marketing of infant formula, a significant victory for the boycott campaign. Activists later charged that the company was reneging on its pledge and announced a resumption of the boycott. Consumers were no longer aware or interested, though, and the renewed boycott never caught on.

The Taco Bell campaign is another, more recent example of the creative interplay of boycotting, protest, and effective use of the media. The campaign was organized by the Coalition of Immokalee Workers, which represents Mexican migrant farmworkers near the town of the same name in southern Florida. The coalition was founded in 1996 in an attempt to end virtual slave labor conditions among the mostly undocumented workers. In one instance, hundreds of workers were held captive by labor contractors and forced to work without pay.[53]

When the coalition learned that Taco Bell was a major purchaser of the tomatoes grown in the surrounding fields, it saw an opportunity. The fast-food chain with stores nearly everywhere presented an ideal target for boycotting. Its huge advertising budget made it vulnerable to negative publicity. As the nation's largest purveyor of Mexican food, it did not want to be seen as exploiting impoverished Mexicans. When Taco Bell refused to ask its suppliers to raise wages and improve human rights for the workers, the coalition launched a nationwide boycott in 2001, focusing on high schools and colleges. Soon "Boot the Bell" campaigns began popping up in schools across the country. Students at twenty-one colleges removed or blocked the food chain from their campuses. Campaigns developed in at least three hundred colleges and universities and more than fifty high schools.[54] Endorsements came in from the National Council of Churches, the United Methodist Church, and other religious and human rights groups. Aiding the campaign was the coalition's clever framing of the wage demand—a pay raise of one penny for every pound of tomatoes picked. The penny-a-pound slogan was easily understood by boycott supporters and became a rallying cry on campuses, in churches, and at protest rallies. The coalition organized a "Taco Bell Truth Tour" which brought dozens of workers to campuses around the country. They also brought their campaign directly to the corporate headquarters of Taco Bell's parent company, Yum! Brands, in Louisville, Kentucky. In March 2005, a protest rally there drew participation from actor Martin Sheen and Kerry Kennedy, daughter of the late senator Robert F. Kennedy. As bad publicity and boycott pressure mounted, the company yielded, signing an agreement that acceded to all of the coalition's demands. It was a remarkable victory that showed the creative power of a successful boycott campaign.

The boycott instrument can be highly effective, but it has limitations. Cesar Chavez and the United Farmworkers Union used the boycott effectively to secure the initial right to organize, but it proved less effective as a means of sustaining those gains or responding to changing circumstances. Once the grape boycott was called off after the initial contracts were signed, it could not be easily resumed. Nor could a tactic developed for one campaign be transferred readily to another. The lettuce boycott, for example, never enjoyed the level of excitement and energy of the grape boycott, and it did not produce as clear a political victory. It was difficult for supporters to keep track of the various starts and stops of the union's boycotts. Many of us were frustrated and uncertain during those days, not knowing whether or when it was permissible to eat grapes or lettuce. Most of us simply refrained from eating either and shunned Gallo wine as well, since we were never quite sure at any given moment which product was being boycotted. The farmworkers union, overwhelmed with constant strikes and attempting to manage new labor contracts, simply did not have the means to communicate its boycott decisions quickly and efficiently to its many supporters around the United States and in Canada.

I am not suggesting here that Chavez and his colleagues misused the boycott instrument. On the contrary, they applied it brilliantly and won important gains as a result. But they may have gone back to the well too many times. And they perhaps placed too much faith in their ability to calibrate and fine-tune the instrument to the changing fortunes of their multifaceted campaigns. The boycott is a blunt instrument, not a refined surgical tool, and it works best as a means of applying general pressure to gain bargaining leverage.

The boycott can be a powerful tool of social change, but it is difficult to develop and sustain. Boycotts depend on the willing cooperation of thousands or even millions of consumers, most of whom have little knowledge of specific developments within the particular campaign involved. People join a boycott only when it is for clear and compelling purposes (justice for farm-workers, independence for India) and when it is supported or sponsored by reputable organizations (unions, religious bodies, established political parties). Consumers cannot be expected to follow the twists and turns of a particular social campaign. Their natural inclination, once a boycott ends, is to go back to shopping as usual. When a movement calls off a boycott, either to declare victory or to enter a negotiating process, it should recognize that resuming the boycott will be very difficult. Once under way, a boycott should be sustained for as long as possible, until concrete changes are secured.

Fasting

Next to the use of the boycott, Chavez is perhaps best known for his frequent resort to fasting. Here again he was strongly influenced by and sought to emulate Gandhi, who fasted more than a dozen times—most often to quell communal violence between Hindus and Muslims. Gandhi's fasts were a mixture of personal penance and political drama. Through voluntary suffering and his willingness to fast even unto death, Gandhi sought to purify himself and increase his spiritual powers, thereby hoping to acquire greater ability to sway the hearts and minds of both his followers and his British adversaries.[55]

Chavez had similar goals in mind: to perform penance for the excesses of his followers or for the social sins of his adversaries, while aspiring to the greater spiritual power that he hoped would enable him to achieve his political objectives. He viewed the fast as a "great communicator," a way of applying what he termed "moral force."[56] Chavez engaged in several major fasts—in 1968 to halt violence by union supporters, in 1970 to support justice for lettuce workers, in 1975 to encourage a stronger California Agricultural Labor Relations Act, and in 1988 to protest the use of pesticides that harm farmworkers. He also engaged in several shorter fasts. Chavez suffered greatly during these ordeals. He

Cesar Chavez, with Senator Robert F. Kennedy and Chavez's wife, Helen Fabela Chavez, in Delano, California, in 1968 at the conclusion of his twenty-five-day fast (photo: George Elfie Ballis).

took many months to recover from the last major fast in 1988. The night he died unexpectedly in his sleep in 1993 he had just ended a fast.

Chavez's first fast was in many respects his most successful. It was aimed at purification, at purging his movement of violence and hatred. Anguished at reports of property damage and acts of sabotage by union supporters, Chavez sharply criticized his followers and insisted that they maintain nonviolent discipline. At an emotional union meeting in February 1968, he announced without advance notice that he had stopped eating food and that he would not eat again until everyone pledged to remain strictly nonviolent. The effect was dramatic and immediate, bringing forth an overwhelming response from union members. Thousands of farmworkers streamed to Delano to pledge their loyalty to Chavez and vow allegiance to his nonviolent creed.[57] The fast was a "defining moment" for the union, guaranteeing that Gandhian nonviolence would be the guiding principle of the farmworkers movement. Its impact was almost miraculous, in the way that Gandhi's major fasts—in 1932 against untouchability, and in 1947 and 1948 for Muslim-Hindu harmony—sparked massive outpourings of sympathy and support. The end of Chavez's 1968 fast was an emotionally charged event that attracted thousands of people, including Robert F. Kennedy, and that solidified Chavez's leadership within the movement.

Chavez's other fasts also attracted outpourings of support, especially the 1988 fast, but their impact was uncertain. His fasts dramatized the plight of farmworkers and the urgency of addressing their concerns. They helped galvanize support for la causa among his followers and the general public. But their broader political effect was limited. Many of Chavez's adversaries were unmoved; some were even angered by his self-sacrifice, and they refused to yield to what they considered psychological pressure. Like Gandhi, Chavez claimed that his fasts were transcendental in nature, but they also had a coercive element that sometimes clashed with his deeper spiritual aspirations.

Many other social activists have resorted to fasting as a technique of social protest.[58] In the 1980s, Mitch Snyder of the Community for Creative Nonviolence in Washington, D.C., went on a hunger strike to demand shelter for the homeless. Snyder's personal witness was effective in attracting attention to the problems of the homeless and shamed local officials into opening a major shelter near downtown Washington. In South Africa, more than six hundred imprisoned UDF activists went on a coordinated and disciplined hunger strike in 1989. As the strike continued for weeks, more than one hundred prisoners had to be hospitalized. The strike brought increased international attention to the depth of government repression and the scale of popular resistance in South Africa, and it led to the eventual release of the prisoners.[59] One of the most prominent hunger strikes in U.S. history was that of Ethel Byrne, Margaret Sanger's sister, who was arrested in January 1917 for illegally distributing information about birth control and went on a hunger strike to protest her imprisonment. Byrne nearly died from the ordeal, taking a year to recover, but her resistance attracted widespread public attention and sympathy. Said Sanger, "no single act of self-sacrifice in the history of the birth control movement had done more to awaken the conscience of the public and to arouse the courage of women."[60]

The women of the suffrage movement were among the first to use fasting as a tool of mass protest. The tactic emerged in England in 1909 when suffragist Marion Wallace Dunlap was arrested for writing on the walls of the House of Commons. When her request to be treated as a political prisoner was refused, she defiantly announced that she would forego all food and water. Her condition rapidly deteriorated, and she was released after ninety-one hours. Other women followed her lead, committing civil disobedience and going on hunger strikes after their arrests. American women followed the example of their British sisters and engaged in a number of high-profile hunger strikes. Police authorities in Britain and the United States responded to the militancy of the suffragists by instituting the gruesome practice of forced feeding, which meant immobilizing the victim and forcing down milk, eggs, and stimulants, often through a rubber tube reaching into the stomach. The cruel procedure became the subject of extensive press attention and aroused widespread public indignation. The spectacle of the suffragists being violated in this manner generated outrage and solidarity among a growing number of women. For some, the brutal invasion of women's bodies had haunting parallels to rape.

The use of hunger strikes generated both support and opposition for the women's movement. Many male politicians resented the method, vowing not to give in to such pressures. But hunger strikes were an undeniable success in drawing press attention to the demand for women's rights. Because they were part of a mass movement and delivered a clear and compelling moral message, the hunger strikes were an effective method of social action. They demonstrated dramatically the willingness of women to suffer and risk death for their cause. They showed the determination of women to win political freedom regardless of cost and against all odds.

Fasting is a controversial and uncertain tactic that works only in special circumstances. While fasts are generally employed within the context of nonviolent action, they contain an undeniable coercive element. Gandhi insisted that his fasts were for personal religious purposes, but he realized that his adversaries might find them coercive.[61] Gandhi scholar Judith Brown writes that his fasts "exerted a moral pressure for which nonviolence was a dubious description."[62] But coercive elements do not necessarily disqualify a tactic as nonviolent, provided there is no physical harm to the adversary. The more uncertain question is political viability. Fasting works when it is part of a truly massive popular struggle, such as the suffrage movement, or when those who employ it command broad public respect and recognition, such as Gandhi. Fasting also depends on effective communications strategies that frame the sacrifice as an expression of compelling moral urgency. The cause must be widely understood and broadly shared within society. These conditions do not often coincide, but when they do, as in Chavez's struggle for farmworker rights, fasting can be a highly effective method.

Chapter 5

Dorothy Day: A Mission of Love

When Dorothy Day joined dozens of other suffragists for a demonstration at the White House in November 1917, she was barely twenty years old. She decided to join the action on a whim only the night before.[1] She was restless, bold, and actively committed to progressive political causes. When Day and the other women approached the White House, they were taken into police custody and released. When they returned to the picket line, they were rearrested and refused to post bail, at which point they were taken to the penal workhouse at Occoquan in northern Virginia, then as now a grim place of suffering for imprisoned men and women. When the demonstrators demanded to be treated as political prisoners and were refused, they began a hunger strike. The resulting ordeal was Day's first personal experience with oppression.

The women were dragged roughly and jammed fifteen at a time into rooms meant for two. When Day tried to get to a friend, guards grabbed her and twisted her arms painfully. As she struggled to free herself, she was thrown to the floor. When another friend tried to rescue her, "we found ourselves in the midst of a milling crowd of guards being pummeled and pushed and kicked and dragged, so that we were scarcely conscious, in the shock of what was taking place." As the hunger strike began,

Day suffered "days and nights in darkness, cold, and hunger."[2] Food was proffered to tempt the women, but otherwise they faced only monotony and fear. Day writes eloquently of the ordeal in her autobiography, *The Long Loneliness*:

> Those first six days of inactivity were as six thousand years. To lie there through the long day, to feel the nausea and emptiness of hunger, the dazedness at the beginning and the feverish mental activity that came after.... I lost all consciousness of any cause.... I could only feel darkness and desolation all around me.... That I would be free after thirty days meant nothing to me. I would never be free again, ... when I knew that behind bars all over the world there were women and men, young girls and boys, suffering constraint, punishment, isolation and hardship for crimes of which all of us were guilty.... Never would I recover from this wound, this ugly knowledge I had gained of what men were capable of in their treatment of each other.[3]

After six days, as the hunger strike began to take its toll, the women were placed in hospital cells where they could at least enjoy light and warmth. Some of them were subjected to forced feeding. Twice a day, orderlies came to an older woman next to Day. "Holding her down on the bed, they forced tubes down her throat or nose and gave her egg and milk. It was unutterably horrible to hear her struggles, and the rest of us lay there in our cubicles tense with fear."[4] As the hunger strike continued and controversy mounted, the White House became increasingly worried about adverse publicity. On the tenth day the government announced that the demands of the suffragists would be met. The strike was called off, and the women were transferred to the city jail to be treated as political prisoners, their civilian clothes returned and mail service provided. It was another victory for the suffrage movement and an important event in shaping Day's commitment to social justice.

Conversion

A gifted writer and committed political activist, pacifist, suffragist, and ardent advocate for the poor, Dorothy Day has been described as "the most significant, interesting, and influential person in the history of American Catholicism."[5] She was also

Dorothy Day in 1917 as correspondent for the New York Call *(photo courtesy of the Marquette University archives).*

one of the twentieth century's most important practitioners of nonviolent social change. Her commitment to social justice emerged in the heady atmosphere of early twentieth-century radicalism. As the daughter of a journalist, she was inevitably attracted to the power of the word. She was thrilled by the writing of Jack London, Upton Sinclair, and the Russian anarchist Peter Kropotkin. Later she befriended playwright Eugene O'Neill and went drinking with him in Greenwich Village taverns, where they read poetry together and discussed politics and art.[6] In Chicago as a girl, she spent long hours walking through the West Side neighborhoods that Sinclair immortalized in his classic, *The Jungle.* She was seized by the plight of the poor and determined even then, at the age of fifteen, that "my life was to be linked to theirs. . . . I had received a call, a vocation, a direction to my life."[7] She became deeply committed to activist causes. She briefly joined the Socialist Party and later signed up with the Industrial Workers of the World led by labor organizer Bill Haywood. She worked for the *New York Call* and also wrote for *The Masses,* along with the radical authors Max Eastman and John Reed. She opposed World War I and worked for the Anti-Imperialist League against U.S. military intervention in Central America.

During these tumultuous political times, Day lived a turbulent personal life. A love affair led to unwanted pregnancy and an abortion in 1919. She briefly married Barkeley Tobey, founder of the Literary Guild, and she had a longer and deeper relationship with Forster Batterham, who was the father of her daughter Tamar. She had hoped to marry Batterham, but he could not accept her growing interest in the church and was unwilling to make a commitment to her.[8] Unlike many of her friends, Day was not satisfied with the bohemian life. In her later years, she looked back with regret at this "disorderly" period, the heavy drinking and the "loose moral standards" of her radical friends.[9] She longed for a more stable, anchored existence. She sought solace and order in her life. "I wanted to obey."[10] Her colleagues could be sustained by a commitment to politics or the arts, but Day needed something more, a deeper spiritual foundation. She found herself increasingly called to the Christian faith.

The moment of her conversion came with the birth of Tamar in 1927. She turned to faith not in anguish but in happiness, in the celebration of the miracle of life. The birth of her daughter produced "so vast a flood of love and joy" that she felt the "need to worship, to adore."[11] She was drawn to the Catholic Church because it was the church of the masses, the home of immigrants and the poor. In Lower Manhattan parishes she found the same community of workers she was attempting to reach as a political activist. She discovered in the message of the Gospels "an understanding of human liberation, a sense of community and solidarity much larger than politics alone could provide."[12] She was attracted, according to editor Robert Ellsberg, by Christianity's "theology of immanence, God's indwelling presence in the world."[13] The Gospel teaching that Jesus came to preach good news to the poor perfectly matched her political commitment to social justice. She became a devoted Catholic and defender of the faith for all of her remaining fifty-three years.

Day loved the Catholic Church and was totally committed to its teaching and discipline, but she was also critical of its failure to serve the needy. When she first entered the church, she felt like a hypocrite, because it "was lined up with property, with the wealthy, with the state, with capitalism, with all the forces of reaction."[14] She was troubled by a church that professed concern for the poor but did not raise a cry against their exploitation.[15] "When I see bishops living in luxury and the poor being ignored or thrown crumbs, I know that Jesus is being insulted."[16]

Nor was Day content with church-sponsored charities such as soup kitchens or shelters for the homeless. Charity is not enough, she insisted. She considered charity "a word to choke over."[17] Being generous to the needy leads some to accept poverty, to see it as a natural condition that can be ameliorated through the palliative of charity. Day was too close to the poor, too familiar with their suffering, to accept such a view or to settle for the meager efforts of church charity. What was needed was justice, she believed, a social order in which there would be less need for charity. She wanted to overcome the structural violence that denies so many people the opportunity for decent employment, education, health care, and housing. She wanted to challenge the institutional forces that give rise to poverty. This sometimes meant challenging the church itself. She said that "one must live in a state of permanent dissatisfaction with the Church."[18]

Many present and former Catholics have felt that dissatisfaction acutely. At times the church has acted as a bastion of backwardness, a citadel of male privilege and prejudice. During the Vietnam War, the official church was unsympathetic to those of us who spoke out against the war, more an obstacle than an ally to the cause of peace. Many are troubled today by the Catholic Church's continued opposition to contraception and sex education (although these are proven means of reducing unwanted pregnancies), its refusal to accept the ordination of women, and its insistence on celibacy for priests (which some link to the pedophilia crisis that has gripped the American church). On the other hand, the church has been a defender of the right to life and a protector of the needs of the poor and underprivileged. On international issues it has become a leading voice for peace, nuclear disarmament, and reduced military spending. Some conservative Catholic writers have complained of the "de facto pacifism" of the Vatican. The official position of the church is "just war" doctrine, not pacifism, but in practice the Vatican has been a frequent opponent of war. It was particularly vociferous in condemning the U.S. invasion of Iraq, labeling the March 2003 attack an act of "aggression."

The Catholic Church thus represents an ambiguous social force, simultaneously reactionary and progressive. Day faced similar ambiguities in her time. A church that extolled the rights of labor and the needs of the poor did little to address the underlying injustices that consigned millions of workers to unemployment and poverty during the Great Depression. She was deeply troubled by the church's accommodation of fascism during the 1930s and its complacency about the plight of the Jews.[19] Yet she continued to stand with the church, out of deep devotion to the underlying faith. She hoped that it would come to embody more completely the Christian message of love and that it would make a greater commitment to peace and social justice.

Day's religious conversion marked a turning point in her life, but she did not abandon her previous commitments. As psychologist and author Robert Coles writes, "Aspects of her past ... persisted as strengths in her later life."[20] She remained a committed political activist and brilliant writer with the "same awareness and ideals." She was always a woman "prepared to break ranks."[21] She was an uncompromising champion of the downtrodden, an advocate for the dignity of labor, an opponent of war and violence. The message of Christ reinforced Day's devotion to serving the poor and opposing war, and her belief in the necessary connection between the two. She was heir to a rich, if often-neglected, tradition of Catholic social teaching in support of the poor and the rights of labor. She embodied the original, now frequently forgotten Christian commitment to nonviolence as the true way of Christ. Day's life in the Catholic Church was a constant affirmation of Christ's call to serve the poor and put away the sword. She became a modern-day saint for an age ravaged by poverty and injustice and threatened by war and nuclear annihilation.

The *Catholic Worker*

Day was strongly influenced by Peter Maurin, an itinerant worker, writer, and social reformer whose eclectic philosophy combined Catholic social teaching and anarchism.[22] Maurin's indefatigable zeal matched Day's restless energy. Each was committed to radical social activism through nonviolent means. Maurin spoke of

GETTING CLOSE TO NATURE'S HEART
Dorothy Day, youthful author, discarding feminine frills and frivolities at
her tiny Staten Island bungalow, where she keeps house and writes novels.
(Kadel & Herbert.)

Early photo of Dorothy Day in front of her Staten Island bungalow in 1924 (photo courtesy of the Marquette University archives).

the need for a new society that would transcend the limitations of both capitalism and communism. He envisioned a future that was less competitive, with fewer smokestacks, where life would be simpler, where it would be, as he put it, "easier for people to be good."[23]

Day and Maurin wanted to create a new kind of social movement, one that was based on the teachings of Christ. They believed that social change must be rooted in sanctity and community.[24] Together they founded the Catholic Worker movement. They launched the *Catholic Worker* newspaper in May 1933 during the depths of the Depression, charging a penny a copy. The paper began with a print run of 2,500 but by 1936 was selling 150,000 copies per edition.[25] Day and Maurin also opened a series of "houses of hospitality" that provided shelter, food, and mercy for the poor and the unemployed. Dozens of

Catholic Worker houses sprang up in New York and other cities, and many continue today.

The Catholic Worker movement drew from two seemingly contradictory impulses: the Christian belief in the sacredness of life and the communist commitment to empowering workers and the poor. Day saw convergence, not contradiction in the messages of Christianity and communism.[26] Christ had driven the money changers from the temple, she recalled.[27] Christian teaching calls us to serve the poor and the needy, not just in charity but through justice.[28] Day admired the left for being on the front lines of the struggle to overcome the structures of oppression. Although she never joined the Communist Party and strongly opposed its atheism and violent methods, she refused to condemn or disassociate herself from her leftist friends. "I loved the Communists," she said. "They helped me to find God in His poor, in His abandoned ones."[29] She believed that the Marxist ideal, "from each according to his ability, to each according to his need," was borrowed from the teachings of Christ.

A Gandhian Faith

Day had much in common with Gandhi and was thoroughly familiar with his life and writings. She was greatly impressed by Louis Fischer's 1950 biography, describing it as "a wonderful study for all who are seeking peace in the world."[30] She saw in Gandhi's style of leadership a role for herself.[31] She shared his belief in nonviolence and the power of love. True faith, she said, is expressed in our love for others, especially our love for the "least of these." Her eulogy at the time of Gandhi's death portrayed him as a Christlike figure. "There is no public figure who has more conformed his life to the life of Jesus Christ than Gandhi, there is no man who has carried about him more consistently the aura of divinized humanity." He was assassinated, she wrote, "because he insisted that there be no hatred, that Hindu and Moslem live together in peace." She described him as a "pacifist martyr."[32]

Day shared Gandhi's commitment to an ascetic lifestyle. She had few possessions and lived most of her life in Catholic Worker communities, sharing the tasks of cooking and serving the needy, very much in the manner of Gandhi. She also shared

Gandhi's commitment to celibacy, according to Coles. After her conversion to the Catholic Church and the founding of the Catholic Worker, she lived her life "poor, chaste, and obedient."[33] She had no romantic involvements after Batterham, according to her longtime disciple Tom Cornell. She was under "spiritual direction" and devoted herself completely, body and soul, to her mission of Christian witness.[34]

Unlike Gandhi, Day was no prude. She chose celibacy for herself, but she did not demand it of others. "It is not idealism as against sensuality," she told Coles. "God . . . certainly put us here to enjoy our sexual lives."[35] When sexual love is genuine and faithful, it is a beautiful thing, she said. It is a "mating of spirit and flesh," a symbol of divine love. "It is the foretaste we have of heaven." But when sex is careless and exploitative, it "takes on the quality of the demonic, and . . . is a foretaste of hell."[36] Day called for a greater commitment to love and responsibility, not only in society but also in the social justice movement. She believed that the personal is political, although she didn't use that phrase. She urged higher standards of morality and mutual respect among activists. "I don't think the moral life of a social activist is a separate matter," she told Coles. "If we exploit each other personally and keep holding our placards and proclaiming our ideals to the world, then we've become hypocrites."[37] The idealism of our politics must be matched by idealism in our personal lives—our love and respect for others reflected in our private deeds as well as our public words.

For Day as for Gandhi, the decision to forego sexual relations was directly linked to the commitment to nonviolent struggle. Gandhi put on the loincloth and became celibate as he launched his satyagraha movement in South Africa. Day turned toward a more ascetic life as she founded the Catholic Worker movement. Both felt the need for greater spiritual discipline as they assumed the rigors of leading epic struggles for social justice. Gandhi sought spiritual power to achieve greater influence in his fight for political freedom and ethnic harmony. Day yearned for divine assistance as she faced the trials of serving the needy during the Depression and espousing nonviolence during World War II and the cold war. She considered her leadership in the Catholic Worker an indication of God's will, and she felt the need for an ascetic lifestyle to remain worthy of what she considered a sacred calling.[38]

Day also shared Gandhi's commitment to nonviolent action as a force for social change. Gandhi gained respect and support, Day wrote, because "he led his people to independence" and showed "that nonviolence worked" to achieve political change.[39] In a series of articles in the *Catholic Worker* in 1949 and 1950, Robert Ludlow described satyagraha as a spiritual discipline rooted in religious values and a social method for addressing questions of power and political conflict.[40] Gandhi showed that it is possible to confront and transform social evil through disciplined struggle and suffering. Day understood that the success of nonviolent action depends on the willingness to sacrifice. "The strongest wars in history," she wrote, are fought by activists with "no weapons but those of suffering."[41] She spoke of "the necessity ... and the glory of suffering for a cause."[42] She recognized, as other prophets of nonviolent action have emphasized, that attacks from the adversary are to be expected and even welcomed as indications of one's impact. She and her Catholic Worker colleagues viewed suffering as a spiritual act made possible by divine grace. They rejoiced at being "accounted worthy to suffer."[43]

Like Gandhi, Day became a revered figure among her colleagues and contemporaries. Even those who disagreed with her usually respected her profound religious faith and deep commitment to social justice. Just as Gandhi was called mahatma, or "great soul," Day was often considered a saint. Soon after her death, in fact, a movement to canonize her began, and in March 2000, New York's Cardinal John O'Connor formally opened sainthood proceedings.[44] Day probably would have disapproved. She bristled at talk of her saintliness, just as Gandhi disliked being called mahatma. "Don't call me a saint," she insisted. "I don't want to be dismissed so easily."[45]

Despite these many similarities, Day gave little indication of being directly influenced by Gandhi. Her voluminous writings rarely mention him and give no indication that she borrowed much from either his philosophy or method. Her most important articles on violence in the 1930s make no mention of Gandhi.[46] In her autobiography, Day reports reading Fischer's biography, but she says nothing about Gandhi himself.[47] Day did not need to rely on Gandhi. She went over his head, so to speak, to the original source: a religious commitment to love and truth as expressed in the teachings of Christ. She needed no other authority or inspiration for her commitment to non-violence and a lifetime of service to others.

A Peace Devotion

Day was a persistent critic of war and absolute pacifist throughout her life. She believed that a Christian could never kill under any circumstances. She even refused to support World War II, which cost the *Catholic Worker* many subscriptions and subjected her to widespread criticism and misunderstanding. Day was not neutral in the struggle against Nazism, however. She was a founder of Catholics to Fight Anti-Semitism in 1939 and lobbied the Roosevelt administration to lift quotas for Jewish immigrants from Europe. She challenged the anti-Semitic broadcasts of Father Charles Coughlin, the populist Catholic priest from Detroit who stoked the flames of intolerance in the United States during the 1930s. She reviled fascism and all it stood for. But she could not bring herself to endorse the mass slaughter that was engulfing the world. She feared that unleashing the forces of militarism would lead to ever more terrifying forms of destruction.[48]

The development of the atomic bomb seemed to prove Day's worst fears. She vigorously opposed this new means of annihilation. Day and others in the Catholic Worker movement launched a campaign to oppose civil defense air raid drills. In those days of cold war anxiety, when schoolchildren were instructed to "duck and cover" as protection against nuclear attack, the federal government ordered communities to practice air raid drills. When the state of New York announced a mandatory drill in June 1955, Day and her colleagues decided to disobey the order. At the appointed hour, when people were ordered to scurry into subways and basement shelters, Day and a few other determined activists sat conspicuously in City Hall Park and refused to budge. Their statement declared, "We do not have faith in God if we depend upon the atomic bomb."[49] Day and her colleagues were arrested and jailed. The protest was small and at first failed to arouse much response, but Day persisted. "Silence means consent, and we cannot consent to the militarization of our country."[50]

The air raid shelter protests continued through the 1950s. As public concern about nuclear testing and radioactive fallout increased, the protests began to draw attention. In 1960, a thousand people joined Day in defiance of the air raid drills. In 1961, two thousand people joined the protests, and all over New York the air raid sirens seemed to call people into the streets for protest rather than into the subways for protection.[51] As people in New York and across the country began to defy the civil defense drills, the program was quietly dropped. Day and her colleagues had helped spark a movement for nuclear sanity.[52]

Day was outraged by the war in Vietnam and deeply troubled by the prowar stance of many Catholic bishops, especially the ardent appeal for "total victory" of New York's Francis Cardinal Spellman. As a pacifist Day was opposed to all war, but she was particularly horrified by the massive U.S. military assault against this poor peasant nation. She supported the nonviolent witness of activist priests Daniel and Phillip Berrigan and Catholic war resisters, although she opposed efforts by the Berrigans and others to destroy Selective Service System records. Day never accepted property destruction as a legitimate form of nonviolent struggle, even if the property in question was part of the war machine. She had personal experience in suffering property attacks from hostile right-wing groups, which over the years burned Catholic Worker houses and barns and destroyed the organization's lists and records. She believed that property attacks were a violation of Gandhi's call for openness and truth. She also worried that they would lead to more destructive acts by less disciplined activists.

Nonetheless, Day greatly admired the willingness of Catholic activists to accept prison terms as the price of their antiwar discipleship. Day had no compunction about counseling individuals to disobey the law. As Vietnam-related draft calls began to increase, Day called on young men to refuse conscription. At a draft card burning in New York in the fall of 1965, she intentionally broke the law by publicly counseling men to resist the draft, thus sharing the legal jeopardy she was urging on others.[53] She encouraged Tom Cornell and others to found the Catholic Peace Fellowship, which assisted draftees in registering as conscientious objectors.

It is hard to evaluate the impact of Dorothy Day. She helped found a new movement for justice and peace and published a newspaper that reached hundreds of thousands, but she was not a political organizer in the traditional sense. She did not mount large-scale strategic campaigns in the manner of Gandhi, King, or Chavez to achieve specific political objectives. She was not credited with major transformations such as the political independence of India or the end of legal segregation in the United States. She did not strive for immediate results the way most activists do. Her purposes were different. She sought to shape attitudes and moral principles.[54] Her definition of success was more personal. Although she addressed huge social issues and challenged the very foundations of poverty and war, her primary goal was to bring about a spiritual revolution. She did not measure success by the number of laws that are passed but by the number of hearts that are transformed. In her case, that transformation took the form of a deeply felt religious devotion. Her faith helped her achieve personal and spiritual fulfillment, and it strengthened her commitment to social justice. She applied her faith both personally and socially, and in the process she created a new community of love.

Chapter 6

The Power of Nonviolence

Several years ago, I was invited to give a presentation on "Martin and Malcolm" before an audience of mostly African American inmates at a federal prison in Ohio. My audience was a well-educated and highly motivated group, participants in a college credit program. They had strong opinions on the contrasting philosophies of Martin Luther King Jr. and Malcolm X. All expressed great respect for King, but almost to a man they favored the philosophy of Malcolm X. "There's a war against the black man in America," one exclaimed. "The white power structure will only respond to the militant methods of Malcolm." Nonviolence is nice in theory, several said, but it cannot work against a heartless, brutal opponent. Heads nodded as I read Malcolm X's assertion: "Tactics based solely on morality can only succeed when you are dealing with people who are moral or a system that is moral."[1] When confronted with unrelenting oppression and institutionalized racism, they argued, the only response is "by any means necessary."

Many activists have similar doubts about the effectiveness of Gandhian methods. Some globalization protesters justify the trashing of property and even attacks against police as necessary to overcome the world domination of corporations and government. Even among peace and human rights activists, violence is sometimes considered acceptable if it is part of a revolutionary movement. While not appropriate for the streets of the United States, armed insurrection may be seen as legitimate for liberation fighters in the third world.

A certain degree of revolutionary romanticism exists among some American progressives. During the Zapatista "Intercontinental Encounter" in 1996, movie director Oliver Stone was photographed atop a horse carrying a rifle and wearing the trademark mask of Zapatista leader Subcomandante Marcos. Violent and destructive methods are sometimes seen as necessary to liberate the oppressed.

The question at the root of these concerns is a legitimate one: Should the victims of brutal tyranny be expected to maintain a strictly nonviolent response? When a legitimate popular movement striving for justice has attempted every nonviolent form of redress yet faces relentless repression and terror, must it maintain a purely nonviolent form of struggle? This is the challenge King faced from Malcolm X and later from the advocates of black power in the United States. The same challenge was posed by third world revolutions and African liberation movements. Nelson Mandela concluded in the early 1960s that armed struggle was necessary to overcome the brutalities of apartheid, although the resistance movement in South Africa ultimately succeeded in the 1980s mostly through nonviolent methods. Andrew Young wrote in his memoir that, while he always emphasized the advantages of nonviolence, he "refused to condemn those leaders who felt they had run out of nonviolent options."[2] Young argued that King also saw a difference between violence that is aggressive or retaliatory and that which is purely defensive. King vigorously condemned the former, insisting that we must break the action–reaction cycle of violence by refusing to retaliate against provocation. But he was willing to accept certain forms of defensive violence, citing the case of a black woman in rural Georgia who fired on Ku Klux Klan terrorists as they attempted to break into her home.[3]

Gandhi also faced the question of whether violence may be necessary at times and can be legitimate, but he was more uncompromising (some would say more dogmatic) in his response. The toughest challenge to Gandhi and his philosophy of nonviolence was posed by the Nazi Holocaust. Jewish leaders at the time questioned whether the Gandhian method was appropriate or even possible in the face of Hitlerism. In response to several queries, Gandhi wrote in 1938 that the Jews of Germany could resist nonviolently: "I am convinced that if someone with courage and vision could arise among them to lead them in non-violent action, the winter of their despair can in the twinkling of an eye be turned into the summer of hope."[4] Martin Buber replied sharply to Gandhi in a widely quoted letter: "In the five years which I myself spent under the present regime, I observed many instances of genuine satyagraha among the Jews.... Such actions, however, apparently exerted not the slightest influence on their opponents.... A diabolical universal steamroller cannot thus be withstood."[5] Judah Magnes, the outspoken Jewish educator and pacifist, himself a disciple of Gandhi, also responded skeptically, doubting that nonviolent action could be used effectively against Nazi barbarism.[6] In reply, Gandhi continued to insist that nonviolent action was appropriate for the Jewish community and that while many would suffer in such resistance efforts, in the end "Herr Hitler will bow before the courage" of satyagraha.[7]

Gandhi was quoted by Louis Fischer as saying that the Jews should commit collective suicide, which would arouse the people of the world to Hitler's violence. George Orwell was contemptuous of such thinking. "One has the impression," he wrote, "that this attitude staggered even so warm an admirer as Mr. Fischer."[8] Gandhi could not answer the question "What about the Jews?" because he did not understand the true horrors of totalitarianism. He could not comprehend the enormity of the evil perpetrated by that "diabolical universal steamroller." He was molded by his experience with the British, who could be brutally repressive in suppressing Indian nationalism but who never matched the ruthlessness and barbarity of the Nazis. Gandhi and his colleagues were always able to attract public attention and press coverage. But how can one "arouse the world," Orwell asked, when there are no outlets for free speech, and when regime opponents are taken away in the middle of the night and disappear without a trace?[9]

The experience of the Nazi Holocaust or Stalin's terror may indeed be the type of extreme case in which strictly nonviolent means will not work, at least not on a large enough scale to end systems of mass tyranny. This is the conclusion that Dietrich Bonhoeffer reached reluctantly, despite his pacifist convictions.

A religious leader and author of *The Cost of Discipleship* and other influential books, Bonhoeffer joined with theologians Karl Barth and Martin Niemöller to found the Confessing Church in Germany, which served as a voice of Christian opposition to Nazism and the suppression of Jews. Bonhoeffer believed passionately in the Sermon on the Mount and Christ's teaching to love even our enemies, but he could not stand aside in the face of Nazi tyranny. He concluded that violence was necessary to stop Nazism, and he joined the plots to assassinate Hitler, for which he paid with his life.

Nonviolent action may not be viable in every situation, but there are examples of nonviolent success even in the most extreme conditions. Gene Sharp and other scholars have documented examples of successful civil resistance to Hitler in Norway and other occupied countries.[10] Perhaps the most striking example of nonviolent resistance to Nazism occurred in the heart of Berlin in February 1943. When the Gestapo launched the final roundup of Jews, arresting thousands who were married to non-Jewish German spouses, it sparked an extraordinary protest.[11] When the family members, mostly women, learned that their loved ones were interned at a Jewish community building on a street called Rosenstrasse, they went there spontaneously, initially one by one or in small groups, and found themselves unexpectedly part of a growing crowd. They returned again the next morning and began to shout in unison, "We want our husbands back." The crowd grew to nearly one thousand people. Unauthorized public gatherings had been banned in Germany for nearly a decade. A Gestapo headquarters office was right around the corner. In the nearby Reich Security Main Office, where Adolf Eichmann worked, Nazi officials debated whether to crack down on the women or make an accommodation. Traffic on Rosenstrasse was diverted, and the nearby elevated train station was closed, but the spouses continued their daily vigil. After a week, Propaganda Minister Joseph Goebbels stepped in to end the standoff. The continuing protest was unacceptable at a time when the regime was mobilizing for "total war." Goebbels ordered the release of between 1,700 and 2,000 Jews. His deputy said in a postwar interview that "Goebbels released the Jews in order to end the protest." Even at the center of Nazi power in Berlin, protest was possible and effective.

Orwell argued that Gandhian methods could not work against Stalinism, yet several attempts at mass resistance were made in Eastern Europe during the cold war.[12] The entire Soviet system collapsed in the late 1980s under the weight of mass nonviolent protest and noncooperation. The "velvet revolution" that swept through Poland, Hungary, East Germany, and into the Soviet Union itself was completely unprecedented and unexpected—the greatest wave of nonviolent political change in history. Yet even this great success does not guarantee that nonviolence can work in every case, especially in circumstances of unrelenting repression. There are numerous examples—Kosovo in the early 1990s, China in 1989, the Burmese democracy movement since 1990—where nonviolent methods have been tried but have been unsuccessful. The potential for nonviolent resistance exists in every case, but the actual conditions for its development may not be present.

My own belief is that one's reply to these difficult questions is inevitably conditioned by personal circumstance. For myself, as a white, middle-class North American who has never faced terror or the threat of death because of my political activities, I do not feel in a position to insist to a Palestinian militant in the West Bank or a black activist in south central Los Angeles that she or he must always renounce violence. Yet I can and will insist for myself and colleagues who share a similar social experience that nonviolence is indispensable, and that the method pioneered by Gandhi and developed by King is morally and politically superior to other forms of social struggle.

Challenges to Nonviolence

In the United States, the viability of nonviolence was strongly challenged in the mid- to late 1960s. After the halcyon days of the civil rights movement, when nonviolent campaigns in Birmingham and Selma helped bring down the system of segregation, respect for the Gandhian method began to fade. King's strategy of nonviolence and respect for the law was sharply challenged by student activist Stokely Carmichael and the black power movement. Particularly in the urban north, African Americans saw little or no improvement in their lives from the victories of the civil rights movement. Most continued to chafe under grinding poverty, rampant police brutality, and an utter lack of opportunity for advancement. Many were angry at the oppressive white power structure and eager for faster, more radical change. For the critics of nonviolence, the choice seemed to be between a meek plea for justice on the one hand and a strong and forcible demand for power on the other. Respect for nonviolence was also undermined by the culture of violence bred by the escalating war in Vietnam. The corrosive consequences of the war were captured in King's famous 1967 address at Riverside Church in New York:

> As I have walked among the desperate, rejected and angry young men I have told them that Molotov cocktails and rifles would not solve their problems. I have tried to offer them . . . my conviction that social change comes most meaningfully through nonviolent action. But they asked—and rightfully so—what about Vietnam? They asked if our own government wasn't using massive doses of violence to solve its problems. . . . Their questions hit home, and I knew that I could never again raise my voice against the violence of the oppressed in the ghettos without having first spoken clearly to the greatest purveyor of violence in the world today—my own government.[13]

When I entered the antiwar movement in the late 1960s, this mood of frustration and militancy was plainly evident. As a naive, recent convert to the movement, I expected peace activists to be loving and gentle, perhaps a bit like politicized hippies. Instead, there was divisiveness, anger, and revolutionary rhetoric. Many of us were turned off by the militant sloganeering and radical posturing, but we understood and shared the anguish that many felt about the intractability of the war and the apparent inability of all the marches and demonstrations to stop it. It was easy to see why many activists longed for more effective and forceful means of opposition. Within the antiwar movement, as among civil rights activists, there was a palpable desire for more assertive forms of nonviolent resistance.

Barbara Deming and Revolutionary Nonviolence

Into the fray stepped Barbara Deming with her seminal essay, "On Revolution and Equilibrium," published in *Liberation* magazine in February 1968. King scholar Stewart Burns described

Barbara Deming of the War Resisters League at a peace rally in 1968 (photo: Dorothy Marder).

Deming's essay as "the decade's most persuasive intellectual challenge" to the call for violence.[14] Deming offered an eloquent defense of the Gandhian method and issued a passionate plea for more forceful but still nonviolent forms of resistance. A writer and critic by profession, a member of the War Resisters League, the Committee on Nonviolent Action, and many other activist groups, Deming was deeply involved in the civil rights movement (arrested in Birmingham in 1963), the Vietnam antiwar movement (arrested during the 1967 march on the Pentagon), and the disarmament campaigns of the 1980s (a founder of the Women's Peace Camp in Seneca, New York). She was also an outspoken feminist and defender of lesbian rights. Her writings offered vivid and penetrating insights into the world of activism and the meaning of nonviolence. Deming deserves to be better known than she is today. She transformed and modernized the Gandhian method by developing a systematic argument for nonviolent action that rested entirely on pragmatic rather than religious foundations. She stretched the limits of nonviolence to mold it into a militant and revolutionary form of social change.

Deming's embrace of nonviolence followed a trip to India in 1959. The journey aroused her interest in Gandhi and set her on a path of discovery.[15] "It was after the visit to India," she recalled, "that I began to read Gandhi. Realized that I was in the deepest part of myself a pacifist. Read more and more by him and about him. Became at once deeply committed to nonviolent struggle."[16] Prior to that she described herself as being "vaguely liberal."[17] Afterward she became a radical activist, and her subsequent life was a whirlwind of demonstrations, marches, and civil disobedience on behalf of nuclear disarmament, civil rights, peace, women's liberation, and gay and lesbian rights.[18]

Deming's study of Gandhi was important to her activist transformation, but the decisive factor in her personal journey was a 1960 trip to Cuba. It was during that trip and an impromptu interview with Fidel Castro that Deming's emerging commitment to social activism crystallized.[19] During the interview, Deming questioned why it was necessary for the revolution to kill its adversaries. Castro responded sharply by asking Deming where she was staying in Havana (it was a luxury hotel) and whether she had seen the poverty and desperation of the Cuban people (she had not). Taken aback and perhaps a bit embarrassed, Deming set out on a journey of discovery across the island. She saw firsthand the misery of the population and heard testimony from the victims of the former Batista dictatorship's brutal policies.[20] She encountered poverty as she had never seen before, and she was deeply moved. This daughter of privilege (her father was a corporate attorney) felt that she could no longer remain neutral in the struggle against oppression. She vowed to commit herself to the struggle for justice and peace, but to do so nonviolently.

Deming's philosophy tried to combine Gandhi and Castro. She sought to reconcile the seemingly contradictory impulses of nonviolence and revolution. She embraced and celebrated the principles of Gandhian nonviolence, but she also believed in the necessity of revolution. She urged revolutionists to see the potential of nonviolent means, and she challenged nonviolent activists to adopt ever more powerful means of disruption and noncooperation. "This is how we stand up for ourselves nonviolently," Deming said. "We refuse the authorities our labor, we refuse them our money, ... we refuse them our bodies (to fight in their wars)."[21] Those who employ nonviolent methods have "simply never gone as far as they could in this direction."[22]

Deming insisted that nonviolent action is not merely prayerful protest. It is much more than a means of persuasion and moral appeal. It can be, and in her view must be, a form of coercion, a means of exerting power. "To resort to power one need not be violent, and to speak to conscience one need not be meek. The most effective action *both* resorts to power *and* engages conscience."[23] If properly applied, Deming argued, nonviolent action can be highly effective. In fact, it is more effective than violent methods. The choice is not between accepting oppression and resorting to violent resistance. Revolutionary nonviolence provides a third way. It allows us to be, in the words of author Albert Camus, neither victim nor executioner.

Deming wrote "Revolution and Equilibrium" partly as a response to the highly influential book *The Wretched of the Earth,* written by Frantz Fanon, the West Indian psychologist and radical opponent of colonialism. Fanon extolled revolutionary violence as a liberating, "dizzying" step toward freedom for the oppressed. Violence is necessary, Fanon asserted, to create a new consciousness of liberation, to empower the oppressed to break the chains of bondage. Deming agreed with Fanon that a revolution is needed against the structural violence of the status quo, not only in the third world but in the United States as well. She also agreed with black power advocates in the United States that the protests of the civil rights and antiwar movements were often ineffectual, and that the progressive movement in America must go beyond mere symbolic action to bolder and more creative forms of resistance. But she insisted that armed struggle is not the best means of achieving these ends. The resort to violence is no guarantee of success.[24]

Violence can exact a severe toll, not only on those who tremble under its fury but on those who use it. Fanon wrote that the resort to violence can lead to "an attack of vertigo," creating doubt and anguish about the consequences of one's actions. Deming seized on this concept, insisting that we must avoid the dizzying effects of violence. "If ... we will wage battle without violence, we can remain very much more in control—of our own selves, of the responses to us which our adversaries make, of the battle as it proceeds, and of the future we hope will issue from it."[25] Through nonviolent resistance, we can wage revolutionary struggle against war and oppression yet maintain the personal and social balance necessary for a just outcome. Deming insisted that the methods of mass noncooperation and civil resistance pioneered by Gandhi and King were capable of challenging the most powerful and entrenched systems of oppression and were the most effective means of bringing about a more just and peaceful society. Her colleague Dave Dellinger agreed. Nonviolence uses strikes, boycotts, civil disobedience, and mass noncooperation to undermine the oppressor's ability to commit injustice. In the process it creates an "adjustment of grievances through mutual respect."[26]

To the skeptics who argued that nonviolence has been tried and found wanting, Deming replied, "It has *not* been tried. We have hardly begun to try it. The people who dismiss it ... do not understand what it could be."[27] Gandhi himself said, at the end of his life, that the "technique of unconquerable nonviolence as a weapon of the strong has not been discovered as yet."[28] Dellinger said that nonviolence was at a "primitive state of development" roughly equivalent to the harnessing of electricity in the early days of Edison. Because of our limited experience so far, we don't yet know its full potential and limitations.[29] Throughout history violence has been the usual means of revolutionary change. Nonviolence is the new and still-undeveloped method. Only at the beginning of the twentieth century, with Gandhi's campaigns of mass noncooperation in South Africa and India, did nonviolent action begin to emerge as a viable means of social change. While examples of nonviolent action can be found throughout history, as Sharp documented, it is only in the last century that the nonviolent method has made a contribution to revolutionary change.[30] Gandhi's great innovation, later enlarged upon by King, was to elevate nonviolence into a tool of mass action. Many of the previous historic approaches to nonviolence were individualist in nature. With the mass social action campaigns of Gandhi, King, and others, the nonviolent method began to be applied systematically on a broad scale.

As Walter Wink observed, mass-based nonviolent action has become a frequent tool of social change in recent years. In the South African freedom struggle, during the overthrow of communism in Central and Eastern Europe, in the "people power" revolution in the Philippines, and in countless other social struggles, the nonviolent action methods of Gandhi and King have been applied with growing frequency and success. Wink exulted, "never before have citizens actualized this potential in such overwhelming numbers or to such stunning effect. And yet 'people power' is still in its infancy!"[31] Nonviolent action also played a crucial role in the political transformations that rocked Serbia, Georgia, and Ukraine in 2000, 2003, and 2004.[32] Compared to the previous sweep of history, these recent applications of nonviolent action are but a fleeting moment. The lessons to be learned have yet to be distilled and applied. As Deming correctly observed, nonviolence is still "in the process of invention."[33]

Popular culture and the dominant symbolism of society have yet to catch up with this nonviolent awakening. Apart from the national holiday for Martin Luther King Jr. in the United States, there are few occasions for acknowledging the power and importance of nonviolence. The cultural images and media messages we receive from an early age tend to glorify war and military conflict. The statues in the parks and the heroes celebrated on civic occasions are mostly warriors. Christ's teaching to love our neighbors or turn the other cheek may intrude during Sunday morning church services, but the underlying message of nonviolence is otherwise ignored or suppressed. Conventional wisdom continues to uphold war and military violence as the natural and even virtuous way of resolving conflict. The nonviolent heroes who sacrifice to uphold peace and human rights have yet to be recognized as the pioneers of a new, more creative means for achieving justice. Nobel Peace Prize winner and Holocaust survivor Elie Wiesel told an interviewer in 1994, "For centuries we've been glorifying war.... Why not give a medal to those who oppose and prevent war? Give *them* the medal of honor."[34]

Coercion

To be politically effective, nonviolent action must be able to challenge power. Symbolic protest is not enough. One must also confront and undermine oppressive power with forceful action. The key to assertive social action, Deming argued, is acknowledging and even embracing the coercive elements of nonviolence. Coercion means forcing another to act against his or her will. Through mass noncooperation and actions that disrupt business as usual, nonviolent resisters can limit an adversary's freedom of movement. By directly intervening in the social, economic, and political functioning of the system, activists can undermine authority and create new realities that must be accommodated. Nonviolent resisters employ social force when they blockade an intersection or occupy a building. They exert economic force when they engage in boycotts or strikes. They use political force when they defy orders or refuse to participate in institutions. These and other forms of nonviolent action, elaborately enumerated by Sharp,[35] constitute the coercive elements of nonviolence. They challenge power by altering or restraining the adversary's options, physically intervening to prevent certain oppressive actions. Such actions are more than an attempt to persuade. They actually undermine and impede the exercise of power.

Deming had none of Gandhi's ambiguity about the coercive elements of nonviolence. Like King, she had a more pragmatic and realistic approach to the question of coercion. Entrenched privilege cannot be overcome merely with persuasion. Pressure and forceful action are often necessary to bring about political change. Deming shared King's interest in developing more assertive forms of Gandhianism that rely less on persuasion and more on coercive pressure. She urged the strongest possible methods of nonviolent action. In the process, she stretched the definition of what is nonviolence. The difference between violence and nonviolence, she argued, is not in the use of force but in the prevention of physical harm. Any form of action is permissible, she believed, as long as it does not cause physical injury to another person.

Deming's standard raises moral and political concerns, however. Some forms of nonviolent action may avoid direct injury to another but nonetheless impose serious harm and suffering. If noninjury is to be the criterion for judging whether an action is violent or nonviolent, indirect effects also must be taken into account. As Niebuhr pointed out, a boycott can deprive a community of its livelihood and, if maintained long enough, may even lower living standards to the point of threatening life.[36] In international affairs, economic sanctions can be harsh and deadly instruments that impose their greatest harm on the most vulnerable.[37] General trade sanctions on Iraq contributed to severe malnutrition and disease, resulting in hundreds of thousands of preventable deaths.[38] Nonviolent protest actions, such as a blockade or obstruction of traffic, may severely infringe upon the freedom and well-being of others, and they may even cause harm to those in need of emergency services. Such actions pose moral dilemmas and may also create political problems by generating a backlash of public resentment.

When disruptive actions are indiscriminate and cause severe hardships for innocent or vulnerable populations, they lose their moral legitimacy and political support. If coercive action is to be effective and morally legitimate, it must be targeted to apply pressure on those responsible for injustice, while limiting harm to innocent bystanders. The targeted boycotts of the civil rights movement sought to limit collateral damage and direct coercive pressure against those most responsible for segregation (and also most capable of bringing about change). Few, other than the wealthy individuals targeted by such action, could have moral objection to the use of targeted boycotts or strikes to bring about social justice. At the United Nations, international policymakers have increasingly turned to targeted or smart sanctions as an alternative to general trade sanctions. Through such measures as arms embargoes and the freezing of financial assets, UN officials have sought to direct coercive pressure against decision-making elites while avoiding harm to innocent or vulnerable populations.[39]

Property Damage

A more complicated question concerns the issue of sabotage and property damage. Gandhi ruled out sabotage and objected to any actions that lead to physical destruction. Day also objected to property damage. But Sharp included sabotage in his listing of legitimate nonviolent action methods. Deming had a more nuanced view. She believed that some forms of property damage may be acceptable if such actions avoid personal injury and do not create a political backlash. Deming distinguished between property that is an extension of a person, such as a home, and that which is destructive, such as a factory producing nuclear missiles. She justified sabotage against the latter as a legitimate means of disabling an instrument of mass annihilation.[40] Acts of sabotage should be directed only against "property that is by its nature deathly or exploitative, and unambiguously so."[41] But she cautioned that such acts must not harm people and must have popular support. "As we strike at the machinery of death, we have to do so in a way that the general population understands, that encourages more and more people to join us."[42]

During the Vietnam War, resisters inside the U.S. military occasionally resorted to sabotage in an attempt to disable the war machine. The most spectacular incidents occurred in July 1972 when two of the navy's aircraft carriers, the U.S.S. *Forrestal* and the U.S.S. *Ranger,* were put out of action by sailors aboard ship.[43] On the *Forrestal,* sailors set fire to the admiral's quarters and extensively damaged the ship's radar center. On the *Ranger,* a paint scraper and two twelve-inch bolts were dropped into one of the ship's main engine gears. These incidents disrupted naval war operations, especially in the case of the *Ranger,* without causing bodily harm to anyone. Senior officers decried the destruction of navy property, but no tears were shed among enlisted sailors who opposed the war and welcomed the chance to stay home. Acts of antiwar sabotage encouraged other forms of resistance within the ranks and contributed to the general malaise that undermined military effectiveness and hastened the war's end.

The question of property damage has become a pressing concern for the global justice movement. Although only a tiny fraction of global justice activists actually engaged in destructive acts, the behavior of that small minority became a large issue for the overall movement. In the wake of the vandalism and street fighting that occurred during protests in Seattle in 1999 during the World Trade Organization meeting and Genoa in 2001 during the G-8 summit, many activists began to debate the issues raised by destructive acts.[44] Throwing bricks or fire bombs at the police was clearly beyond the bounds of nonviolence, but what about the breaking of windows at a Starbucks? Some anarchists justified the trashing of stores as a legitimate tactic in the struggle against corporate globalization.[45] Others worried that property destruction could escalate into fanaticism and violence against people.[46]

Pacifists have sometimes engaged in property damage—the destruction of military draft records at Catonsville, Maryland, in 1969, the hammering of nuclear nose cones during the Plow-shares actions in 1993 and 1998. How is this different from vandalizing a multinational company that exploits workers and despoils the environment? One important distinction is that the pacifist resisters who destroyed draft records or ham-mered nuclear missiles were accountable for their actions and in most cases accepted arrest and imprisonment to underscore their readiness to sacrifice. They remained at the scene of their "crime" to face arrest and explain their actions. In so doing they communicated to the public and sought to bring more people into the circle of resistance.[47] In the manner of Gandhi and King, they maintained a spirit of love and respect for their adversaries. Accepting the penalty of the law, they expressed their support for the higher principles of justice and peace that law is supposed to uphold. By contrast, the anarchists who trashed stores in Seattle and Genoa wore masks and fled from the scene to avoid apprehension. They were neither accountable nor loving in their behavior and acted more as rioters than protesters.[48] Such ac-tions have little in common with the principles of nonviolence.

Pragmatic considerations also enter into this equation. The resort to vandalism and street trashing can turn off potential supporters and distract media attention from a movement's core message. In Genoa the main news story was not debt relief for the world's poor but street battles between police and anarchists. When property destruction is wanton and indiscriminate, as it was in Genoa, it creates negative media images and popular revulsion. When the Genoa protests turned ugly and violent, even many movement supporters stayed away.

Ecoterrorism has become a concern for the environmental movement. Groups such as the Earth Liberation Front (ELF) and the Animal Liberation Front (ALF) have damaged ski resorts and housing developments, attacked animal farms, fire-bombed genetic engineering labs, and spiked trees (hammering large nails or spikes into trees so that they won't be cut).[49] Some of these actions, especially tree spiking, pose risks to human life. Liberation Front militants claim that mainstream environmental groups have been too timid, which is true in some cases, and that more forceful methods are needed to save the Earth from ruin. The global environmental crisis is indeed grave, and there is a clear need for more effective and assertive action, but eco-terrorism is not the answer. ELF and ALF actions have sparked a strong political backlash in the United States, especially in the wake of the terrorist attacks of 9/11. There is little public sympathy for such action, even among those who support the cause of saving forests and protecting animals. The cause may be just, but the means are not.

Individual terrorist acts cannot stop the juggernaut of environmental ruin caused by irresponsible corporate and government behavior. Developers may be temporarily inconvenienced by incidents of "ecotage," but they are usually able to roll over their opponents and continue despoiling the Earth. When it comes to saving the environment, there is no alternative to the difficult and often-frustrating tasks of consciousness raising and political organizing. Terrorist acts make such work more difficult. They may also discredit direct action environmentalism, as practiced by groups such as Greenpeace. The latter is completely nonviolent in nature and is a legitimate and often effective means of environmental action. It includes tree sitting, blockading, trespassing, and other forms of noncooperation or nonviolent intervention. Groups such as Greenpeace may disobey the law during such actions, but they avoid property damage or any risk to other humans. They operate openly and are willing to face the consequences of their action. They enjoy considerable public sympathy and are often successful in building public opposition to destructive corporate and government practices. They are more effective at protecting the environment than ecoterrorists.

The problem with sabotage is that it is born of frustration, driven by a desperate desire to speed the pace of change. But there is no shortcut to progress. Acts of destruction by a few cannot substitute for action by many. Progressive change requires a democratic process that invites and wins broad public support. As Deming wrote, the new world we seek "can only be built in the company of a great many people."[50]

The Two Hands

Deming emphasized the importance of maintaining control during a conflict. By keeping our equilibrium and avoiding the dizzying effects of violence and chaos, we can better control our own reactions and those of the adversary. We can put more effective pressure on and control the responses of an adversary for whom we show respect and concern. It is the combination of solicitude for the person and determined opposition to his policies that gives the nonviolent activist a special degree of control. This is what Deming called the "two hands" phenomenon: respect for the person combined with defiance of his policies. Together they are "uniquely effective":

> The more the real issues are dramatized, and the struggle raised above the personal, the more control those in nonviolent rebellion begin to gain over their adversary. For they are able at one and the same time to disrupt everything for him, making it impossible for him to operate within the system as usual, and to temper his response to this.... They have as it were two hands upon him—the one calming him, making him ask questions, as the other makes him move.[51]

By assuring the personal safety of the adversary and refusing to respond in kind to repression or attack, the nonviolent activist constrains or limits the level of violence in a dispute. The usual action–reaction cycle of escalating violence is broken. Niebuhr identifies this "spiritual discipline against resentment" as one of the greatest advantages of the nonviolent method.[52] Violent attack inevitably creates resentment and the desire for revenge. The bullets and shells fired in war sow the seeds of continued violence in the future. Nonviolence cuts across this tendency. It conveys a message of respect and concern. It offers reassurance against personal harm. It cools the desire for retaliation.

The unique duality of nonviolent action—concern for the person, but defiance of authority—throws the adversary off balance. The adversary may respond harshly at first, but the lack of retaliation by the challenger upsets the usual emotional and psychological response pattern. The challenger's readiness to accept punishment without retaliation robs repressive methods of their bite and makes them counterproductive. Sharp and others refer to this as "political ju-jitsu."[53] Just as the agile fighter causes his stronger opponent to lose physical balance, so the nonviolent challenger causes the adversary to lose moral and political footing. Gandhi invoked the image of a strong man striking water with a sword. The water remains as before. The man's arm is hurt.[54] The adversary's physical power is of no use and may even be a detriment. Meanwhile, the challenger maintains equilibrium and control. The goal in all this, said Deming, is to blow the opponent's mind, to shake up the adversary and induce a process of questioning and reappraisal.[55] This is possible because one expresses concern for the adversary's personal safety, while displaying determined opposition to unjust policies.

Creative Energy

When we are challenged physically, our usual response is anger and hostility. In nonviolent struggle this normal reaction pattern is disrupted. As Richard Gregg emphasizes, the controlled demeanor of the nonviolent activist alters the dynamic flow of emotional and psychic energy during a conflict. The intense energy burst that comes in response to attack is tempered. The desire to strike back is frustrated, and the emotional response of the adversary becomes confused and uncertain. There may even be an involuntary, sympathetic response to the challenger's willingness to suffer.[56] Gregg believes that these unfamiliar responses revert back on the adversary and upset normal cognitive processes. The adversary may begin to have doubts and start to see the issues in a new light.

Nonviolent action is a unifying force. Instead of energies clashing as they do in violent conflict, the contending forces in a nonviolent struggle interact and are able to learn from one another. Gregg emphasizes that the flow of energy in nonviolent action can be creative and mutually reinforcing, leading to synthesis and reconciliation. The spirit of love within nonviolence creates greater understanding and peace.[57] Violence repels and divides. Love attracts and unites.

Because nonviolent action reduces animosities to a minimum, it allows for what Niebuhr called "a certain degree of objectivity in analyzing the issues of the dispute."[58] In a violent conflict, hatred clouds our perceptions and prevents us from seeing the other side's perspective. Rage blinds our vision. The nonviolent method, by contrast, allows the contending parties to engage in dialogue more readily and facilitates understanding. Violence makes communication and dialogue more difficult and impedes the reconciliation of contending viewpoints. Nonviolence keeps the lines of communication open and allows for mutual understanding and reconciliation.

Nonviolence enables us to distinguish between person and function, to hate the sin but not the sinner. Deming emphasized the importance of differentiating between the adversary as a person and his or her role in the machinery of oppression. We must attempt to separate the social evil of an oppressive policy from the persons who carry out that policy. Niebuhr sharply differentiates personal and social immorality. "Individuals are never as immoral as the social situation in which they are involved."[59] We must treat our opponents not as parts of a machine but as people capable of compassion and change.[60] Of course we can never completely disassociate social evil from the persons who practice it, but as a practical matter, attempting to separate the two helps minimize animosities and resentment and places the principal focus on the issues involved, not on personalities.

The nonviolent challenger seeks to get through to the adversary's other side, to address constituencies within the opponent's power base. This is possible because nonviolent action minimizes the likelihood of a rally-around-the-flag effect, which often occurs in wars or in cases of physical coercion. Where there are no casualties and no one suffers physical harm, there is less pressure to close ranks behind the leader. People are more likely to hear the message of the challenger. The discussion of the issues is more open. The challenger may even have the opportunity to appeal directly to the adversary's constituency. Gandhi did this with consummate skill in his visit to England during the roundtable conference in 1931. He spent more time outside the conference meeting with ordinary people and political and cultural luminaries than he did negotiating with British officials. In the process, Gandhi won great popular sympathy and respect, even among the mill workers in Lancashire who were being put out of work by the Indian boycott of British cloth. Through these encounters with the British people, Gandhi did more to undermine the authority of British rule than was accomplished in the fruitless discussions with Lord Irwin.

Martin Luther King Jr. followed a similar script and successfully appealed to key constituencies within the white power structure, not only in the South but throughout the United States. He cultivated close relationships with white churches, the Jewish community, trade unions, and other key constituencies within the Democratic Party and thereby exerted pressure on the Kennedy and Johnson administrations.

An obvious advantage of nonviolent struggle is that it pro-
duces fewer casualties. The problem is that they're all on the
side of the movement. This is hard to accept. During the civil
rights struggle, dozens of activists and even innocent children
were killed, while the terrorists who perpetrated these crimes
suffered no harm and in most cases were not even brought to
justice. In nonviolent struggle the battle is completely one-sided.
The burden of physical suffering falls completely on the side
of the nonviolent challengers. For many people it seems wrong
and even immoral that those who are struggling for justice
should suffer casualties while the oppressors escape harm. Yet
this seemingly perverse imbalance is to be expected. As Sharp
emphasized, the adversary's resort to violence is a sign of weakness and desperation. It may indicate that the balance is ready
to tip in the challenger's favor.[61] The greater the suffering by
nonviolent challengers, the more likely they are to gain sympathy and support from bystanders. In the upside-down world of
nonviolent struggle, victory has nothing to do with punishing
the adversary. The goal is not to defeat or humiliate the opponent, said King, but to bring about reconciliation. As Deming
observed, "vengeance is not the point; change is.... A liberation
movement that is nonviolent sets the oppressor free as well as
the oppressed."[62] It liberates the adversary from enemy status,
and it frees both parties from the state of enmity. It changes the
relationship between challenger and adversary, thereby altering
the political position of the adversary.

The Third-Party Effect

Perhaps the most important feature of the nonviolent method
is its ability to win the sympathy and political support of those
who were previously uncommitted. Deming called this "the
special genius of nonviolence."[63] Sharp referred to it as the art
of winning over uncommitted third parties.[64] Dellinger said
that the success of nonviolence depends on winning the support of those who were previously hostile or neutral.[65] This
alters the political and moral dynamics of a struggle and tips
the balance of power toward the nonviolent challenger. If the
adversary is unjustifiably harsh or repressive in responding
to nonviolent action, support for the challengers may increase

while the adversary's own base of support shrinks. As Gandhi emphasized, power ultimately rests on the consent of the governed. Even in the most dictatorial of regimes, leaders depend on the support or acquiescence of the people to remain in power. That support can begin to erode, however, when authorities abuse their power, and especially when they are unjustifiably brutal toward nonviolent challengers. People who were previously indifferent or on the sidelines may be moved by such unjustified brutality to support the nonviolent challengers.

As a general rule, nonviolence attracts support, while violence repels it. When social activists resort to violence, they usually turn off potential supporters and push third parties into the camp of the adversary. Street fighting and vandalism at globalization protests have alienated potential allies and undermined the effectiveness of the global justice movement. During the Vietnam antiwar movement, the violent actions of a few turned off the many who otherwise opposed the war and supported the goals of the peace movement. On the other hand, when unprovoked violence is employed by the adversary, support for the movement increases, as those on the sidelines are motivated by sympathy and/or shock to become allies. This was dramatically illustrated in India during the great salt satyagraha of 1930, when hundreds of Gandhian activists were beaten by police at the Dharasana salt works. Hour after hour, volunteers courageously stepped forward to enter the salt works, only to be clubbed by steel-sheathed police batons. The spectacle of police officers raining blows on the heads of defenseless protestors shocked world opinion and generated widespread support for the Gandhian movement in India and in Britain itself. According to Louis Fischer, the incident "made England powerless and India invincible."[66]

The same phenomenon occurred during the civil rights movement in the United States. The violence unleashed against the freedom riders in May 1961 generated widespread public revulsion and swelled the ranks of the movement. In Birmingham in 1963, Police Commissioner Bull Connor unleashed dogs and fire hoses on defenseless marchers, including many children. The public response was shock and increased sympathy for the movement. In Selma in 1965, Sheriff Jim Clark fired tear gas and sent horse-mounted police against demonstrators crossing the Edmund Pettus Bridge. Dramatic scenes of the police brutalizing nonviolent protesters were broadcast to the world on television and had a powerful impact on public opinion, generating widespread sympathy and increased support for the demands of the civil rights movement.

The use of excessive force often undermines the legitimacy of the adversary's authority. As Niebuhr writes, unjustified brutality "robs the opponent of the moral conceit" that identifies his interest with the larger good of society. He describes this as "the most important of all the imponderables in a social struggle."[67] In the wake of Gandhi's great satyagraha campaigns, says Niebuhr, British fulminations about law and order lacked "moral unction." The legitimacy and pretense of British rule were challenged by the massive scale of Indian noncooperation, by the dignity and discipline of those who participated, and by the brutal excesses of British repression at Dharasana and elsewhere. In the wake of these events, public sympathy within India and around the world shifted decisively against continued British rule. The intransigence of Winston Churchill and the Tories could delay but not prevent the transition to Indian independence. In the civil rights movement as well, the ugly displays of segregationist violence in Birmingham, Selma, and elsewhere, combined with the unflagging courage and dignity of African American protestors, rapidly undermined the seemingly impregnable power of southern hard-liners and generated an overwhelming national consensus in favor of civil rights.

The presence of an audience is crucial to the workings of the third-party effect. The moral and political dynamics of nonviolent action are greatly magnified when there are onlookers. This means that effective press relations and media communications are extremely important to the success of nonviolent action. Press coverage is necessary to create the audience, which enlarges the role of potential third parties.[68] Media coverage acts as a kind of mirror, reflecting the contrast between the harsh behavior of the adversary and the sacrifice of the challengers.[69] Gandhi and King were keenly aware of the importance of an audience, and they arranged their most important campaigns so as to maximize press coverage. Gandhi was a master at ensuring widespread press coverage for his campaigns of civil resistance, even in the years before broadcast journalism. The attempt to enter Dharasana salt works in 1930 was announced in advance to the press, and many important reporters were present to witness and write about the gruesome display of police brutality. United Press correspondent Webb Miller described the scene in words that were published in two thousand newspapers and read aloud in the U.S. Senate.[70] They shocked readers throughout the English-speaking world: marchers "went down like ten-pins ... the sickening whack of clubs on unprotected skulls."[71]

The civil rights movement was able to take advantage of the power of television journalism. It was the first activist movement in history to unfold before the modern news media.[72] The movement used the media to its advantage not only in Birmingham but during the "bloody Sunday" incident at the Pettus Bridge in Selma. The unprovoked police attack on civil rights marchers that Sunday was broadcast to the nation and the world. This was just at the time when the national news networks were beginning to introduce immediate live coverage of breaking news events. By ironic coincidence on that Sunday night, ABC television was broadcasting the movie *Judgment at Nuremberg.* The film was interrupted several times with updates and replays of the police attack. Television viewers were appalled by the graphic film footage of the police assault on the peaceful marchers. As Andrew Young wrote, "The violence in Selma was so similar to the violence in Nazi Germany that viewers could hardly miss the connection."[73] According to John Lewis, who was severely beaten in the march, the images of Selma "touched a deeper nerve" than any previous event. The spectacle of "troopers ... on horseback rolling into and over ... stoic, silent, unarmed people" was unprecedented. It was a vivid face-off between dignified, composed demonstrators and "the truly malevolent force of a heavily armed, hateful battalion."[74] The carnage of Bloody Sunday created an immediate national and worldwide revulsion against segregationism and generated enormous sympathy and support for the civil rights movement. The response, said Lewis, was "greater than anything I'd seen ... greater than the freedom rides, greater than the March on Washington, greater than Mississippi Summer. The country seemed truly aroused."[75]

President Lyndon Johnson in the White House was also deeply moved. On Monday, 15 March, just eight days after Bloody Sunday, he gave a nationally televised address before a joint session of Congress. It was the first time in nearly twenty years that a president had addressed a joint session on domestic issues. The viewing audience was estimated at seventy million. Seized by the powerful images from Selma and the vast wave of sympathy for civil rights that was sweeping the nation, Johnson gave one of the most memorable speeches of his career. Selma was a milestone in the nation's history, he said, an event comparable to Lexington, Concord, and Appomattox. It was a place where "history and fate meet in a single time in a single place to shape a turning point in man's unending search for freedom." Johnson paused and then declared "we shall overcome."[76] Watching on television in Selma, King was moved to tears, according to Lewis. As historian David Garrow observed, "it was an emotional peak unmatched by anything that had come before, nor by anything that would come later."[77] In that highly charged atmosphere, Johnson introduced the Voting Rights Act, which was passed by Congress a few months later. Practically overnight, the civil rights movement achieved a historic advance for racial equality.

The "Great Chain of Nonviolence"

Johan Galtung postulated the theory of the "great chain of nonviolence" to explain how third-party involvement helps bring about social change.[78] The process can be compared to the laws of physics, Galtung argues. For a physical object to move another, it must act on it in proximate space and time or through an intervening field in which energy is transmitted. The force of nonviolence is similar. It has to be applied directly or from group to group until it reaches its intended target, the decision-making elite. Nonviolent pressure is transmitted not through spatial distance but social distance. The shorter that distance, Galtung contends, the more effective the action. Political change thus depends on closing the social space between victim and oppressor, which can be accomplished through the effective action of intermediary groups that support the victimized population.[79]

Galtung goes so far as to claim that political change does not result from the resistance of the oppressed themselves but from the action of others who intervene on their behalf. Groups that intercede for the oppressed are largely responsible for ending systems of oppression, he contends. Change is created "*for* them, *on behalf of* them ... but not primarily *by* them."[80] This part of Galtung's hypothesis is overstated. It discounts the value of direct resistance struggles. In most examples of progressive change, the oppressed themselves are primarily responsible for their own liberation. In many of the examples we have examined—the U.S. civil rights movement, the farmworkers movement, the freedom struggle in South Africa—it was the effective social action of the oppressed populations—African Americans, farmworkers, and native Africans—which brought about social change. In each case, third parties and intervening groups also supported the struggle for justice, but it was the action of the oppressed population itself that was the decisive factor in achieving progress. Indeed, it was the effective strategy and sacrifice of the oppressed population that attracted third-party involvement.

Galtung nonetheless makes a helpful contribution in identifying the important role of third parties in assisting the process of social change. Third-party intervention is especially important in closing the social space between oppressors and their victims. It helps overcome the psychological mechanisms that oppressors utilize to justify their exploitive policies. Many analysts have noted that oppressors dehumanize their victims. Southern racists considered blacks subhuman. During the Vietnam War, soldiers called the Vietnamese "gooks." In Iraq, American troops label their opponents "terrorists." Oppressors see their victims as objects, not subjects. They consider themselves superior to and socially distant from those they oppress. This distance begins to narrow when third parties intervene on behalf of the oppressed. The victims are no longer as isolated or vulnerable as they were. This is especially important when the third-party interveners are of the same social milieu as the oppressing class. The white student activists, clergy, and others who participated in the civil rights movement fundamentally changed the social dynamics of the struggle. So did the many labor, religious, and other social activists who stood with Cesar Chavez and the farmworkers. The struggle was no longer white against black or brown. It was no longer possible for the oppressors to dismiss the opposition as entirely "other." It now included an element of "self." Intervention by these intermediary groups thus helped transmit the pressure of social resistance directly to the oppressors. The power of nonviolent action is enhanced when third parties join the struggle and intervene on behalf of those who are struggling for justice.

The significance of the third-party effect cannot be overemphasized. It bridges the apparent gap between the spiritual emphasis of Gandhi and Deming's plea for more forceful and assertive forms of nonviolence. It combines both principled and pragmatic nonviolence. We don't have to assume, as Gandhi did, that all humans will respond to generosity and appeals of morality. Even if some hearts are simply too cold and cannot be warmed even with the most loving and long-suffering appeals to conscience, nonviolence can still be effective. We don't have to win over the heart of every adversary. We can go over or around the opponent to win the sympathy of his or her allies and potential supporters. Even if the adversary remains absolutely unmoved personally, nonviolent action can appeal to the hearts of those on whom the exercise of power depends. It can alter public sympathies and erode an opponent's power base, thereby generating pressure for a change in policy. The effectiveness of nonviolent action thus becomes less a question of moral persuasion and more a matter of influencing third-party opinion and undermining the adversary's legitimacy and public support. The essential considerations become tactical and strategic rather than philosophical. The emphasis shifts to a pragmatic calculation of the most effective ways to divide the loyalties of the opponent's constituency and to win the sympathy and support of bystanders. The news media amplify these effects and create important strategic possibilities for winning third-party support.[81]

Perhaps it is possible after all to reconcile Martin and Malcolm. If I were to meet those prison inmates in Ohio again, I would explain how Martin's call for reconciliation and Malcolm's challenge to power are connected. They are part of the same process of nonviolent revolution. We can combine love and the spirit of nonviolence with determined and forceful resistance to injustice. Nonviolence enables us to preserve our moral principles while achieving concrete political change. It is the bridge between belief and practice, the glue that holds together our conflicted yearnings for morality and practicality. It enables us to strive simultaneously for peace and justice.

Chapter 7

Learning Lessons

A Tale of Two Cities

They were two of the most segregated cities of the Old South: Albany in southwest Georgia, Birmingham in northern Alabama, both bastions of white racial hatred. They also witnessed two of the most important resistance struggles of the civil rights era. The campaigns had many similarities. Thousands marched in protest. Jails filled to overflowing. White-owned businesses were idled by effective boycotts. For weeks, even months, demonstrations and mass meetings occurred almost daily. Nonviolent discipline was maintained throughout. Yet the results were very different. The Albany movement failed to achieve any significant desegregation of local facilities, despite months of bitter struggle. The movement in Birmingham scored a historic victory, forcing the desegregation of downtown stores and exerting influence through the Kennedy administration that transformed the national debate on race.

Two cities, two campaigns. One a disappointing failure, the other an inspiring triumph. Why the contrasting outcomes? The difference was not in the commitment or depth of sacrifice of the activists involved. In both cities dedicated heroism was the norm among thousands. Rather, the difference lay in the strategic choices made by movement leaders. The lesson of Albany and Birmingham is that strategy matters, that decisions made about goals, leadership, tactics, and operational planning are crucial to the success of nonviolent action.

The Albany movement began in the fall of 1961 when twenty-two-year-old Charles Sherrod and eighteen-year-old Cordell Reagon arrived in town to mount a frontal assault on the imposing edifice of local segregation. The two young organizers from the Student Nonviolent Coordinating Committee (SNCC) had few contacts in Albany and were initially viewed with suspicion by some of the city's established black leaders. Sherrod and Reagon quickly gained the confidence of young people, however, and began challenging segregation in local transportation facilities.[1] When students were arrested for attempting to desegregate the bus terminal in early December, local residents responded with mass meetings and protest marches, leading to hundreds of arrests. Martin Luther King Jr. was invited to speak at a mass rally, and he, too, was arrested after joining a protest march.

The initial demonstrations prompted negotiations between the Albany movement and white officials, resulting in a settlement just before Christmas that proved highly controversial. Marches and protests were halted. Hundreds of demonstrators were released from jail, although charges were not dropped and each person had to pay bail. City officials promised a future dialogue to address the movement's demands. Nothing was put in writing, however, and the mayor and local police chief denied that any concessions had been made. In fact, nothing changed in Albany, and local segregation laws remained as rigid as ever. Local and national press rightly portrayed the result as a "devastating loss of face" for King and the civil rights movement.[2] The demonstrations and marches were resumed a few weeks later, and they continued into the summer of 1962. Hundreds of additional arrests occurred, and boycott activity continued, but the local authorities successfully parried the protests and refused to yield. After so much sacrifice and effort, the Albany movement ended in failure.

The defeat in Albany prompted intense soul-searching by King and his lieutenants, who gathered in Dorchester, Georgia, in January 1963 to draw lessons from the experience. The stakes were extremely high. King and his colleagues desperately needed a victory to reenergize the movement and build momentum for national civil rights legislation. King already had his sights on Birmingham as the next major battleground, but before launching a new campaign, he needed to understand and overcome the failure in Albany.

The first problem, King believed, was the lack of focused objectives. The Albany movement tried to do too much. The goals were too numerous and diffuse. It would have been better, he argued, to attack segregated lunch counters or buses rather than all forms of segregation.[3] By concentrating on a specific, focused objective the movement would have increased its chances of success. The gains thus won would have given people a lift in morale and thereby motivated them to continue the struggle to achieve additional goals.

The next lesson was the need to prioritize the boycott of downtown stores. Albany would have been a greater success, King believed, if the movement had targeted the city's business leaders rather than elected officials. Blacks had little political power, due to restrictions on their voting rights, but they had substantial economic leverage through their patronage of downtown stores. Boycott efforts in Albany were effective but too limited. The protest marches should have focused on the downtown stores rather than city hall.[4] "You've got to center in the area where you have power," King argued.[5] Exerting pressure on the economic power structure would have applied pressure on the political power structure as well, since the two were closely linked.

Third was the lack of organizational unity. Tensions between the student activists of SNCC and the more established leaders of the local NAACP hampered the movement. When King and the SCLC were called in to help, this development further complicated the picture. SCLC became involved, without planning or strategic forethought, only after King was arrested. Public attention centered on King rather than the lesser-known student activists who initiated the campaign. The organizational problems in Albany were exacerbated by the outsider status of the SNCC organizers. Activists are most effective when they have contacts and credibility within the community they are attempting to organize.[6]

Last was the opposition's coolness under fire. Albany police chief Laurie Pritchett restrained his officers throughout the months of demonstrations, protests, and arrests. He carefully avoided violent confrontations with the protesters. Pritchett had read King's *Stride toward Freedom* and knew that excessive police harshness would play into the hands of the movement.[7] Pritchett also frustrated the movement's attempts to "fill the jails." When the Albany jail quickly reached its capacity in the early days of the movement, Pritchett transported inmates to jails in surrounding communities. The Albany movement never had the opportunity for the kind of dramatic confrontation that could turn the political tide in its favor.

Project "C"

From this analysis of the Albany movement, King and his lieutenants entered the Birmingham campaign with a carefully developed strategy and plan of action. It was a campaign, according to Andrew Young, that King "anticipated, planned, and coordinated from beginning to end."[8] The objectives of the campaign were narrowly focused on the desegregation of downtown stores. The ultimate purpose, of course, was to end segregation throughout the city, and indeed in the entire country, but the immediate goals of the Birmingham campaign were more limited and specific: the desegregation of downtown stores, including lunch counters, restrooms, and fitting rooms; the upgrading of store employees and a program of nondiscriminatory hiring; and the creation of a biracial committee to deal with other desegregation issues. SCLC leaders calculated (correctly, as it turned out) that victory on these seemingly modest demands would have far-reaching consequences, creating a new political dynamic in Birmingham and breathing new energy into the wider civil rights struggle.

Given the goal of desegregating downtown stores, the Birmingham campaign placed major emphasis on the use of an economic boycott. The start of the boycott and the larger campaign was timed to coincide with the busy Easter shopping season, when African Americans traditionally buy new clothes. An Easter season boycott had been used effectively in the Nashville movement of 1960, and it proved successful again in Birmingham. The lack of customers during one of the most important shopping seasons of the year dealt a severe blow to downtown business interests. The constant picketing, demonstrating, and marching that went along with the boycott added to its effectiveness, creating something of a siege environment downtown and driving off white as well as black customers. In the final days of the campaign, demonstrators eluded police barricades and brought their protests into the middle of the business district. Police responded by lobbing tear gas and attacking the demonstrators, creating a scene of turmoil and chaos. This further disrupted sales and commercial activity. By bringing their protests to the center of the economic power structure, the movement exerted effective pressure on the white establishment.

The Birmingham movement benefited from coherent leadership and unified organization. The campaign was conceived and executed entirely by the SCLC and its local affiliate, the Alabama Christian Movement for Human Rights (ACMHR), the city's only major protest group.[9] Reverend Fred Shuttlesworth, a veteran civil rights campaigner and a founder and board member of SCLC, was the president of ACMHR. King and Shuttlesworth maintained constant direction over the campaign. They selected SCLC director Wyatt T. Walker to head the campaign and placed a large staff at his disposal.

The Birmingham campaign also succeeded in provoking an overreaction from local police officials. The city was notorious as a site of frequent Ku Klux Klan violence and was derided by local blacks as "Bombingham."[10] Walker referred to the Birmingham campaign as Project "C"—C for *confrontation*.[11] Walker hoped to take advantage of the mercurial and violent nature of the local police chief, Bull Conner. The goal was to provoke Conner into attacking the movement, thereby setting up a dramatic confrontation that would attract public support and force a negotiated settlement. Walker and his colleagues hoped that this would focus public attention on the brutalities of segregation in Birmingham and arouse the sympathy and concern of bystanders far and wide. As Walker later commented, "We ... calculated for the stupidity of a Bull Conner."[12]

The Birmingham campaign got under way with a series of demonstrations and sit-ins in early April 1963. As the marches spread, hundreds were arrested, including King, who spent his time behind bars writing the ineffable "Letter from a Birmingham Jail." Brimming with eloquence and passionate insight, King's letter has become a classic of American literature. It is also an important guide to social action. In the letter King describes the essential four steps of a nonviolent campaign, which can be paraphrased as follows: collect the facts, engage in negotiation and dialogue with the adversary, purify yourself and prepare for sacrifice, and take direct action.[13]

Action is the last step, not the first. Like Gandhi, King believed that activists must first get their facts straight. Before taking action, they should research and publicize the issues. They should present their demands to the adversary in an attempt at negotiation and dialogue. When the initial dialogue proves fruitless, as it often does in the early stages of a campaign, the activists then pause for reflection and training before taking action. Activists must "purify" themselves by preparing to sacrifice and pledging to maintain nonviolent discipline. They must free their hearts of selfishness or animosity toward the adversary. Only after all these steps have been taken does direct action begin. As the demonstrations, sit-ins, and other forms of pressure work their magic, the process is then driven back to the bargaining table for the negotiation of a final settlement. All of these steps were carefully followed in Birmingham.

As the weeks passed and the number of arrests climbed (eventually surpassing 2,600), the campaign strategy seemed to be foundering. Conner had not yet been provoked into overreaction, and the numbers of people willing to face arrest began to dwindle. In a bold escalation of tactics, organizers called on schoolchildren to join the marches. Hundreds of students eagerly responded and, like other demonstrators, were promptly hauled off to jail. The students brought increased numbers and enthusiasm to the campaign. Their presence was the straw that broke the back of Conner's patience. On Friday, 3 May, as hundreds of students and other demonstrators approached Kelly Ingram Park near downtown, Conner unleashed police dogs and fire hoses, and a gruesome display of police brutality unfolded before television news cameras. Shocking images of police dogs tearing at pant legs and fire hoses slamming children to the ground were broadcast that evening to the nation and the world, becoming indelibly imprinted in public consciousness. This was a decisive turning point in the Birmingham campaign, and indeed the entire civil rights movement. It led quickly to a negotiated agreement in Birmingham and prompted the Kennedy administration to begin work on national civil rights legislation.

Civil rights demonstrators brace themselves against fire hose spray strong enough to rip bark from trees, Birmingham, Alabama, May 1963 (photo: Bettmann/CORBIS).

One of the crucial elements in the success of the Birmingham campaign was the movement's effective use of the media. A major purpose of the campaign was to portray the ugliness of racial segregation before the court of public opinion. All elements of the campaign, including King's letter and the confrontation in Kelly Ingram Park, were designed for that purpose. According to Young, "[It was] important to us that the demonstrations be understood by the media.... I had impressed on Martin the importance of crafting a message that could be conveyed in just 60 seconds for the television cameras.... That 60 seconds was what we were demonstrating for."[14]

The media strategy was a brilliant success locally and nationally. The images of disruption and mass protest contributed to the crisis atmosphere in the city and motivated white political leaders, especially the downtown store owners, to accept a negotiated settlement. At the national level, the Birmingham events had a dramatic effect on the political climate, prompting

President Kennedy to deliver a nationally televised speech on civil rights, and providing the impetus for the development of civil rights legislation. Walker later boasted, "There never was any more skillful manipulation of the news media than there was in Birmingham."[15]

The success of the Birmingham campaign holds many lessons for the strategy of social change. By focusing on limited objectives, applying pressure on the economic power structure, and maintaining organizational unity, King and his colleagues exerted effective control over the campaign. Their expectations that Conner would overreact were fulfilled, and they effectively used the media to expose the brutality of segregation to world opinion. The Birmingham campaign inspired increased activism and nonviolent protest across the South. In the three months that followed, according to government figures, more than 750 demonstrations occurred in 186 cities, with 15,000 arrests.[16] Perhaps the most important lesson of Birmingham is that ordinary people have power and can sometimes effectively organize themselves to change the course of history. The Birmingham campaign was a dramatic victory, brought about by the heroic sacrifice of thousands of local citizens and by the development and implementation of wise strategy.

The Success of the Unruly?

During the sit-ins, freedom rides, and street demonstrations of the civil rights era, the disruptive effects of protest were pivotal to political effectiveness. The strategy of the civil rights movement in Birmingham and elsewhere was to generate "creative tension" that would expose the injustices of racial segregation and force the political system to respond to the demand for change.[17] To confront social evil, it is sometimes necessary to disrupt the normal functioning of society through civil disobedience, mass arrests, and, as we have seen, the conscious provoking of police brutality.

In his classic study *The Strategy of Social Protest*, sociologist William Gamson demonstrates that political effectiveness depends on "the willingness to break rules and use non-institutional means, ... to use disruption as a strategy of influence."[18] Scholars Frances Fox Piven and Richard A. Cloward likewise argue in their book, *Poor People's Movements,* that protest is most likely to succeed when it disrupts the normal functioning of society. From their examination of the unemployed and industrial workers' movements of the 1930s and the welfare rights and civil rights movements of the 1960s, Piven and Cloward conclude that "the most useful way to think about effectiveness of protest is to examine the disruptive effects."[19]

Disruption does not necessarily mean violence, however. According to Gamson, it is not violence but "feistiness" that accounts for the success of the unruly.[20] A movement can disrupt the functioning of society without resorting to violence. The Gandhian movement in India and the civil rights and farm-workers movements in the United States frequently employed disruptive methods (boycotts, mass marches, civil disobedience, strikes), but they never strayed from their commitment to non-violence. As Gandhi, King, Chavez, Deming, and so many others emphasized, violence is counterproductive, undermining a movement's ability to claim the moral high ground and alienating third parties whose support may be crucial to political success. Disruptive methods are most effective when they remain strictly within the framework of nonviolence.

During the Vietnam antiwar movement, when some groups employed "street-fighting" tactics and a few even resorted to bombings and overt violence, the peace movement lost support. While only a few out of the millions involved in the antiwar movement used such tactics, political opponents exploited these incidents to discredit the entire antiwar cause. Destructive methods played into the "law and order" appeal that put Richard Nixon in the White House. It was a frustrating time. The antiwar message was finally getting through to the American people, as opinion polls showed growing majorities in favor of the immediate withdrawal of U.S. troops. But politicians used distorted claims of anarchy in the streets to undermine the peace movement.[21] The image of the movement suffered, as did our political effectiveness.

One of the surest ways for adversaries to undermine a social movement is to portray it as violent. This was the strategy of the Nixon administration against Vietnam Veterans against the War (VVAW). In 1971, antiwar veterans were at the forefront of the peace movement.[22] The medal-throwing ceremony of that year, in which hundreds of veterans defiantly threw back their war medals at the steps of the U.S. Capitol, was described by *Time* magazine as perhaps the most important demonstration of the era.[23] White House officials feared the veterans' movement ("they're killing us" in the media, complained Nixon aide H. R. Haldeman) and were determined to subvert it.[24] The FBI sent agents, informers, and provocateurs into the organization and gained control over several regional branches. In July 1972, the federal government issued an indictment against eight VVAW leaders on charges of conspiring to attack the Republican national convention in Miami that year. The charges were a sham. The so-called conspiracy consisted of a beer-drinking, pot-smoking, weekend camping trip replete with late-night braggadocio. No acts of violence were actually planned or carried out. At their trial in Gainesville, Florida, the veterans were acquitted on all charges. But the endless hours and huge financial resources devoted to the legal defense drained the organization and contributed to its decline. Even when they are false, charges of violence can have a detrimental effect on social activism.

Nonviolence and the Global Justice Movement

The way in which violence and destruction can damage a successful protest is illustrated in the global justice movement[25] that surfaced in Seattle in 1999 and that emerged as a powerful presence at subsequent gatherings of world leaders and international institutions. Tens of thousands of environmentalists, trade unionists, religious activists, farmers, advocates for indigenous people, and self-styled anarchists gathered in city after city to challenge the global dominance of multinational corporations. Major protests occurred in Seattle (World Trade Organization, November 1999), Washington, D.C. (World Bank and International Monetary Fund [IMF], April 2000 and September 2001), Prague (World Bank and IMF, September 2000), Quebec (Free Trade Agreement of the Americas, April 2001), and Genoa (G-8 summit, July 2001). Through demonstrations and civil disobedience actions, protesters focused worldwide attention on the damaging consequences of unbridled capitalism. They demanded trade policies that are more equitable, democratic, and environmentally sustainable. "Fair trade," as AFL-CIO president John Sweeney framed it in Seattle, "not just free trade."

The movement's effectiveness was jeopardized, however, by the destruction and violence that sometimes accompanied the protests. The bulk of the violence came from the police. Dressed in menacing Darth Vader–like uniforms, police forces unleashed clouds of tear gas and volleys of rubber bullets, pepper spray, and concussion grenades in vicious attacks against mostly nonviolent civil resisters.[26] Some demonstrators made matters worse, though, by resorting to vandalism and physical attacks. In Seattle, it began with the breaking of windows at a McDonald's and the trashing of a Starbucks and other downtown stores. With each succeeding demonstration, the level of violence seemed to increase. In Prague, demonstrators hurled paving stones and Molotov cocktails, injuring dozens of police officers. In Genoa, street battles between anarchists and the police resulted in the death of one protester and hundreds of injuries.

One of the key groups involved in these confrontations was the black bloc, an amorphous group of activists, often dressed in black bandanas and army surplus gear, who have appeared at demonstrations throughout the world. Many black bloc activists espouse revolutionary politics and are dedicated to a variety of social justice causes. They defend property destruction and even violence against the police as necessary to counter the pervasive poverty and suffering that result from government and corporate exploitation. Black bloc members wear masks to assert their anonymity and as a way of rejecting hierarchy and prioritizing the group over the individual. They see police violence as endemic and believe they are justified in forcefully confronting state repression. In response, the police have become increasingly violent in attempting to counter the globalization protests. In Genoa, local police mounted a midnight raid against a school complex used as a movement headquarters and dormitory, brutally beating dozens of activists and sending many to the hospital.[27]

In Seattle, the anarchists who trashed downtown stores on the second day of the protests claimed to be responding to an unprovoked police attack earlier that morning. The police attack was indeed unjustified and disproportionate, but this was no excuse for the vandalism that followed. The question of who struck first is irrelevant. As Gandhi and King taught, a nonviolent activist does not retaliate or use violence under any circumstances, no matter what the provocation. Even if the police did start the troubles in Seattle, which is debatable since the trashing of McDonald's occurred the previous afternoon,[28] this point does not matter. A disciplined activist always remains nonviolent and never concedes or reacts with violence to the abuses of the adversary.

The effectiveness of social protest depends on attracting the support of third parties. As one participant in the Quebec demonstrations put it, "The movement is about winning the hearts and minds of the tens of millions of working families who must be persuaded to support necessary political change."[29] When nonviolent activists display a willingness to sacrifice and remain dignified and disciplined in the face of repression, they are often able to win sympathy and political support from bystanders. This is what Deming called the "genius" of nonviolence, what Chavez termed its "chemistry"—the ability of dignified suffering to attract sympathy and political support. Violence, by contrast, turns off potential supporters and pushes third parties toward the sidelines or the other side. Street-fighting tactics jeopardize the moral integrity and political legitimacy that are necessary for political success.

The contrast between the anarchical images of vandalism in Seattle and Genoa and the dignified demeanor of civil rights demonstrators forty years before is striking. Students in Nashville in 1960 sat at lunch counters wearing dresses and suits, strictly nonviolent despite the blows and curses of racist thugs. Careful training and nonviolent discipline enabled them to withstand attack without retaliation. The civil rights protesters maintained the moral high ground and preserved their ascendancy over the segregationists who attacked them. By contrast, the actions of black bloc vandals in Seattle and Genoa blurred the distinction between the movement and its repressive adversaries. Attacks against the police created negative media images and provided an excuse for even harsher repression.

Activists complained about the biased media coverage they received in Genoa and other cities, but such bias should come as no surprise. The media are inevitably attracted to controversy and mayhem. If a hundred people are sitting in peacefully at a street corner, but five are smashing windows nearby, the cameras will cover the latter. The mass media rarely provides a fair or accurate picture of protest movements that challenge the status quo. As social critics Noam Chomsky and Edward Herman observed in

Manufacturing Consent, the major news organizations reflect the biases of the powerful multinational corporations that own them. In Seattle television networks broadcast more images of broken glass than of tear gas, although the latter was far more prevalent. The media focus on vandalism and street fighting diverted attention from the movement's underlying message of concern for the poor and the environment.

Some anarchists argued that since the corporate media often ignores protest movements, property destruction is an effective means of attracting press coverage. One activist marveled that "the first time I saw someone break a window at a demonstration ... suddenly we were all on the six o'clock news."[30] Street trashing can certainly attract coverage, but the image conveyed is of lawless rampaging rather than concern for global justice. In Seattle, this behavior diminished rather than increased support for the movement's goals.[31]

Even before Genoa, global justice activists were beginning to question the resort to vandalism and street-fighting tactics. The death in Genoa catalyzed the soul-searching and prompted calls to distance the larger movement from the destructive fringe. In Seattle, Sierra Club director Carl Pope and other organizational leaders vigorously condemned attacks against property.[32] Some activists even went to the commercial district to protect downtown stores and prevent further vandalism. In Genoa, some protesters demonstrated against the vandals and chased them away. Maria Grazia Franceschato, the head of Italy's Green Party, urged the movement to rethink its entire strategy. "We can't be responsible for devastating entire cities every time we hold a demonstration." U2 rock star Bono declared, "It's okay banging your fist on the table. It's not okay to put your fist in the face of an opponent."[33]

Some activists countered that nonviolent methods are too weak, that more militant forms of disruption are needed to bring about social change. They were right to strive for more assertive methods but mistaken in equating disruption with violence. In Seattle, Quebec, and other cities, global justice demonstrators developed innovative urban lockdown methods. Groups of civil resisters occupied major intersections, immobilizing themselves and refusing to leave even in the face of often-brutal police attack. Demonstrators managed to remain in the streets and maintain their blockades long enough to disrupt official proceedings.

These were effective tactics. They had nothing to do with the trashing of stores and the throwing of bricks and fire bombs.

Innovative forms of disruptive action also emerged in response to the invasion of Iraq in March 2003. In the days following the outbreak of war, activists blocked traffic and blockaded government buildings in dozens of cities. In San Francisco, antiwar demonstrators shut down thirty intersections and blockaded a dozen buildings in the downtown financial district. Employing the methods of globalization protestors, the demonstrators used mobile civil disobedience tactics "to an extent never before seen in the Bay Area."[34] Small groups of activists armed with cell phones flitted from corner to corner, closing down intersections and then fleeing to other locations as police arrived to make arrests. Some demonstrators chained themselves together, forcing police to use saws to separate them. The combination of mobile civil disobedience tactics and constant police action caused widespread chaos. The disruption was so severe that police asked motorists not to enter the downtown area. These methods proved to be an effective form of disruptive action, an example of the more assertive forms of nonviolence advocated by Deming. In the San Francisco antiwar actions, however, as in the globalization protests, some activists resorted to street-trashing methods. While most demonstrators were peaceful, some scuffled with police, smashed windows, and heaved newspaper racks and debris into the streets.[35] These actions detracted from the overall effectiveness of the antiwar protest.

In the wake of Genoa protests in 2001, many global justice groups called for a greater commitment to nonviolence. The Mobilization for Global Justice, one of the leading U.S. groups, issued a "visions for action" declaration in August 2001, stating, "We envision a nonviolent world; we will use means consistent with this vision." But the mobilization statement also said, "These are not philosophical or political requirements or judgments; there are many ways to resist corporate globalization." This phrasing reflected a rather tepid commitment to nonviolence and suggested a tolerance for destructive tactics that seemed contrary to the declared goal of upholding nonviolence. Within the global justice movement as a whole, there has been some reluctance to publicly disavow vandalism and street fighting. It is impossible to control the actions of everyone who participates in a demonstration, of course, but more vigorous efforts to ensure nonviolence and prevent destructive behavior are possible and necessary. A 95 percent commitment to nonviolence is not enough. The discipline must be total if the political benefits of the nonviolent method are to be realized.

The most important step, nonviolence trainer George Lakey advises, is to "fully commit to strategic nonviolent action explicitly."[36] Movement leaders must insist on an unambiguous code of nonviolent conduct among those who participate in global justice demonstrations. In August 2001, a group of U.S.-based activists issued a nonviolent declaration specifically renouncing all forms of violence in future globalization protests. The proposed declaration pledged "we will not harm people or property" and will "treat everyone with goodwill and respect." Supporting such a declaration does not mean abandoning civil disobedience or urban lockdown tactics. The search for more assertive and disruptive forms of nonviolence can and should be encouraged, but this should not be confused with vandalism and violence. Attacks against other persons are unacceptable under any circumstances and must be actively opposed.

The question of property damage is more ambiguous. Some forms of damage against destructive forms of property, such as hammering the nose cones of nuclear missiles, may be morally appropriate if conducted in a Gandhian spirit of respect for the adversary. Deming wrote of the need at times to "shock" people but at the same time to provide reassurance against harm and to act in ways that encourage more and more people to support the movement. This is a far cry from the hit-and-run tactics and random trashing of cars and stores that have marred globalization protests. The indiscriminate vandalism that occurred in Genoa and other cities should have no place in a movement that espouses global justice.

The choice of nonviolence, says George Lakey, should not be left to chance. It should be integrated into every action and publicly proclaimed as the movement's guiding principle and method. The most radical and effective forms of social action are those that maintain nonviolent discipline and that heighten the contrast between the just demands of the global justice movement and the brutal reactions of the police.[37] Only by preserving nonviolent discipline can the movement occupy and hold the moral high ground and win support for the necessary social change.

Part of the crowd of nearly one million people at the Rally to Halt the Arms Race, held in New York City, June 1982 (photo: Jenny Warburg).

Polite Rebels

Far from being disruptive, some social movements are positively polite.[38] This was the case with the nuclear freeze movement of the 1980s. The Nuclear Weapons Freeze Campaign was a populist prairie fire that swept through American society and implanted itself in politics and culture. Millions of people voted in electoral referenda and joined in vigils, demonstrations, and grassroots lobbying. The peak of the movement came in June 1982 when nearly one million people gathered in New York's Central Park for a rally to "freeze and reverse the arms race." It was the largest political demonstration in U.S. history. That same year eighteen million Americans in nine states and dozens of cities went to the polls to vote on nuclear freeze referenda, 60 percent voting in favor of a "mutual, verifiable halt to the nuclear arms race."[39] In these and other freeze movement activities, disruptive action was almost entirely absent.

The only example of mass civil disobedience during the freeze campaign occurred at the Nevada test site near Las Vegas, where thousands of demonstrators were arrested over the course of several years in attempts to shut down nuclear weapons testing. Even these efforts were rather tame, however. I participated in several of the Nevada demonstrations and was arrested twice for attempting to enter the test site. It was an orderly and ritualistic affair devoid of drama or confrontation. On one occasion more than a thousand of us were arrested, but the police handled our detention and processing smoothly. We were herded into police vans, given citations, booked, and then released, in some cases after being driven more than one hundred miles to isolated locations far from the test site. We were in police custody only a few hours and faced no mistreatment—a far cry from the harsh conditions civil rights activists often faced during the 1960s.

The freeze movement worked its influence in subtle but significant ways. As I argue in *Peace Works,* disarmament activism in the 1980s helped shape the political climate of the United States, generating opposition to the Reagan nuclear buildup and convincing a reluctant White House to negotiate with the Soviet Union for arms control.[40] Popular opposition stopped the MX basing system, which would have covered large areas of the Great Basin in Utah and Nevada with roadways and shelters for mobile missiles. The Stop MX campaign also reduced the missile production program to one-quarter its original size. Along the way political pressures were created by arms control Democrats in Congress that forced the White House to alter the U.S. negotiating position with the Soviets in Geneva. Thousands of leading scientists signed a Pledge of Non-participation, vowing not to accept research money for missile defense and helping to derail the Reagan Star Wars program. Demonstrations at Nevada and an extensive citizen lobbying effort convinced Congress to cut off funds for nuclear testing. These and other citizen actions during the 1980s had significant results. The nuclear freeze campaign is an example of a movement that influenced politics and culture without causing social disruption.

Toward the Mainstream

Movements are most successful when they reach toward the political mainstream. They arise naturally on the left, but their effectiveness depends on reaching across the political spectrum.

In earlier decades, peace activists often suffered from a kind of ghettoization—dismissed as soft-headed dreamers, hippie leftists, or, worse, Communist sympathizers and dupes of dictators. This was never a fair or accurate depiction of the many serious-minded people who spoke out against the Vietnam War or campaigned for disarmament, but it was an image problem that stuck and that hindered political outreach and movement building. This began to change with the nuclear freeze campaign and disarmament movements of the late 1970s and 1980s, when large numbers of peace activists in the United States and Europe demonstrated against Soviet as well as U.S. nuclear missiles. A growing number of activists began to link peace with human rights and freedom.

This maturation of the peace movement continued during the Iraq antiwar movement. The vast majority of those who opposed the war condemned the brutal policies of Saddam Hussein, while sympathizing with the Iraqi people. We supported UN inspections and targeted sanctions as alternatives to war and effective means of keeping Iraqi military ambitions in check. This allowed us to cast the opposition to preemptive war in a broader international security framework. It also enabled us to build a more mainstream antiwar coalition. This was our strategy in creating Win Without War.

As the buildup to war intensified in 2002, many activists called for a broadly based national effort to oppose the Bush administration's war policy. In August I wrote an article for *The Progressive* magazine, "Stop the War before It Starts," arguing for a mainstream movement that could "capture the patriotic wave" and reach beyond the usual peace movement constituency. Many of us recognized the need, and the opportunity, for building a large opposition movement. Opinion polls showed that most Americans opposed a war fought without major allies and without the authorization of the UN Security Council. Many opinion leaders and policy experts were expressing concern and skepticism about the consequences of an invasion and occupation of Iraq. The moment was ripe for seizing the initiative to create a new antiwar movement. In October 2002, representatives of more than fifty peace, religious, and social justice organizations gathered in Washington and agreed to create the United for Peace and Justice coalition. Several of us who attended the meeting gathered for dinner later that evening to discuss the need for a parallel coalition of mainstream national organizations that would have a more focused agenda and a streamlined decision-making structure. We wanted to create a new kind of coalition that would reach beyond traditional peace movement constituencies to speak to and for the majority of Americans who opposed the march toward war.

The Win Without War coalition was founded with several principles in mind. The first was the need to develop a positive, proactive message: The United States and the UN could disarm Iraq and enhance security through vigorous UN weapons inspections and continued containment. We accepted the argument that "doing nothing about Saddam Hussein is not an option," but we proposed concrete alternatives to war. We wrapped ourselves in the flag (the opening line of the founding statement read, "We are patriotic Americans ... "). We kept our message narrowly focused on stopping the war and avoided other issues.

The coalition also sought to enlist large membership groups and constituency organizations that were not the usual peace movement suspects. Two of the founding coalition members were new, rapidly growing Internet-based organizations: MoveOn, which reached two million members by the time war began, and True Majority, which grew to more than half a million members. Another founding member was Working Assets, a progressive telecommunications and wireless company with hundreds of thousands of subscribers. Among the other organizations that agreed to come together in the new coalition were the National Council of Churches, Sojourners, the Sierra Club, the National Organization for Women, and the NAACP.

The Win Without War coalition also developed a streamlined decision-making structure. We sought to avoid the tedious process and internal bickering that sometimes plague activist coalitions by giving decision-making authority to a small steering committee that included the coalition's largest and most influential member groups. The coalition developed professional leadership by hiring Tom Andrews, a former congressional representative and member of the House Armed Services committee, as national director. Andrews brought unaccustomed political experience, strategic acumen, and communications skills to the antiwar movement. The coalition employed innovative tactics that went beyond mass demonstrations. A de facto division of labor emerged, with United for Peace and Justice focusing on rallies and demonstrations, and Win Without War using the tools of the Internet to activate citizens in their homes and at the local level.

Among the most successful Win Without War actions were the "Virtual March on Washington" in February 2003, when an estimated one million people sent antiwar messages to Congress and the White House on a single day, and the vigils that took place in more than six thousand communities all over the world on the eve of war in mid-March. The Win Without War coalition also placed a major emphasis on effective media communications. We recognized the power of the media as a means of political influence, and we were determined to use the techniques of public relations to communicate our message to the public. These approaches, combined with the massive mobilization of grassroots protest through United for Peace and Justice, helped build one of the largest antiwar movements in U.S. history.

Winning While Losing

Despite its massive scale in the United States and around the world, the antiwar movement was unable to prevent the Bush administration from launching its preplanned invasion and occupation of Iraq. The fact that this enormous effort could not prevent war reflected not the weakness of the movement but the failings of democracy in the United States and the entrenched power of American militarism. Although the antiwar movement did not stop the war, it nonetheless achieved significant gains. Public pressure forced the White House to take its case to the United Nations, which slowed and complicated the preparations for war. When the Bush administration sought Security Council authorization for war in February 2003, it was decisively rebuffed. The United States could muster only three votes on the Council (Britain, Spain, and Bulgaria) for its proposed resolution authorizing military action. This was a humiliating defeat for the White House and a major victory for the antiwar movement, one that robbed the Bush administration of the international legitimacy it sought. It was, according to scholar Immanuel Wallerstein, "the first time since the United Nations was founded that the United States, on an issue that really mattered to it, could not get a majority on the Security Council."[41]

Thousands gather on the Washington Mall for a candlelight vigil, March 2003 (AP photo: Evan Vucci).

The war was lost politically before it ever began militarily. The Bush administration succeeded in starting a war but lost the larger and more important struggle for hearts and minds. Meanwhile, the peace movement gained unprecedented legitimacy and public support.

Social movements have impacts even when they fail to achieve their main purpose. The lack of legitimacy and political support for Bush's war had direct bearing on the conduct of the war and the military occupation that followed. Washington's defeat at the Security Council undermined the legal standing and political legitimacy of American policy. When the invasion began, no major government other than Britain agreed to participate. This added greatly to the U.S. military and financial burden. Washington's efforts to recruit international partners for the occupation were largely unsuccessful. Allied troops were insignificant in number and made only minimal contributions to military operations. Washington's "coalition of the willing" soon began to unravel as Spain, Ukraine, and the other erstwhile partners withdrew their forces in response to domestic political concerns. The United States was left increasingly alone in dealing with the violent and chaotic aftermath of its ill-advised policy. Washington paid a high price for alienating international opinion and rejecting the global plea for peace.

The interplay between the antiwar movement and United Nations deserves special comment. A creative dialectic developed between the Security Council and global antiwar forces. Most governments on the Security Council did not favor an invasion, but they faced intense arm twisting from the United States to support the proposed resolution. Their resolve to resist U.S. pressures received a boost from civil society. The stronger the voice of citizen opposition around the world, the greater the determination of UN diplomats. The resistance of the Security Council in turn bolstered the antiwar cause. Citizen groups used the lack of UN authorization as a major argument against the war. The stronger the objections at the UN, the greater the legitimacy and the political impact of the global antiwar movement. It was a unique and unprecedented form of global political synergy.

The UN's rejection of the Iraq war was one of the world body's finest moments. Bush administration supporters criticized the UN for "failing its responsibilities," but many of us were heartened by its stand against unprovoked aggression. Some on the left hoped that the UN could do more to stop the war, but the Security Council by its very design is a captive of its permanent members. When the most powerful state is bent on aggression, the UN is helpless to prevent it. The United Nations has one important power, however: the authority to confer or withhold international legitimacy. By refusing U.S. demands, the Security Council denied that legitimacy to the Bush administration's invasion. In doing so it displayed unaccustomed political courage. All of this was made possible in part by the worldwide public outcry against war.

The global impact of the Iraq antiwar movement shows the value of linking citizen action campaigns across borders and connecting with multilateral institutions such as the United Nations. In today's wired and interdependent world, the prospects for transnational activism are greater than ever. International linkages are sometimes necessary to resolve political grievances. Injustices that exist within a particular country are often linked to conditions in other nations. For environmental, human rights, antiwar, and other social movements, international partnerships are increasingly necessary to achieve success and are an essential component of nonviolent strategy.

Iraq: The Continuing Struggle

The antiwar movement faced new challenges as it campaigned to end the military occupation and bring U.S. troops home. Organizations opposed to the war remained active but were unable to replicate the historic outpouring of protest that occurred in the weeks before the invasion. Movements inevitably face cycles of ebb and flow, and it was only natural that levels of activism would diminish, at least for a while. A contributing factor was the uncertainty many opponents of the war felt about abandoning the people of Iraq to the horrors of terrorism and civil conflict. Everyone agreed that the war was wrong, but many worried that a precipitate U.S. withdrawal would make matters worse. Nonetheless, antiwar groups managed to work together amicably in efforts to increase pressure on the Bush administration. All agreed that military withdrawals should begin immediately and that the United States should abandon plans for maintaining permanent military bases in Iraq.

Demonstrations against the war continued at the local and national level. In October 2004, coordinated vigils were held in nearly a thousand communities to mark the grim milestone of one thousand U.S. troops killed in Iraq. Another wave of nearly a thousand vigils occurred in the United States in March 2005, with hundreds of parallel demonstrations across the world, to commemorate the second anniversary of the invasion. In September 2005, more than 150,000 people descended on Washington, D.C., in an impressive display of the continuing strength of organized antiwar sentiment.[42] It was the largest protest rally since the beginning of the war. Meanwhile, Win Without War and MoveOn continued to sponsor media campaigns to undermine further the Bush administration's declining credibility.

Gold Star mother Cindy Sheehan at "Camp Casey" outside President Bush's home in Crawford, Texas, August 2005 (photo: Jeff Paterson).

Significant new antiwar voices emerged within the military community. Cindy Sheehan, whose son Casey was killed in Iraq in 2004, captured public imagination in August 2005 with her dramatic vigil during President George W. Bush's vacation at his home in Crawford, Texas. She and other mothers who lost loved ones in Iraq formed a new organization, Gold Star Mothers for Peace. Together with Military Families Speak Out and Iraq Veterans against the War, they added legitimacy and moral credibility to the antiwar cause. Military family members and veterans became heroes of the movement and played a vital role in communicating the antiwar message. Their influence resembled that of Vietnam Veterans against the War three decades earlier. The personal witness of those of us who were veterans and active duty soldiers during Vietnam helped expose the lies underlying U.S. policy and gave validity to the call for peace. This enabled the movement to reach audiences that otherwise might not listen. The same was true with Cindy Sheehan and the military families and veterans during Iraq. Authenticity and credibility are crucial requirements for the effectiveness of social protest. This factor is especially important in antiwar movements, where the other side invariably responds with "support our troops." The family members and war veterans are able to deflect this message: "We are the troops and the family members. Support our troops by bringing them home."

Despite continuing antiwar protests, the Bush administration pretended to ignore the demands for military exit. Many protesters felt frustration and grief at their inability to stop the bloodshed. They could not see that their efforts were already having an effect. The political ground was moving under the president's feet, even as he put up a facade of imperturbability. The combination of continuing antiwar criticism and the relentless flow of hellish images from Iraq eroded public support for U.S. policy. Public approval ratings for Bush's handling of Iraq steadily dropped, and the White House found itself increasingly on the defensive. Political pressures for the beginning of troop withdrawals steadily mounted.

The ways in which social movements influence policy are not always readily apparent. They often emerge in unanticipated form or have impacts far into the future. "It is always too early to calculate effect," writer Rebecca Solnit observed.[43] We can never know today how our actions may influence events tomorrow. Movements can win even as they appear to lose. Politicians try to throw us off balance by claiming to ignore our efforts. They hope we will lose heart and give up. Yet we persist, because we believe in the cause and the urgency of change. We carry on the fight even in the absence of tangible victories. During the civil rights movement, there were many moments of despair, when the sacrifice and suffering of so many thousands seemed for nothing. Yet the dawn of a better day eventually arrived—not just in Birmingham, but in Albany and throughout the South. The movement won not only because of wise strategy but because of persistence. This is perhaps the most important lesson. Persistence is the value that makes all others possible.

Chapter 8

Gender Matters

Gandhi's fame and success attracted the interest of social reformers from all over the world. His ashram at Wardha, India, was like a magnet, drawing visionaries from many different countries and causes. They came to sit with the great soul, sharing ideas and basking in his glory.

One of the most prominent but unlikely Americans to make the trek was Margaret Sanger. At the time of her visit in 1936, Sanger was renowned as the world's leading crusader for birth control and women's rights. A few years before, H. G. Wells had acclaimed her the "heroine" of civilization, the founder of a movement that would become "the most influential of all time."[1] When Sanger received an invitation to speak from the All-India Women's Conference, she immediately wrote to Gandhi and asked for a meeting. Gandhi readily agreed, and the stage was set for an encounter between two of the most important leaders for social progress of the twentieth century.

Gandhi and Sanger shared a commitment to social justice, but on issues related to women and sexuality, they were polar opposites: he, the prudish ascetic who would confine women to home and hearth; she, the sexually liberated proponent of women's emancipation. Sanger believed that economic and social advancement depended on freeing women from the tyranny of constant childbirth.[2] Overpopulation was the cause of poverty and human misery, she believed, the source of fodder for war. Birth control was absolutely necessary for the freedom of women and the progress of human civilization.[3] Gandhi, on the other hand, considered birth control a Western vice and saw no relation between sexual liberation and the struggle for India's emancipation. He considered sexual abstinence the only solution to India's crushing population problem. "Self-control," he believed, "is the surest and only method of regulating the birth rate."[4]

Sanger knew full well of Gandhi's narrow views on birth control and sexuality, but she came to India in the hopes that she might open his mind. She had corresponded with him in 1925 in response to his article condemning contraception,[5] and he responded graciously at the time that he was open to education on the subject.[6] Sanger had no illusions about the chances of changing Gandhi's mind. She nonetheless hoped to win at least some support for her campaign to liberate women, and she knew that merely meeting with Gandhi would advance her prestige and that of her cause.

Like Gandhi, Sanger was a pacifist and radical social activist, but the influences that shaped her political commitments were very different from those that inspired Gandhi. Religious beliefs held no sway over Sanger. She shared the anticlerical views of her Irish immigrant father, and she struggled throughout her life against religiously motivated intolerance and prudery. The Roman Catholic Church was her nemesis and constant antagonist, and she bitterly condemned what she called the church's "barbaric and savage" views on birth control.[7] She had a profound reverence for life, but this regard came not from religion but from her experience in nursing and caring for oppressed women.

Sanger's political beliefs evolved from her immersion in New York's community of radical socialists prior to World War I. The living room of her uptown apartment became a gathering place for liberals, anarchists, and socialists.[8] From such luminaries as anarchist Emma Goldman, writer John Reed, and labor organizer Bill Haywood, Sanger absorbed the spirit of radical activism.[9] She was especially influenced by Goldman's revolutionary philosophy of sexual liberation and the political empowerment of women.[10] Goldman was one of the first to proclaim a woman's right to control her own body. She helped

Mahatma Gandhi and Margaret Sanger in India in 1936 (photo: Anna Jane Phillips, courtesy of the Sophia Smith Collection, Smith College).

Sanger see the connection between personal liberation and economic and social justice. Sanger was hired briefly by the Socialist Party to promote the vote for women, but she considered suffrage of secondary importance. Like Goldman, she believed that the franchise was not enough. Social transformation was also needed. Sanger sought to create a new movement that would concentrate on women's personal and social liberation.[11]

Sanger did not employ the mass organizing methods of Gandhi but focused instead on building alternative institutions. She founded the American Birth Control League, which later became the Planned Parenthood Federation, and she created numerous birth control clinics. The first clinic opened in Brooklyn in 1916, which led to her arrest and famous trial of 1917. Over the years, as Sanger crisscrossed the country to inspire local audiences, the clinics gradually spread. By the mid-1930s, some three hundred clinics were in operation in the United States.[12] She also helped establish clinics in Japan and India. Through her clinics Sanger established new forms of social organization that helped liberate and empower women.

Sanger did not promote mass civil disobedience as Gandhi did, but her intentional violation of the law helped spark a movement and catapulted her into the national limelight. Sanger and her sister, Ethel Byrne, were arrested in 1916 for violating the infamous Comstock laws that prohibited the distribution of birth control information. The court trials of the two sisters, and especially Bryne's ten-day hunger strike, became a cause célèbre that attracted widespread publicity for the cause of birth control. Byrne's ordeal was front-page news in the *New York Times* and countless papers across the country. (Among the writers covering the story was the young reporter for the *New York Call*, Dorothy Day.)[13]

Sanger had what her biographer Ellen Chesler described as a natural talent for public relations. She knew that the power of her birth control campaign lay in its public impact, and she "ingeniously courted the attention of the popular media." She understood the "value of public relations over conventional political organization" and carefully cultivated her public persona.[14] In this she was very much like Gandhi. When the two met in 1936, each had a personal stenographer to record the conversation and report it to the awaiting world press. Their encounter was as much political theater as intellectual exchange. Each knew that their words would be read and pondered far beyond Gandhi's modest ashram.

Of Love and Lust

Sanger began their meeting by linking the movement for reproductive freedom to the struggle for India's liberation. "I believe no nation can be free," she told Gandhi, "until its women have control over the power that is peculiarly theirs ... the power of procreation."[15] Drawing on her nursing experience with women in the tenements of New York, and recounting her observations of the shanties in Bombay, Sanger pleaded for the right of poor women to escape the burdens of constant childbirth and child rearing. She relayed the successful experience of clinics in the United States and Europe where education and birth control helped liberate women and enhance their welfare and self-reliance. Gandhi recognized the need to limit population, but he insisted that sexual abstinence was the only way to eliminate unwanted pregnancies. "We will have no birth control problem in India," he argued, if women "will only learn to say no to their husbands when they approach them carnally."[16] If women do not want more children, he said, they must learn to resist their husbands. Sanger asked Gandhi whether he recommended that the women of India engage in marital civil disobedience. "Yes, I do," he replied. "That advice is not practical," Sanger objected. "It means a revolution in the home. It leads to divorce."[17] Gandhi would not hear of it. If a woman simply says no, he insisted, there will be no bitterness or trouble from the husband.

Not only were Gandhi's views on birth control unrealistic, but they placed the burden for preventing conception on women. He advocated sexual abstinence for both men and women, but he viewed birth control as primarily a woman's responsibility. It was up to her to say no, to resist even natural marital urges and expectations. He did not consider that a woman might have sexual desires and needs of her own. "There are times when wives desire physical union as much as their husbands," Sanger told him.[18] Gandhi was unmoved. He seemed to believe that a woman has no role in sexual matters other than to say no.

Sanger tried to persuade Gandhi that lovemaking between consenting, mutually committed adults is a healthy and spiritually fulfilling experience. "Mr. Gandhi, do you not see a great difference between sex-love and sex-lust?"[19] Gandhi admitted the difference but could not shake the belief that all sex is mere animal passion. "It becomes a lustful thing when you take love for your own satisfaction. It is just the same with food. If food is taken only for pleasure it is lust."[20] Sanger respectfully but forcefully disagreed. "I think that is a weak position, Mr. Gandhi." Sexual love is a force of respect, consideration, and reverence, she said. "Sex-love makes for oneness, for completeness between the husband and wife and contributes to a finer understanding and a greater spiritual harmony."[21] Sanger described mutual sex-love as a form of evolution toward higher consciousness, as perhaps "the stepladder to God."[22] When sex-love is truly faithful, when it is for the pleasure and mutual satisfaction of both partners, it becomes a transcendent experience.

Sanger was unable to convince Gandhi. The great prophet of nonviolence, who so selflessly dedicated himself to others, never appreciated the full dimensions of human love. He never understood that sexual love can be a source of strength, not weakness.

Although Sanger did not persuade Gandhi to support her cause, she benefited greatly from the encounter. As Chesler noted, "the glamour of her personal association with the legendary Indian nationalist far outweighed any philosophical differences between them."[23] News stories and photographs of their meeting ran in major newspapers in the United States. Her fame increased even further, and she gained special recognition as a significant player on the international stage. During her visit to India, she spoke at forty public meetings and helped create organizations and clinics that still flourish today. The trip solidified her reputation as a significant social reformer. Feminist author Gloria Steinem writes, "She pioneered the most radical, humane and transforming political movement of the century."[24] She may not have swayed Gandhi, but she influenced and helped liberate tens of millions of women all over the world.

Elevating Women

Gandhi's beliefs on gender were a unique, sometimes-contradictory, blend of modernity and tradition. On the one hand, he campaigned vigorously for women's legal and political rights. Gandhi did more to advance women's freedom in India than any other single individual in four thousand years of India's history, according to Stanley Wolpert.[25] Judith Brown calls Gandhi a "very considerable champion" of Indian women.[26] He promoted equality for women as one of the essential pillars of his agenda for India's advancement. "I have ever believed," Gandhi wrote, "that the salvation of India lies in the elevation of her women."[27] He fought against the rigid and often-cruel patriarchal customs of traditional Hinduism. He railed against child marriage and defended a widow's right to remarry. He accepted women as political equals. "Women must have votes and an equal legal status," he wrote.[28] He rejected the traditional view of women as sex objects and subordinates to their husbands. Women are equal to men, he insisted, possessing an independent free will and capable of participating fully in public life. Movements for women's rights in India preceded Gandhi's involvement, mostly due to the work of English suffragists, but these efforts were apolitical and focused primarily on the concerns of urban upper-class women.[29] Gandhi supported and broadened the campaign for women's rights, extending it to all classes and communities and linking it to the demand for independence. Freeing women from the bondage of traditionally prescribed roles was essential to his vision of social change.

Gandhi did not devalue "women's work." He fully embraced it as the duty of men as well as women. He organized social life in his ashrams so that the work of cooking and cleaning was divided equally between men and women. He elevated supposedly feminine tasks—spinning, protecting cows, and cleaning—to the status of spiritual, even patriotic, duty.[30] Among the many reasons Gandhi emphasized the importance of spinning (the image of the spinning wheel was incorporated into the new flag of independent India in 1947) was to acknowledge and appreciate the role of women in the country's economic and social life.

Under Gandhi's leadership and with his encouragement, women played a major role in the independence movement. The contribution of women to the great salt satyagraha of 1930–1931 was particularly significant. Much of the credit for the successful boycotts of British cloth and liquor, he believed, belonged to women. "The part played by women," he declared in a 1931 speech, "is indescribable. When the history of this movement comes to be written, the sacrifices made by the women of India will occupy the foremost place."[31] In another speech that year, he repeated his praise of women: "The women in India . . . came forward to work for the nation. . . . They manufactured contraband salt, they picketed foreign cloth shops and liquor shops and tried to wean both the seller and the customer from both. . . . They marched to jails and they sustained lathi blows as few men did."[32]

Women also played a prominent role in Gandhi's "constructive program," the promotion of economic self-sufficiency, literacy, sanitation, and communal harmony at the village level. Gandhi's encouragement of women's participation in the movement made him a hero and political mentor to many of his female supporters. Through his support for women's rights, notes Wolpert, Gandhi "launched as potent a social revolution in India as the political revolution he'd started a decade and a half earlier."[33] Women were extremely loyal to him and essential to his vast public following.[34]

Gandhi's support for women's rights was part of a conscious political strategy to identify with and appeal to the margins of society. It is well-known and has been commented on frequently that Gandhi transformed the Indian Congress from a society of urbanized lawyers into a mass movement encompassing workers and peasants, and reaching into the country's vast expanse of rural villages. He communicated with the unlettered masses in uniquely creative ways: by adopting their dress, becoming a traditional Hindu ascetic, and traveling in third-class compartments. He identified with minorities and the most excluded—untouchables and women—to build the base of his successful mass movement.

Gandhi assiduously cultivated his feminine side and aspired toward androgyny. He hoped that men could acquire the traits of women. "Man should cultivate the gentleness and the discrimination of woman," he wrote.[35] He often spoke of his feminine qualities and said that mentally he had become a woman.[36] He considered himself a mother to the young people in his ashram, and many of his followers spoke openly of his maternal traits. According to scholar Sudhir Kakar, this striving for feminine characteristics was part of the Vaishnava culture in which Gandhi was raised.[37] Religious ascetics considered it a form of spiritual enlightenment. Gandhi followed the same path to social enlightenment. He tried to break down gender roles both politically and in the home. He wanted to liberate men as well as women, to transcend gender roles and stereotypes.

Less Than Equal

While Gandhi's support for women's equality was genuine, his vision of female autonomy was limited. He was the product of a rigidly patriarchal society in which women had little or no education or independent identity. Gandhi espoused greater political independence for women, but he saw a more limited social role for women. He had little experience with women as leaders either in the independence movement or in his ashram communities. He supported education for women but favored a very narrow curriculum. His notion of female education was confined to home economics and family health. At an educational conference in Gujarat in 1917, he declared, "They should be taught the management of the home, the things they should or should not do during pregnancy, and the nursing and care of children."[38] Training women for the professions and employment outside the home was anathema. "Equality of the sexes does not mean equality of profession," he wrote.[39] Women should work in the home, he insisted, not in the workplace. "It is not for women to go out and work, as men do ... nor is it for women to go to work in factories. They have plenty of work in their homes."[40]

Gandhi conceived of women's economic and social roles as confined to serving their families. In a speech before Ahmedabad workers in 1920, he said, "They should attend to the bringing up of their children; they may give peace to the husband when he returns home tired, minister to him, soothe him if he is angry."[41] He believed that keeping women at home was good not only for the family but for society. "If women go out to work, our social life will be ruined and moral standards will decline."[42] Even in his promotion of the public role of women, Gandhi often acted in a patronizing and domineering manner. He dictated every detail of ashram life and directly supervised women's participation in public affairs.[43] The independence movement drew women out of their homes and opened their lives to social activism, but Gandhi tried to bind them to traditional economic and social roles.[44]

Gandhi was at times callous and domineering toward his wife, Kasturba, and his three sons. In his autobiography, he confesses that in the early years of his marriage he made Kasturba "thoroughly miserable."[45] He was intensely jealous of the strong-willed young woman who had become his wife, and he tried to educate and control her. "I wanted to *make* my wife an ideal wife" (emphasis in original).[46] Gandhi recounted an incident at his ashram near Durban, South Africa, depicted in Richard Attenborough's film *Gandhi*, in which he angrily harassed Kasturba for refusing to clean a visitor's chamber pot. After shouting at her, he dragged her to the gate with the intention of pushing her out. Tears poured down her cheek as she cried, "Have you no sense of shame?" This scene was one of many, Gandhi admitted. "We have had numerous bickerings."[47] Over the years Gandhi became more tolerant and accepting of Kasturba and stopped trying to be her teacher. After he took the vow of celibacy, he reported that his domestic life became more peaceful and harmonious.

Gandhi subjected his family to "hardship and experimentation," says Brown.[48] He denied his sons the benefits of higher

Gandhi with his wife, Kasturba, on the trip back to India, 1915 (photo: Vithalbhai Jhaveri, courtesy of the GandhiServe Foundation).

education he had enjoyed. His relations with his eldest son, Harilal, were particularly painful. When Gandhi received an offer for the financing of a legal education in London for one of his followers, he turned aside Harilal's entreaties and chose someone else. He said he didn't want to show favor to members of his family. Harilal rebelled against the pressures to conform and had a tortured relationship with his father. His life descended into a miserable existence of alcoholism, sexual philandering, and crime. When his father led a boycott of British cloth, Harilal went into business to sell British textiles. When his mother lay gravely ill, he came to her deathbed drunk.[49] The 1997 play *Mahatma versus Gandhi* portrays this tragic estrangement between father and son.

Gandhi was so intent on saving India and the world that he was unable to care fully for his own family. He considered the demands of his public mission incompatible with the obligations of normal family life.[50] The man of love and nonviolence could be cruel toward those closest to him and was often insensitive to the immediate needs of his wife and sons.[51] At times he displayed greater concern for strangers and outcasts than for his own family. He seemed to believe, George Orwell wrote, that "if one is to love God, or to love humanity as a whole, one cannot give one's preference to any individual person."[52] The Gospel teaches, "Those ... who do not love a brother or sister whom they have seen, cannot love God whom they have not seen."[53] It is through loving other humans that we love God. Gandhi understood this belief in the abstract but had difficulty living it in practice.

The Nature of Women

Gandhi attempted to define what he considered the innate characteristics of women. This is a perilous enterprise for any author, but for one as confused about sex roles as Gandhi, it proved embarrassingly awkward. Gandhi tried to dispel the stereotypical belief of women as inferior, but his attempts to do so only reinforced his prejudices. To refer to women as the weaker sex, he said, is a libel, for women are in some respects stronger than men. "If by strength is meant moral power, then woman is immeasurably man's superior. Has she not greater intuition, is she not more self-sacrificing, has she not greater powers of endurance, has she not greater courage? ... If non-violence is the law of our being, the future is with woman."[54]

Gandhi referred often to the capacity of women to suffer. He thought this quality made women well suited to the practice of nonviolence. "Nonviolent war calls into play suffering to the largest extent," he wrote, and women can suffer "more purely and nobly" because of their experience with the "pangs of labour."[55] "Silent and dignified suffering is the badge of her sex."[56]

Women are indeed effective participants in nonviolent movements, but to base this assessment on the presumed female capacity to suffer is absurd and troubling. To speak of women as somehow naturally suited to suffering is almost to invite such suffering, to accept it as natural. Such a view excludes women who are not mothers, who have not given birth and experienced the "pangs" of labor. This narrow focus on the capacity to suffer also ignores the many other talents women bring to the struggle for social justice—intelligence and specific work skills, leadership, emotional balance, holistic thinking, and so forth. By dwelling on the capacity to suffer, Gandhi devalued the strengths and contributions of women.

Gandhi seemed to hold women to a higher moral standard than men. In his book *Satyagraha in South Africa,* Gandhi recounts an incident in which two young men "looked sinfully at two young girls," thus violating his ashram rules. He punished the girls for tempting the boys, shaving their heads and making them less attractive. It was the girls' responsibility to guard the boys' chastity and moral purity.

Gandhi had little understanding or sympathy for a woman victimized by sexual violence. He seemed incapable of dealing with the horror of rape, just as he was unable to give a satisfactory response to victims of the Holocaust. In addressing rape, he was doubly handicapped. His prejudices against female sexuality blinded him to a woman's plight, and his absolute pacifism precluded the option of fighting back. What should a woman do, he was asked, if threatened by rape? He could only answer with the absurd comment that it would be better for her to die than submit to the act. Moral force would somehow prevail. "I have always held that it is physically impossible to violate a woman against her will. The outrage takes place only when she gives way to fear or does not realize her moral strength."[57] Gandhi placed the responsibility for preventing rape entirely on the woman. "I believe ... that no woman can be absolutely and simply raped. Not being prepared to die, a woman yields to the wrongdoer. But a woman who has overcome all fear of death would die before submitting to the outrage."[58] But what if a woman's moral powers do not prevent the assault? "If such a woman becomes pregnant," Gandhi asserted, "she should not resort to abortion."[59]

Battling Sexuality

Gandhi wrote about sex often and was relentless in condemning sexual desire and promoting chastity. "The sexual act is permitted only when there is a clear desire by both for a child."[60] Sex for any other purpose, he believed, was "a sin against God and humanity."[61] Sexual needs and desires should be suppressed. Gandhi's views seemed to verge on the crackpot at times. He believed that sexual activity saps one's physical strength and moral courage. He wrote of the need for men to "retain and assimilate the vital liquid."[62] Following an ancient yogic faith in the supposedly magical powers of seminal fluids, Gandhi believed that sexual abstinence would increase a man's vital powers and make him a more effective and courageous warrior for justice.[63] The celibate man becomes more powerful, he believed, because his "secretions ... are sublimated into a vital force pervading his whole being."[64]

Gandhi claimed to reject the traditional Hindu view of women as morally weak and fickle, but in its place he constructed an equally false image of women as asexual. He tried to cleanse the female body of all sensuality, confining its function solely to procreation.[65] Female sexuality was a source of temptation, he believed, a moral "contamination" to be cleansed and purified.[66] Erik Erikson wrote that Gandhi considered women a "source of evil."[67] Gandhi could not accept female sexuality or understand a woman's desire to control her own body. The idea of a woman seeking her own sexual fulfillment was alien to him.[68] When he decided to become celibate, he did not consult Kasturba. He simply announced it to her, as if she had no say in the matter.

For Gandhi, the vow of celibacy was intimately tied to his commitment to satyagraha. It was no coincidence that his renunciation of sex in 1906 in South Africa came just as he dedicated himself completely to the struggle for nonviolent social change. As Kakar writes, from the repudiation of sex "the weapon of nonviolence was Phoenix-like born."[69] This may have been true for Gandhi, but as Erikson argues, it is not required for those of us who follow him. There is no need to deny sexual love in order to serve the larger human community.

There was more to Gandhi's celibacy vow than the search for moral virtue. Darker impulses were also at work. According to Erikson, Gandhi's beliefs were rooted in a deep sense of guilt and shame. These feelings came from the emotional trauma of his arranged marriage to Kasturba at age thirteen. He was also haunted by the anguish of giving in to "carnal passions" with his teenage bride while his ailing father was dying in the next

room. Gandhi's relationship with Kasturba was stormy throughout their married life. She constantly bristled at his attempts
to dominate and control her. She also seems to have been a
reluctant sexual partner.[70] The vow of celibacy thus may have
helped Gandhi escape a hurting relationship. He claimed that
his understanding and love for Kasturba increased once their
sexual relations ended.

In *Like Water for Chocolate*, novelist Laura Esquivel magi-
cally portrays the sensual links between food and sex. Writers
and artists of many cultures have delighted in the interplay of
culinary and sexual pleasure. Gandhi, too, saw this linkage,
but in characteristic fashion he fought relentlessly against it.
Gandhi was so single-minded in his zeal to conquer sexual
desire that he also waged war on the pleasures of food. His
voluminous discourses on diet and food were not merely to
uphold the principles of vegetarianism. He also sought to
conquer the libido. Denying the pleasures of food would help
control his sexual impulses. The more tasteless and unappe-
tizing the food, the better. The purpose of eating, he said, was
not gratification but "selfless subsistence."[71] Food was "to be
taken as ... medicine," as a means of maintaining the body
while suppressing desire. His dietary and sexual denial was an
attempt to strip himself of all that he considered a hindrance
to the selfless pursuit of truth.[72] It was all part of his goal to
"reduce myself to zero."[73]

The "Sacrifice"

No facet of Gandhi's life is more controversial than his relationship with young women in his final years. The facts are well-
known. Beginning in 1938 and then continuing in the years
before his death, he "tested" his vow of celibacy by inviting
nubile young women to sleep naked with him. He developed
particularly close relationships with three women, his grand-
nieces Manu Gandhi and Abha (Chatterji) Gandhi, and Sushila
Nayar, sister of his secretary, Pyarelal Nayar. He was closest to
Manu, who was just nineteen years old when she came to accompany Gandhi during his perilous trek through the Noakhali
District in Eastern Bengal in 1946 and 1947. Manu and the
other women often walked with Gandhi as he placed his hand

*Gandhi at Birla-House (Delhi) with his grandniece Abha (left) and his grand-
daughter Manu (right) (photo: GandhiServe).*

on their shoulders for support. Manu and Abha, his "walking
sticks," were at his arm when the assassin's bullets struck him
down in January 1948.

Gandhi claimed that the women brought him warmth (Manu
referred to his "frail, shivering body"[74]), but he also sought to
test his will and the strength of his celibacy.[75] Gandhi wanted to
"put our purity to the ultimate test," Sushila Nayar recounts.[76]
He asked the young women to take off their clothes with him.
Sushila Nayar related a conversation with Manu: "Bapu [Gandhi]
said ... we should now both start sleeping naked. She said 'of
course' and I heard from Bapu's own lips that neither he nor
she felt any sexual desire whatsoever."[77] Gandhi admitted his
intimacy with Manu and the other women but vigorously denied
its sexual character.[78] He was unabashed about his "experiment" and wrote openly and frequently about the practice to
friends and colleagues. In one letter he wrote, "A young girl ...
shares the same bed with me, not for any animal satisfaction
but for (to me) valid moral reasons."[79] To his private secretary

he wrote, "I do hope you will acquit me of having any lustful designs upon women or girls who have been naked with me."[80] Gandhi insisted that he was never aroused when sleeping with Manu, Abha, or Sushila.[81]

This brazen behavior from one who so sanctimoniously preached sexual abstinence was offensive to many. Some of his associates resigned in protest.[82] Colleagues questioned Gandhi for devoting so much time to Manu and the other women at a time of grave social and political crisis for India. At the very moment that his lifelong quest for political freedom was being realized, with the subcontinent facing partition and seething with ethnic conflict, Gandhi spent time in correspondence and intimate relations with young women.

The implications of Gandhi sleeping with young women were not what they may seem. Gandhi rarely slept alone. He usually bedded down in more or less public arrangements in his ashrams or guest homes where he stayed.[83] Others slept nearby or in the same room, and doors were usually open. When Gandhi slept with Manu and the others, it was in such settings. Brown writes that the relationship with Manu was undoubtedly "platonic."[84] The events in question took place in the last years of Gandhi's life. He was a frail old man in his late seventies, hardly one to be embarking on sexual escapades. He had been celibate for more than forty years and was not likely to break his vow after so long a time. This fact may help explain but does not excuse his behavior.

Gandhi's motivations seem to have been more spiritual than sensual. He described the experience as *yagna*, a Hindu concept of sacrifice to the gods dating back thousands of years. The purpose of yagna is the preservation and strengthening of personal piety.[85] Gandhi saw his experiments with the young women in the same way, as a means to spiritual purity and transcendence. By testing his vow of celibacy, Gandhi hoped to gain spiritual sustenance to soothe his political disenchantment.[86] He was deeply anguished by the partition of India and the rising tide of communal violence, and he felt powerless to reverse the course of events. According to Wolpert, Gandhi "believed that this most difficult and challenging test of his celibacy was somehow mystically connected to the purity and perfection of his Ahimsa, and to his power to stop Hindu-Muslim violence."[87] Gandhi's grandson Rajmohan Gandhi offered a similar explanation: the

Mahatma "look[ed] within himself for a weakness to explain the misfortunes around him." He thought that "perfecting his brahmacharya [celibacy], including by testing himself, would enhance his power over events."[88] It was, as Kakar noted, "the prideful vice of an uncompromisingly virtuous man."[89]

Gandhi may have preserved his chastity in these "experiments," but he did so at considerable cost to himself and to the women involved. He used the women for his own purposes, taking advantage of their devotion and loyalty to engage in highly questionable practices. They were objects to be used, not independent subjects with their own wants and needs. Manu showed signs of growing alienation less than a month after joining Gandhi in Noakhali, according to Wolpert. When Manu suggested that they stop sleeping together, Gandhi, in his own words, "readily agreed."[90] Gandhi's Bengali interpreter and assistant, N. K. Bose, charged that the women suffered psychological harm, although none of them complained publicly about their involvement. Harm was certainly done to Gandhi's stature, as many followers gazed in pained puzzlement at his bizarre behavior. Over the decades, as women's issues have moved to the center of social discourse, the questions have increased. Gandhi's practices and beliefs have not stood up well to feminist inquiry. His saintlike image has suffered.

It is important to keep these matters in perspective. Gandhi's great achievements for the independence of India far outweigh these distractions at the end of his life. As offensive as some of Gandhi's behavior and beliefs may have been, they were only a part of his being. They do not detract from his monumental contributions to human freedom or diminish his standing as one of the greatest social reformers in history. They did not prevent him from helping bring down the mighty British raj. Given the enormity of his accomplishments and the extreme austerity of his lifestyle, it would be surprising if he did not have faults and limitations. He was human and flawed as we all are. He was molded by his particular time and culture, and he was unable to heal the psychological and emotional wounds that gave rise to his "irrational Puritanism."[91] As we try to appreciate him a century later in a vastly different cultural setting, we can be understanding, even as we are critical.

Deconstruction can have benefits. By taking Gandhi down from the pedestal, we can begin to see his human side. He becomes

less distant and aloof, more accessible. By examining his vulner-
abilities and weaknesses, we can see our own. We can recognize
him as a man haunted as we all are by personal demons and
insecurities. Gandhi's torments inspired him toward world historic achievement, but they also drove him toward denial of self
and insensitivity toward those closest to him. In his mind, social
activism and personal asceticism were linked, but we are free
to separate them. We can enrich Gandhianism by incorporating
the insights of feminism. Women and men can struggle together,
as genuine equals, to achieve a more just and loving society.

"Fleshly Faults"

Martin Luther King Jr. had none of Gandhi's puritanical tendencies. In fact, on sexual matters King was the complete opposite of
Gandhi. Gandhi was the pious celibate; King was prone to what
David Garrow calls a "compulsive sexual athleticism."[92] King
was sexually active outside his marriage and had "carnal connections" with a number of different women during his frequent
speaking trips away from home. He was "solidly chauvinistic"
toward his wife, Coretta Scott King, and the women who worked
with him in the civil rights movement.[93] It appears that King
needs deconstructing on gender issues as much as Gandhi.

In his important book *I May Not Get There with You,* scholar
Michael Eric Dyson offers fresh insight into King's legacy and
message. He looks past the shallow commentaries that often
pass for remembrance of King's life. Dyson reveals the overlooked political dimensions of King's message. He reminds us
that King was an ardent opponent of militarism and the war in
Vietnam. That he raised a radical socialist critique of capitalist
inequality. And that he became increasingly committed to more
radical forms of nonviolence as he contemplated the challenge
of overcoming what he called the "giant triplet" of racism, poverty, and militarism. King was much more of a political and
economic revolutionary than many of his admirers suspect. But
Dyson also examines King's limitations, including his failings
on gender issues. The picture that emerges is of a great leader
for nonviolence who, like Gandhi, transcended the racial and
political constraints of his time but who, also like Gandhi, could
not escape the bonds of sexism and patriarchy.

Dyson variously describes King's sexual philandering as "rampant womanizing," "prolific infidelities," and "fleshly faults."[94] King was a womanizer in college and continued such behavior even after his marriage. This behavior was not unusual among ministers. John Lewis refers in his memoir to the classic model of the "chicken-eating, liquor-drinking, woman-chasing Baptist preacher." King was not a heavy drinker, but he was certainly fond of women.[95] In addition to his many casual affairs while on the road, King developed "relationships of significant affection with three women," one of whom became his "de facto wife."[96] King preached against sexual promiscuity in his sermons, but in his personal life he could not control his urges. According to Dyson, King sought "to escape through sexual release the magnitude of his duty, the burden of his role, and the unrelenting pace of his quest."[97] According to Garrow, King told a friend concerned about his many affairs that "fucking's a form of anxiety reduction."[98]

King took extraordinary risks in pursuing these sexual encounters. Not only was he a minister of the church and therefore supposedly a paragon of moral virtue, but he was one of the most visible public figures in the country, if not the world. He was also a vigorous critic of U.S. domestic and foreign policy and therefore was considered an enemy by powerful reactionaries and defenders of the status quo. Chief among these was J. Edgar Hoover, director of the FBI, who waged a relentless campaign against King in an attempt to destroy him and the civil rights movement. Hoover directed his agents to wiretap and spy on King. The FBI also spread false information and tried to disrupt the movement. The voyeuristic Hoover concentrated on King's sexual activities, and his agents collected as much incriminating information as they could. King was well aware of Hoover's campaign to destroy him, yet he did not slow the pace of his infidelity.[99] Hoover's attacks against King burst into the open in November 1964, just as King was about to travel to Oslo to receive the Nobel Peace Prize. The FBI director told a group of women journalists that King was a "notorious liar" and "one of the lowest characters in the country."[100] The FBI also sent an anonymous package to the SCLC that contained a tape recording and an anonymous letter threatening King. The tape revealed King and his associates in jocular, ribald conversation the night after the August 1963 March on Washington. Another section of the tape included the sounds of a couple engaging in sex, replete with groans and moans. The recording had been acquired from the FBI's bugging of King's hotel rooms. King invited his top aides to listen to the tape with him. Their response was surprisingly nonchalant. Andrew Young later wrote that the voice on that part of the tape was not King's and that Coretta King was not disturbed by it.[101] "Martin's private sexual behavior was not relevant to the movement, and I never saw any behavior that in any way undermined it."[102]

Yes, King's personal life was his own business, and it did not detract from his commitment to the movement. In that respect Young is right. But if Hoover and the FBI had been more adroit at exposing King's extramarital affairs, his private sexual matters would have had major political ramifications. Fortunately for King, the FBI never succeeded in its attempts to smear him, and he escaped public controversy. Partly this outcome reflects the ethos of the time, when even the president of the United States was known to have carried on affairs and the predominantly male writers of the day saw nothing wrong with such behavior (and may have coveted or engaged in such "conquests" themselves).

In other respects, however, King's infidelity had everything to do with the movement. As women activists assert, "the personal is political." King's behavior was part of a male chauvinist culture that was prevalent not just in the broader society but in the civil rights movement as well. In the patriarchal world of the male preachers who dominated the SCLC, women were looked on as either sex objects or as mothers to care for the children. King was no different. According to his aide, Bernard Lee, King was "absolutely a male chauvinist."[103] He insisted that his wife remain at home and concentrate on raising their four children. Coretta King wanted to be more involved in the movement and had considerable talents to contribute, but her husband was adamantly opposed to her ambitions. As she notes, he "thought in terms of his wife being a homemaker and a mother for his children. He was very definite that he would expect whomever he married to be home waiting for him."[104] Coretta King complained openly about being denied a more active role, but she received little sympathy in the black Baptist church milieu, where women were not expected to be decision makers or leaders. (The same was true in many white churches.) She spoke frequently for the peace movement at rallies against the Vietnam War, but she was not allowed to have an autonomous voice within the civil rights movement.

I raise these critical issues not to condemn King or to suggest any moral judgment on his life. Who among us can presume moral superiority over one who sacrificed and achieved so much? I am not in a position to pass judgment, for I, too, have been unfaithful in marriage. I have more than enough faults to know that it is best to be humble in these matters. As Dyson observes, we should not expect flawless leaders.[105] They have weaknesses as we all do. We may even take some consolation that our heroes sometimes stumble as they strive for greatness. We need not be perfect to qualify as leaders for justice. The point is not to judge but to comprehend, to gain a more complete under-standing of King, with his many strengths and his weaknesses. King did not realize that the giant triplets of which he spoke contain a sibling, sexism. The struggle against racism, poverty, and militarism means struggling against patriarchy as well. All must be overcome if the beloved community is to be realized. That community must be home for women and men alike.

Overcoming Sexism

Within the SCLC and other civil rights organizations, nearly all the top leadership positions went to men. The women who often did all the work were kept in the background. According to Lewis, in many of the places where the movement took root, "it was pri-marily women who had gotten out and done all the grunt work." In most cases, though, "men stepped out front, filled the visible positions and took most of the credit." Because of what he called the "discrimination" within the movement, "there were very, very few women getting credit for their work."[106] Ella Baker was one of the few women who gained prominence, in part because she had already established herself as an experienced organizer years before King arrived on the scene. Despite her long experience (she had been national field secretary and later director of branches for the NAACP), Baker often clashed with the male preachers who dominated the SCLC. Baker said that King expected women to take orders, not provide leadership.[107]

Perhaps the most remarkable testament to the sexism of the civil rights movement is this: During the historic March on

Washington in August 1963, not a single woman was allowed
to give a speech. Every speaker in the three-hour program that
day was a man![108] Rosa Parks, Diane Bevel Nash, and a few
other women activists were introduced, and Marian Anderson
and Mahalia Jackson sang, but no woman was allowed to address the crowd in her own words. Such a blatant display of
gender discrimination would be almost inconceivable today. Few
organizations anywhere, least of all in a politically progressive
movement, could get away with such a one-sided program. In
the 1960s civil rights movement, however, it was typical behavior
and an accurate reflection of the male chauvinism that pervaded
the leading organizations.

Similar problems plagued SNCC. Lewis, the group's chair-
man, described "an attitude of chauvinism among many of
the men" in SNCC.[109] Women in the organization objected to
these conditions and argued for greater gender equality. When
Stokely Carmichael, one of the group's leaders, was asked his
opinion about these concerns, he uttered infamously that the
only position for women in SNCC was "prone."[110] Carmichael
was half joking, but the women were not laughing. Some of the
women in the group staged what they termed a "pussy strike,"
refusing to have sex with any of the men until they were treated
with respect.[111] The pervasive sexism in the movement sparked
a feminist fury that convulsed the civil rights and peace movements and that eventually swept through society to transform
politics and culture.

The sexist culture of the civil rights movement (and the
Vietnam antiwar movement) gave rise to the modern women's
movement. Female activists resented the gender discrimination they were forced to endure and began to argue for a
concentrated effort to eliminate sexism. In a paper that was
later described as "the opening salvo" in the emerging feminist
movement, staffers at SNCC wrote a scathing critique that compared gender discrimination to racial oppression. "Assumptions of male superiority are as widespread and deep-rooted
and every bit as crippling to the woman as the assumptions
of white supremacy are to the Negro," declared activists Mary
King and Casey Hayden.[112] Frustrated and angered by their
encounter with male chauvinism, women of the civil rights
and peace movements turned their considerable organizing
energy to the struggle against sexism. When the war ended,

the women's liberation movement continued and evolved into a broadly based campaign for women's rights, while retaining feminist peace sentiment.[113]

Because of the feminist movement, the rights and roles of women in politics and culture have evolved significantly. Yet for all the advances that have been achieved, gender discrimination remains widespread, within peace and human rights movements as well as in the larger society. This situation is especially awkward in the peace movement, where so many of the local activists who perform the difficult and thankless task of grassroots organizing are women. Yet many of the leaders of the national peace groups are men, as are nearly all of the so-called arms control experts quoted in the media. I have been one of those male leaders, and I struggle constantly with my own chauvinist tendencies. My conditioning as a boy, especially in the patriarchal world of Catholicism, left indelible handicaps that I constantly strive to overcome. Am I too quick to assert my own position, to grab a leadership role at the expense of female colleagues? Am I too silent in the face of discrimination against women coworkers? Do I value women more for their attractiveness than their talents and intellectual ability? In this struggle against sexism, I have found King more a hindrance than a help, an example to be overcome rather than a model to be emulated.

While Gandhi was also limited on matters of gender, he was in some respects more progressive than King. He was certainly far ahead of the patriarchal culture in which he lived. Gandhi championed the rights of women. He encouraged his wife, Kasturba, and other women to participate in the struggle for freedom. He strongly rejected the typical male view of women as sex objects. He supported political equality for women as one of the essential elements of his program for liberation. King, by contrast, said little about the rights of women. In all his writings and eloquent speeches, he never addressed the question of women's liberation or drew the connection between nonviolence and gender equality.

It's ironic that the celibate Gandhi was better able to see women as equal partners than the sexually promiscuous King, but in truth neither had an enlightened view toward women. Neither fully accepted the right of a woman to be autonomous, to control her own body and decide for herself the most important questions of life, family, and society. For all their genius in promoting nonviolence, Gandhi and King did not fully recognize the role of women in creating a more just and compassionate society. Thanks to the women's movement, we can now transcend the limitations of Gandhi and King to realize a more inclusive and genuine form of nonviolence. We can acknowledge and honor the contributions of women to the struggle for a more just and peaceful world.

Nonviolence and Feminism

Many of the early suffragists believed that the political empowerment of women would put an end to war.[114] Jane Addams, the prominent pacifist and social reformer of the early twentieth century, considered militarism and feminism polar opposites. She and others promoted the vote for women as a strategy for achieving global peace. The women's vote did not prevent wars, of course, and feminists today dismiss the "essentialist" idea that women are inherently more nonviolent and peaceful than men. On the other hand, there are indications that the empowerment of women in society is associated with more peaceful governmental policy. Author Virginia Woolf wrote in *Three Guineas* that the way to peace is through the social and economic advancement of women. War has traditionally been the "man's habit, not the woman's."[115] The difference is not necessarily innate, she believed, but is the result of law, education, custom, and practice in traditional male-dominated society. Women could help break the grip of this male propensity to war, she argued, through education and professional employment, which would allow them to become independent of male domination and achieve leadership in society. Woolf believed that women would use their elevated status to cast aside the structures of patriarchy to create a more cooperative, peaceful world.

We have evidence to support Woolf's contention. Recent empirical studies of war-making tendencies among nations show a strong correlation between the empowerment of women and a reduced tendency to engage in armed conflict.[116] Research cited by economist Amartya Sen show that the political empowerment of women is directly related to such variables as a woman's literacy and education, and her ability to find employment outside the home and earn an independent income.[117] Countries in which women are relatively empowered, as measured by education, professional employment, and participation in government are less likely to utilize military force in international relations. The higher the degree of gender equality, the lower the likelihood of armed conflict. Women are also less likely than men to commit violent crime.[118] The higher the female–male ratio in a given population, the lower the murder rate.[119] Perhaps there is something to Woolf's prescription for peace after all. As women are empowered socially and economically, and as they take their rightful place in the councils of government, the tendency to resort to violence and use force as a means of settling differences diminishes.

Dorothy Day believed that women think differently than men and are more inclined toward caring and love for others. "Woman is saved by child rearing," she said, which imposes on her "a rule of life which involves others." Men are not as firmly anchored as women. They think more abstractly and are preoccupied by distant ends, while women are more rooted in the present and are more focused on the practical means of resolving problems. "Women think with their whole bodies," said Day. "More than men do, women see things as a whole."[120] Women are more opposed to war than men and have been at the heart of many peace movements. Studies of public opinion indicate a substantial gender gap on war and military-related issues, with women consistently showing a greater propensity to support peaceful solutions to international crises and greater reluctance to endorse the use of military force.[121]

To suggest a link between feminism and peace is not to say that all women are nonviolent or that women by their very nature are inherently more peaceful than men. As political theorist Jean Bethke Elshtain and others remind us, women have sometimes been supporters, participants, and cheerleaders for war.[122] Philosopher Sara Ruddick writes that the maternal practices of nurturing life, avoiding violence, and resolving conflict reinforce the principles of Gandhian nonviolence, but she is careful to avoid the claim that these are essential traits.[123] "There is nothing in a woman's genetic makeup or history that prevents her from firing a missile or spraying nerve gas over a sleeping village."[124] bell hooks argues that the peaceful woman concept risks "reinforcing the very biological determinism that is the philosophical foundation for notions of male supremacy."[125]

The equation of women with peace is seen by some as a form of subordination, as a way of locking women into roles of power-lessness and passivity.[126] If women are incapable of fighting for what is right, they cannot be trusted with political responsibility. The image of the peaceful woman is often used to keep women "in their place," far from the seats of power.

The flip side of the pacifist woman stereotype is the assumption that males are inherently aggressive. To be sure, the histori-cal connections between patriarchy and violence are pervasive and deeply rooted. Not only are men responsible for most of history's wars, but traditional male virtues are linked to aggres-siveness and the use of force. I witnessed this in my military training during the Vietnam War. Recruits who did not mea-sure up were called "girl" or "faggot." One day during weapons training, our drill sergeant raised an M-16 and declared, "This is my rifle; this is my gun [grabbing his crotch]. This one's for business; this one's for fun." The indoctrination of violence as sexual conquest could not have been more explicit. The count-less other associations between militarism and sexual dehuman-ization—from rape as a weapon of war to prostitution and the abuse of so-called comfort women—corroborate the pervasive historical and cultural links between war and sexism.

To acknowledge these connections is not to assert an inher-ent male disposition toward violence. For men as for women, behavior and thinking are socially constructed and conditioned by political, economic, and social hierarchies. These prejudices can be overcome and transformed through conscious political choice. Feminist author Betty Friedan writes that the men who turned against war during the Vietnam era were defying the masculine mystique as women had defied the feminine mys-tique. Those men "were the other half of what we were doing."[127] Many of us are still struggling to shed the macho stereotypes we learned at an early age and that are constantly reinforced in our sexist culture. It is a continuous struggle to which all men must devote themselves.

Feminism can help in this process. As Ruddick notes, femi-nism helps deconstruct "the sexual fantasies and fears that sustain the culture of violence."[128] Feminism is a negation of the patriarchal hierarchies that are at the root of violence and oppression. It is a struggle against the militarism and domestic violence that most severely affect women. It is an attempt to break the social conditioning that has linked patriarchy and male domination with violence against women and institutionalized war making.[129] Feminism rejects the principles of male-dominated hierarchy and promotes democratic principles of freedom, equality, and self-rule.[130] It denies the power principle of domination and subjugation, and it is linked to the fight against racism.[131] Feminism broadly defined in this way is a form of peace politics. It is an essential component of the struggle for a more just and nonviolent future. It is an ideal for both men and women, a personal and political choice that is available and necessary for all.

Chapter 9

Principles of Action

Gandhi and King were masters at the art of social change and brilliant nonviolent strategists. They were more practitioners than theorists, though, and neither attempted systematically to analyze and catalogue the most important principles of social action. That task was taken up by others, most notably Gene Sharp, whose *Politics of Nonviolent Action* remains the classic. Sharp's ideas also inspired the important volume *Strategic Nonviolent Conflict*, by Peter Ackerman and Christopher Kruegler. By far the most popular and widely read compendium of organizing principles is Saul Alinsky's *Rules for Radicals*, an often-humorous and irreverent attempt to codify a lifetime of organizing experience into a set of tactical rules. In the pages that follow I attempt to integrate these differing works, combining Sharp's principles of strategy with Alinsky's rules of tactics to identify the core principles of effective social action.

Understanding Power

Social activists often have difficulty understanding and accepting the importance of political power. For many, *power* is a negative term. Power is corruption. Power is what we are fighting. "Fight the power," says the character in director Spike Lee's film *Do the Right Thing*. "Speak truth to power" is the Quaker phrase. For many, power is the very antithesis of morality, a means of control and coercion. Yet power is fundamentally important to political change. Social activism is all about power: who has it and how it is shaped. Power is inevitable and unavoidable. It is like gravity, always there, even when we are not conscious of it, constantly acting upon us. It is not something to be feared or shunned but rather to be understood and utilized. "To know power and not fear it," said Alinsky, "is essential to its constructive use and control."[1]

Martin Luther King Jr. described power as "the ability to achieve purpose ... the strength required to bring about social, political, or economic changes. In this sense power is not only desirable but necessary in order to implement the demands of love and justice." King spoke eloquently about the importance of power and the need to combine it with love. "One of the greatest problems of history is that the concepts of love and power are usually contrasted as polar opposites. Love is identified with a resignation of power and power with a denial of love.... What is needed is a realization that power without love is reckless and abusive, and that love without power is sentimental and anemic. Power at its best is love implementing the demands of justice."[2] The problem with power, King wrote, is that it is unequally distributed. To redress this imbalance and achieve justice, the movement must go from "powerlessness into creative and positive power."[3]

Sharp also examined the relationship between power and nonviolence. Drawing on the insights of Gandhi, Sharp looked at power from the bottom up rather than the top down. He viewed power as a relationship between the ruled and the ruler. Political authority is not a static phenomenon that can be measured solely by the number of weapons or the size of an army. Power is a variable phenomenon and has multiple sources.[4] It does not rest only on force or the manipulation of reward and punishment to coerce compliance. Power depends on the willingness of the governed to follow orders.[5] Even under the most extreme forms of totalitarianism, obedience is to some degree voluntary. To Sharp, as to Gandhi, political authority ultimately rests on the consent of the governed. The withdrawal of that consent alters the relations of power. When people refuse to cooperate, the power and legitimacy of authority erode. Even seemingly impregnable dictatorships can be swept aside when the governed refuse to be ruled. This basic concept—the collective withdrawal of consent—is at the heart of the Gandhian method, and it is crucial to the strategy of nonviolent social change.

Organizational Strength

During the 1980s, as nuclear fear gripped American conscious-ness, SANE launched a multiyear plan to increase membership and build organizational capacity. Ronald Reagan was the best recruiter the peace movement had in those days. Reckless and ill-informed statements from the president and his cabinet of-ficers struck terror in the hearts of millions and created an unprecedented opportunity to attract membership support. (A Pentagon directive called for "prevailing" in a nuclear war, and the secretary of state spoke of nuclear warning shots.) Through mailings, door-to-door canvassing, and telephone outreach, SANE's membership increased from 5,000 in the late 1970s to nearly 150,000 by the mid-1980s. Income from membership contributions rose tenfold, with thousands joining as monthly sustainers. The SANE staff expanded to include lobbyists, orga-nizers, and publicists. As our membership in local congressional districts mounted, so did our political influence on Capitol Hill. We created the largest peace membership organization in U.S. history. We didn't realize it at the time, but we were following one of the classic principles of social action: organization building.

Alinsky taught that political effectiveness depends on or-ganizational strength. To overcome the entrenched power of corrupt establishments, social movements need to develop an institutional base capable of applying sustained pressure for change. "Power and organization are one and the same," Alin-sky wrote.[6] Organizational clout is necessary to bring about social change. Activists should not confront their adversaries, he advised, until they have developed a "mass power base."[7] Ackerman and Kruegler emphasized the importance of creating what they call "efficient, fighting organizations."[8] Gandhi placed a strong emphasis on organization building as an essential element of his method.[9] He realized that his views would have no impact without the backing of an organized constituency.

Gandhi transformed the Indian Congress from an elite debating society into a broadly based mass organization capable of mounting nationwide political struggle. He began each of his campaigns with vigorous recruitment and fund-raising drives to build organizational capacity and prepare for the challenges of sustained mass action.[10]

Political power in a democratic society ultimately rests on two factors: money and people. Establishment politicians usually gain their power from money. They use the contributions of wealthy supporters to sway the media and influence large numbers of people. Social change groups do not have the deep pockets of the corporate elite. Their power depends instead on the number of people they can mobilize. The influence of SANE and other disarmament groups during the 1980s proceeded in direct proportion to the growth of our membership. While our numbers were small, we had difficulty gaining access. Instead of meeting senators, we had to cool our heels in the reception area and settle for seeing an aide. When our membership topped a hundred thousand, access and influence improved dramatically. We were invited to meet with congressional leaders and sometimes helped plan legislative strategy.

Some analysts disagree with the strategy of organizational development. Piven and Cloward argue that channeling disruptive protest into organizational development weakens poor people's movements and impedes social progress.[11] Others caution against the institutional sclerosis that can afflict large organizations. Trade unions are the classic example of institutions that can fall prey to corruption and that sometimes need reform movements to hold leaders accountable to the original mission. Trade unions and other large citizen organizations have faults, but they can also play a crucial role in advancing social progress. Trade unions have significantly improved the lives of workers and their families. Large organizations such as the Sierra Club, the National Organization for Women, and the NAACP are stalwart defenders of the environment, the rights of women, and racial justice. Without such institutions, the forces of exploitation and injustice would hold even greater sway, and the prospects for social change would be diminished.

My students sometimes question whether, in today's world of cyber networks and the Internet, Alinsky's focus on organizational development is still relevant. Virtual communities now transcend boundaries, connecting people electronically and offering new opportunities for coordinated action. Traditional hierarchies are fading as interactive communication replaces information control. E-mail and Web sites have greatly advanced the art of virtual organizing. Distributed information hubs and networks now function with efficiency. These trends do not obviate the need for creating effective institutions, however. The organizations of today differ from those of the past—less hierarchical, more horizontal, open to diverse channels of communication—but they have the same essential purpose: to mobilize people and resources for collective action.

Internet Organizing

The Iraq antiwar movement sparked the growth of a new form of organizational clout, what the *New York Times Magazine* called "dot-org politics."[12] The largest and most influential of these Internet-based networks was MoveOn, founded in 1998 by software entrepreneurs Wes Boyd and Joan Blades in response to Republican efforts to impeach President Clinton. In late 2001, MoveOn merged its list with that of "9–11peace.org," a Web site founded by recent college graduate Eli Pariser to advocate a restrained, lawful response to the terrorist attacks against the United States.

When the Bush administration began its buildup toward war in 2002, MoveOn entered the antiwar fray and became a driving force in the burgeoning peace movement. MoveOn was one of the founders of the Win Without War coalition. It generated hundreds of thousands of signatures on an antiwar petition prior to the October 2002 congressional vote authorizing military action. It raised millions of dollars in campaign contributions for key senators who voted against the war resolution. It organized hundreds of local meetings with members of Congress. It generated nearly a million signatures in less than a week on an international petition to the UN in March 2003. It helped organize more than six thousand vigils in 140 countries the weekend before war began. All of this incredible action flowed from an organization with only a handful of staff—an organization with a powerful computer and sophisticated software system but with none of the usual accoutrements of traditional membership associations.

In the six months leading up to the outbreak of war in March 2003 MoveOn's online membership, U.S. and international, grew from approximately seven hundred thousand to nearly two million. The network continued to grow through its involvement in the 2004 election campaign, its ongoing opposition to the U.S. military occupation of Iraq, and efforts to block the Bush administration's reactionary domestic agenda. By the fall of 2005 MoveOn boasted more than 3.3 million "members."

Such rapid organizational growth was without precedent. So was the extraordinary potential represented by the emergence of dot-org politics. MoveOn and other electronically based antiwar groups—including True Majority and Working Assets—served as the backbone of the Win Without War coalition. They gave the coalition an extraordinary capacity to mobilize coordinated international action on a massive scale on very short notice. The emergence of MoveOn reflected the urgency and intensity of antiwar feeling among tens of millions of people in the United States and around the world. People were literally waiting at their computer screens, eager to respond to the next action alert from MoveOn. The experience of the Iraq antiwar movement demonstrated the power of Internet-based networks as significant new organizational tools for achieving justice.

Clarifying Goals

The motivating power of a movement depends on its long-range vision. The more inspiring and worthy the ultimate goal, the more effective a movement will be in communicating its purpose and attracting supporters. Social movements are most successful, according to Jim Wallis, when they emphasize "the transcendent character of moral values."[13] Movements, like religions, attract followers on the basis of moral ideals. The voluntary sacrifice of time, money, and effort that is the lifeblood of social activism comes most readily when a movement appeals to lofty goals. Peace activists are motivated by the vision of a planet beyond war, a nuclear-free world at peace. Martin Luther King Jr. inspired the civil rights movement with the dream of a beloved community based on freedom and racial equality. To motivate its followers and communicate its vision, a movement must espouse long-range goals based on compelling moral principles.

Campaigns differ from movements, however, and they are guided by more limited objectives. While broad ideals such as peace and freedom are essential for building movements, campaigns need clear, focused objectives. As King and his colleagues demonstrated in the civil rights movement, focused goals are essential to effective strategy. The more concrete and specific the objective, the greater the chances of success. At times, sweeping social transformations have resulted from modest demands. When the Montgomery bus boycott began in 1955, King and his colleagues did not call for an immediate end to all bus segregation. The demands were more limited:

- open seating, with black passengers filling seats from the rear and whites from the front, and
- the hiring of black drivers on predominantly black bus routes.

From these modest objectives emerged a powerful mass movement that brought an end to legal segregation in Montgomery and eventually throughout the South.

In Poland during the 1980s, the Solidarity movement did not demand the overthrow of communism, although this was its long-term goal. The immediate objective was free elections. The government responded by permitting elections for one-third of the seats in parliament, a move designed to preserve Communist control. But when Solidarity won every one of the contested seats in the June 1989 balloting, Communist authority collapsed, and Solidarity leaders found themselves forming a new government. Modest objectives sometimes can have far-reaching consequences. What matters most is not the sweep of the demands but the breadth and vigor of the social movement behind them.

Some activists have difficulty accepting the need for limited objectives. They consider anything less than the ultimate goal a cop-out. During SANE's campaign against the MX missile in the 1980s, we were sometimes criticized for focusing on a specific weapon system rather than nuclear disarmament in general. The freeze campaign faced similar criticism from those who considered halting the arms race inferior to eliminating nuclear weapons. There is no contradiction, however, between striving for limited objectives and pursuing ultimate goals. Both dimensions, short- and long-term, are necessary. Ideally, short-term objectives are linked to longer-term goals. Victory on a specific issue builds momentum toward the larger goal and empowers activists to carry on the struggle. It is this interplay between tactical objectives and strategic goals, between demands that are realizable in the near term and goals that are more visionary, that constitutes the art of effective social activism.

Achievable objectives are crucial to the process of empowerment. Alinsky defined empowerment as the art of transforming discontent into conscious political action. Many people don't think about or act on social issues because they feel powerless. Why worry about a problem I can't fix? The best way to overcome feelings of helplessness, said Alinsky, is to assist people in winning "a steady stream of modest, concrete achievements."[14] After people experience an initial success, they are eager to take on more difficult and long-range goals. As Alinsky phrased it, "The people were fighting for hamburger, now they wanted filet mignon."[15]

A marvelous change occurs in people when they join a social movement. I remember a fellow soldier at Fort Bliss—"Speedie," we called him—who despite his antiwar feelings paid no attention to the books and articles we gave him. When he finally came to a demonstration and began acting on his beliefs, though, his indifference vanished. He suddenly hungered for information and understanding. He devoured all the antiwar literature he could get his hands on, despite having only a tenth-grade education. He acquired a newfound sense of direction and purpose. The thrill of making change can open minds to new horizons and provide a sense of courage and conviction.

Sometimes a creative new articulation of an old issue can spark an upsurge of public involvement. Such was the case with the nuclear weapons freeze campaign. The call for a nuclear freeze—a bilateral halt to the testing, production, and development of nuclear weapons by both the United States and the Soviet Union—transformed the public discourse on nuclear weapons issues. Previously nuclear weapons issues had been considered too technical and specialized for ordinary citizens. The horrors of nuclear war led to psychic numbing and an unwillingness to even think about the issue. The nuclear freeze changed all that. The idea of halting nuclear weapons development on both sides was easily understandable. The popularity of the concept made it seem achievable. The nuclear freeze was "user-friendly." One didn't need a Ph.D. in nuclear physics or a degree in international relations to embrace its logic. The ordinary citizen was now empowered to address the most awesome and arguably most important of all issues. Previously an obscure field reserved for experts, nearly all of them white males, the problem of nuclear weapons now came into the province of ordinary citizens. The nuclear debate was radically democratized, as the discussion of nuclear policy moved from the cloistered board rooms of the Pentagon to town squares and city streets. This massive public involvement, encompassing literally millions of citizens, changed the dynamics of the nuclear debate in Washington and created a new political climate conducive to arms reduction and the end of the cold war.[16]

Financing Change

During the Vietnam antiwar movement, after a particularly tedious discussion of politics one evening, an exhausted colleague turned to me and said, "The only line that matters is the bottom line." In this she was both rejecting the movement's preoccupation with political correctness and lamenting its lack of money. Without financial resources, a movement's debates over political objectives are futile. To influence political leaders and reach the public, a movement needs money. The larger the campaign, the greater the financial need. Social change groups must acquire sufficient funding to communicate their message. This is another key advantage of organizational development. It provides the capacity for raising funds.

Many activists dislike raising money or consider it beneath them. They prefer "more important" work. The fund-raising committee often has the fewest volunteers and is the last item on the agenda. But fund-raising is essential to social change. Over the years I've raised millions of dollars for various peace campaigns and events, including the June 1982 disarmament rally in Central Park and the Win Without War campaign against the invasion of Iraq. Writing proposals can help crystallize our thinking about action campaigns. Making a succinct and compelling pitch for donors is good practice for arguing our case to the public. The reverse is also true. Action plans can and should be translated into fund-raising appeals. By mailing and telephoning our members, we not only raise money but encourage them to take action in their community.

Fund-raising is organizing. When we ask someone to contribute, we are seeking an investment in the cause. We are selling the mission and asking for support. This is what organizing is all about—motivating others to take a stand. Most of us express our politics by giving money. We're usually too busy with other duties and obligations to have much time for activism, so we give a donation, as large as possible, so that others can do the necessary work. Giving money is what we do during religious services, as an expression of our faith. It is also what we do at activist events, as an expression of our political commitment.

The greatest organizers for social change were also the best fund-raisers. Gandhi was not only the moral leader and chief strategist of the Indian independence movement but also its key fund-raiser. His success, writes Judith Brown, was due to his "skills as a fundraiser and repute as an honest trustee of public funds."[17] He kept meticulous records and was extremely careful in spending and accounting for the funds entrusted to him. In his initial campaigns in South Africa, Indian merchants hired him to represent and defend the Asian community. As his campaigns expanded and developed, he recognized the need for a broader financial appeal. He became adept at raising money not only from people of means but from workers and peasants. He especially appealed to women, calling on them to hand in their jewelry or bring saris that could be sold. It was ironic that this man of voluntary poverty, who had stripped himself of nearly all possessions and even clothes, constantly asked for money. But Gandhi and his colleagues were unabashed in seeking funds for the liberation movement. A wealthy supporter once quipped, "It takes a lot of money to keep Gandhi in poverty."

King, too, was a master fund-raiser, not only for SCLC but the entire civil rights movement. His many speeches across the country were not only brilliant oratory but essential means of raising funds, often thousands of dollars at a single event. Through his hundreds of speaking events each year, King raised substantial funds for the civil rights movement. He also raised money from wealthy individuals, foundations, trade unions, and churches. King was not only the indispensable voice and strategist for the movement but its chief fund-raiser. Like Gandhi, King had little personal wealth, although at least he had a modest home and was well clothed. King earned a salary of $5,000 a year, which was about median income at the time. For his wife, Coretta, raising four children alone and meeting the demands of public life, King's limited income was a hardship. But King gave all the money he received, including the $54,000 Nobel Peace Prize, to the movement.

The Power of the Media

A few days after the 12 June 1982 disarmament rally in New York, I received a call from media guru Tony Schwartz. Schwartz was famous for creating the "daisy ad" in the 1964 presidential campaign that helped Lyndon Johnson win a landslide election victory. (The television spot began with a little girl innocently pulling petals from a daisy, continued as an ominous voice counted down to a rocket launch, dissolved into a mushroom cloud nuclear explosion, and ended with serene reassurances from Johnson.) In his typically gruff manner, Schwartz asked, "How much did you spend on that Central Park rally?" "Half a million dollars," I replied. "You wasted your money," he barked. "If you'd put that amount into advertising you'd have done more for the nuclear freeze." Schwartz invited me to his New York studio and dazzled me with stories and examples of his media wizardry. I came away unconvinced that the rally was a waste but very much impressed with the need for greater attention to the media's role in social change.

No aspect of political reality in contemporary society is more important than media communications. This point is evident in the vast sums that political candidates of all parties pour into advertising and public relations. The power of the media has become a dominant factor in shaping politics, society, and culture. Despite the centrality of communications, however, progressive social change groups often devote too little attention to press and media affairs. Environmental, human rights, and peace groups tend to hire more researchers, organizers, and lobbyists than media specialists. Nonviolent activists devote fewer resources to the media than their corporate or government adversaries, and they are less sophisticated in their use of the media. This is a weakness that must be overcome if challenger groups are to be more effective in achieving their goals.

Ronald Reagan was called the Great Communicator, but it was White House counselor Michael Deaver who orchestrated Reagan's media image. When I interviewed Deaver after he left office, I asked him to describe the process by which presidential decisions and activities were planned. "The first question," said Deaver, "was, What do we want the newspaper headlines and the evening news to say the next day? Then we worked back from there." During the 1985 Reagan-Gorbachev summit, for example, the White House wanted to avoid substantive discussion of arms control and to project instead a human interest "get-acquainted" angle. Reagan was to be shown as the equal of the formidable new leader of the Soviet Union. There would be no questions about test bans, strategic arms reduction, or other nettlesome details. Reporters were fed carefully staged images of the president and the Soviet leader chatting amiably, while news of the actual discussions was blacked out.

Citizen groups do not have the media power of the White House and may find such blatant manipulation offensive, but greater efforts to integrate media planning into campaign strategy are both possible and necessary. Before a campaign even begins we should ask, as political image makers do, How do we want the media to present our message? What is our story and human interest angle? How do we want to frame our message? Are there news pegs on which to hang our story? What actions will best convey our message? These are vital questions to be considered at the outset of every action campaign.

As William Gamson emphasizes, all aspects of a social movement's experience—recruitment, organization, strategy, and tactics—are affected by media communications. Without an effective press and media strategy, a nonviolent social movement cannot expect to win the broad public support needed for political success. Positive press coverage helps attract members and contributions. Media coverage is also essential for gaining the sympathy and support of third parties. All dimensions of the strategy of social change depend on gaining favorable media coverage. In Gamson's words, "the media have become the central battleground which challengers ignore at their peril."[18]

The most important dimension of media relations is the framing of messages. The work of linguist George Lakoff has helped many activists recognize the need for framing public debates in the context of widely shared moral values.[19] Every political contest is at its core a struggle over the meaning of ideas and the framing of issues. According to Gamson, the images and metaphors activists convey to the media are central to their prospects for political success.[20] Ideas such as justice, peace, and freedom do not exist in a vacuum, in some purified form that everyone automatically accepts. Their meaning is shaped by the social and political context in which they are communicated.[21] The role of the activist is to create that context. It is not enough simply to gain press coverage or to inform people. Activists must also offer compelling phrases, symbols, and images that capture public imagination. They must define issues and provide content for the values they espouse. Those who are most effective at these "symbolic" contests are likely to be most successful at achieving political change.

The antiwar movement lost the fight to prevent war in Iraq, but it won broad public recognition and support for its message: that the dangers of terrorism and weapons proliferation can be met more effectively through diplomatic means. Our ability to communicate was aided by the creation of Win Without War, which framed the movement as mainstream and patriotic. By capturing the flag early in the debate, the movement inoculated itself against the usual charges of aiding the enemy. We made explicit our rejection of Saddam Hussein's policies and rule. We supported vigorous UN inspections and containment as constructive alternatives, in the best tradition of Alinsky.

Through all this we were aided by the most extensive public relations and media advertising campaign in the history of the peace movement. Managed by Fenton Communications, organized and funded mostly by MoveOn and True Majority, greatly aided by the participation of Hollywood artists and pop musicians, the Iraq antiwar media effort generated hundreds of millions of viewer impressions, spending more than a million dollars on paid and earned media. Most of the media messages were communicated under the Win Without War banner and hewed to a consistent message: inspections, not war. Antiwar activists found themselves in the unaccustomed position of being the center of media attention. For the first time in history, observes writer Rebecca Solnit, the peace movement was portrayed in the media as "diverse, legitimate and representative," which was a "watershed victory" for the movement's long-term prospects.[22] The movement's media effort did not sway the unlistening Bush administration, but it significantly influenced public opinion. The debate on the fundamental issue—cooperation versus unilateralism in international affairs—continued after the war began. The Win Without War coalition remained an important voice in the contest for hearts and minds.

One of the ways in which social movements shape the course of history is by setting the terms of the debate and forcing issues and images into the collective consciousness. When Margaret Sanger and her colleagues coined the term *birth control,* they injected an electrifying new phrase into the public discourse that quickly gained broad popular support. When Martin Luther King Jr. and Cesar Chavez brought southern blacks and western farmworkers into the political limelight, they forced the nation to hear new voices and to face the plight of its poorest and most oppressed citizens. The mere presence and visibility of these new participants on the political stage was itself a significant achievement. The nuclear freeze movement was inherently subversive of the Reagan administration's nuclear weapons buildup. By providing constant reminders of the potential for nuclear holocaust, which Pentagon policymakers sought to deny, the freeze campaign helped set the terms of the debate. One of the most important successes of the environmental movement has been the creation of a broad public recognition that ecological consequences matter. The very fact that environmental considerations enter into political and economic decision making is a victory for the green movement. These are examples of the important but often-unappreciated ways in which social movements achieve success. By forcing issues onto the public agenda, by defining the meaning of actions and policies, activists can shape the terms of the debate and steer the public agenda toward new conceptions of human progress.

Evaluating Tactics

When Congress party leaders of India decided to launch a massive noncooperation campaign in 1929, they turned to Gandhi to devise a campaign plan. Gandhi retired to his ashram near Ahmedabad and waited for an inspiration. Suddenly the idea hit him. He would march to the sea and openly defy the British salt laws. The plan was inspired. It electrified the country, captured the world's imagination, and sparked one of the greatest nonviolent resistance campaigns in history—moving millions of people into open defiance of British authority. Making salt illegally became a patriotic duty, an exciting and enjoyable act that even the poorest peasants could understand and replicate. When Gandhi's supporters escalated tactics by marching on the Dharsana salt works in May 1930, the government responded by viciously clubbing hundreds of unarmed, nonresisting demonstrators. The resulting public outcry prompted even greater defiance of British authority, as the campaign snowballed and shook the foundations of British rule. British leaders could not understand how something so trivial as the defiance of salt laws could spark mass revolt. An American newspaper editorialized, "As Britain lost America through tea, it is about to lose India through salt."[23]

Gandhi's salt campaign met many of the classic criteria for effective tactics. These are defined by Ackerman and Kruegler as being creative and original, easily replicable without the need for extensive training, within the experience of your constituency, enabling the movement to seize the initiative, and part of a sequence of actions that can build momentum toward larger objectives.[24] The idea of defying the salt monopoly was brilliantly innovative. Everyone, even the most unlettered villager, could follow Gandhi's example of resistance to British authority. Everyone knew the importance of salt in India's torrid climate, and the injustice of a foreign power profiting from so vital a commodity. It was, wrote Brown, "a tax by an alien power on a basic necessity of life, on which there was a long tradition of Indian political opposition."[25] As millions joined the campaign, the independence movement gained enormous political momentum and moral authority. The salt campaign successfully mobilized the nation and made the independence of India virtually inevitable.

The closest thing to a catalogue of nonviolent action techniques is Sharp's listing of 198 methods in *The Politics of Nonviolent Action*.[26] First developed in the early 1970s, Sharp's listing is infinitely expandable. Dozens of additional techniques could be added from the experience of social movements in recent decades. Sharp's listing is most valuable as a framework for understanding the different categories of action and the relative impact of each. Especially helpful are the three broad categories he identifies: (1) protest and persuasion, (2) noncooperation, and (3) nonviolent intervention.

As one moves along the continuum from persuasion to nonco-operation to intervention, the forcefulness and coercive impact of the various techniques increases. The first category, protest and persuasion, is primarily symbolic in nature, communicating a movement's message and demands. When Barbara Deming called for more assertive nonviolent action, she was urging ac-tivists to go beyond mere protest and persuasion. The second category, noncooperation, is more forceful. It is the act of with-holding cooperation or obedience to authority. Sharp divides the noncooperation category into three subcategories—economic, social, and political—and further subdivides the economic cat-egory into strikes and boycotts, as outlined here:

Methods of Nonviolent Action[27]
I.   Protest and Persuasion
II. Noncooperation
       Social
       Economic
          Boycott
          Strike
III. Political Intervention

The last stage in the progression toward more forceful action is nonviolent intervention. This approach means interrupting business as usual and disrupting the normal functioning of society. This category also includes actions to create alternative institutions, to replace the power of the adversary with parallel forms of people power.

The most powerful methods are those of noncooperation and intervention. Noncooperation and intervention are the techniques of "nonviolent obstruction" to which Deming re-ferred—assertive and constructive actions that confront those in authority with unexpected realities to which they must respond.[28] The greatest advances for social justice have come through the application of these methods. Noncooperation in the form of economic boycotts was important to the success of the civil rights and farmworker movements. Intervention played a key role in the civil rights struggle in the form of sit-ins that disrupted lunch counters and freedom rides that defied segregated travel. Social movements around the world have been most effective when they have developed creative means of defying illegitimate authority and obstructing the function of repressive power. The methods of protest and persuasion are also important, especially to win the support of third parties and shape the terms of public debate, but the exercise of political power ultimately rests on a movement's ability to organize mass noncooperation and nonviolent intervention.

Alinsky's Rules

Selecting the right tactic for a particular social setting is the key to effective activism. There is no universal guide to the choice of tactics, since each political situation is unique, but Alinsky produced the most useful and authoritative set of principles for social action. His *Rules for Radicals* offers thirteen rules of tactics, which are reinterpreted and consolidated into the following nine principles:[29]

- Never go outside the experience of your people.
- Wherever possible go outside the experience of the adversary.
- Make the adversaries live up to their own rules.
- Ridicule is a potent weapon.
- A tactic that drags on too long becomes a drag.
- A good tactic is one that your people enjoy.
- Keep the pressure on.
- The threat may be more terrifying than the thing itself.
- The price of successful attack is a constructive alternative.[30]

Gandhi's salt campaign is a perfect example of the first two rules. Making salt was well within the experience of the Indian people. The specter of an entire population defying authority was certainly not in the experience of British colonial authorities. The combination of the two created enormous energy and enthusiasm for the resistance campaign. The salt campaign "generated an atmosphere of contempt for government and a moral enthusiasm for breaking laws seen as oppressive."[31] It placed British officials in the awkward position of having to apply repressive force to retain an increasingly tenuous grip on political power. The campaign was also successful at arousing moral outrage and activating the widespread public indignation at the tax on salt. Gandhi's dramatic march to the sea and defiance of the salt laws touched a latent spark of popular resentment and ignited a social revolution.

Making adversaries live up to their own rules enables a movement to seize the moral high ground and use the power of moral urgency to its advantage. The civil rights movement employed this principle brilliantly. Indeed, the movement could be interpreted as a vast attempt to force local authorities in the South to live up to the 1954 Supreme Court ruling, *Brown v. Board of Education,* that outlawed segregation. The decision of the nation's highest court declaring segregation unconstitutional created a significant political opportunity for civil rights advocates. They now had the power of the constitution behind them. As King declared during the Montgomery bus boycott, "If we are wrong, the Supreme Court is wrong. If we are wrong, the constitution of the United States is wrong." By appealing to the federal courts, the civil rights movement positioned itself as defending the rule of law.

One of the great challenges of social activism is developing tactics that are enjoyable, creative, and even humorous. Too often, as Alinsky wrote, worn-out methods become a drag. Peace movements often have difficulty devising creative and effective tactics. During the Vietnam antiwar movement, the usual approach was to organize mass demonstrations, either nationally or regionally, in the spring and fall of each year. Hundreds of thousands would gather in Washington, New York, or San Francisco to condemn the war and demand the withdrawal of U.S. troops. The demonstrations had some political impact,[32] but they consumed an enormous amount of energy and became a drag, a stale and overused tactic that seemed to lose punch as time went on. In the fall of 1969, activists developed a new approach: the Vietnam moratorium. People stayed in their communities and organized rallies, teach-ins, prayer services, and vigils at their schools, workplaces, and houses of worship. Business as usual came to a halt that 15 October, as millions of people paused to plead for peace in Vietnam. The moratorium was designed to give local groups flexibility in deciding the form of their participation, with events tailored to the interests and needs of the community. Even troops in Vietnam participated, with many soldiers wearing black armbands or peace symbols as a show of solidarity with their sisters and brothers marching for peace back in "the world."

Hundreds of thousands of demonstrators gather at the Washington Monument for the Moratorium Day peace rally to protest the Vietnam War on November 15, 1969 (AP photo).

Activist groups have recently developed the social forum concept to supplement the traditional model of demonstrations. In November 2002, more than half a million people marched in Florence, Italy, as part of the European Social Forum against war in Iraq. In January 2003, tens of thousands participated in the World Social Forum at Porto Alegre, Brazil. The social forum events featured hundreds of workshops and a wide range of cultural activities in addition to political demonstrations and speeches. In the United States, by contrast, most of the initial demonstrations against war in Iraq offered the traditional menu of endless political speeches with little cultural entertainment. In January 2003, Working Assets, California Peace Action, and the Sierra Club tried to spice up the antiwar demonstration planned for that month in San Francisco. On the day of the 18 January rally, more than five thousand people attended an "environmentalists against the war" rally and alternative energy fair at the steps of Grace Cathedral. Afterward, an ecocaravan of hybrid and electric cars proceeded down to the main protest rally. Bumper stickers on the vehicles read "Go Solar, Not Ballistic" and "Real Patriots Drive Hybrids." The environmental event highlighted the importance of energy efficiency and reduced oil dependence as peace issues. The September 2005 mobilization against the war in Washington featured an "Operation Ceasefire" festival that followed a short program of opening speeches and a long protest march. The festival combined music and speeches in a concert atmosphere that continued late into the night.[33] Many activists in the assembled crowd welcomed the creative combination of entertainment and culture as a marked improvement over the usual menu of hard-core political rhetoric.

Social movements by their very nature address serious social problems. Dealing with nuclear proliferation, environmental pollution, or AIDS can be deeply depressing. It is difficult to find a creative or humorous way to address such problems. The *Bulletin of the Atomic Scientists* has developed the famous doomsday clock as an effective way of illustrating the global danger of nuclear conflict. The image is not humorous, of course, but it is attractive and appealing, a more effective and universally recognized way of depicting the nuclear danger than the many learned reports and pamphlets of peace and disarmament groups. AIDS activists developed the AIDS quilt as a creative way of highlighting the grim toll of the epidemic and the need for greater efforts to care for the afflicted. The AIDS quilt is a giant mosaic of creative expression commemorating the lives of the many thousands who have died from AIDS. When it was first displayed behind the White House in Washington, D.C., covering almost the entire Ellipse, it had a powerful effect in dramatizing the enormous scale of the AIDS crisis. Tens of thousands of people came to view the quilt, learning firsthand of AIDS' devastating impact, contributing money to the quilt project, and volunteering to join the campaign to find a cure. The AIDS quilt subsequently went on the road to communities across the United States, serving as an effective and creative means of public education.

The need for a constructive alternative is critically important to the success of social action campaigns. Protesting an objectionable policy is not enough. It is also necessary to propose alternatives. Opponents of nuclear power plants must do more than highlight the risks of accidents and radiation leaks. They must also propose alternative ways of meeting electrical power needs, through greater energy efficiency and renewable energy production. Opponents of war must do more than criticize the costs and consequences of military action. They must also provide answers to the security concerns that prompt the consideration of military force. Offering constructive, viable alternatives is crucial to a movement's public legitimacy and its ability to attract third-party support.

In the case of Iraq, opponents of the initial invasion argued that viable alternatives were available—intrusive UN inspections and targeted sanctions—to counter the potential military threat from Iraq. Later, as groups campaigned against the U.S. occupation, differences emerged about whether to advocate constructive alternatives. Some demanded the immediate withdrawal of all foreign troops, without regard for the nuances of policy or the consequences of abrupt exit. Others argued for phased withdrawal, linked to substantial economic assistance and international efforts to stabilize Iraq. All factions wanted the U.S. military to withdraw as soon as possible, but they differed on how best to achieve this. The "out now" faction argued that social movements generate pressure for change by raising maximum demands. The role of activists is to force politicians to act, not to devise alternative policies. The advocates of "phased withdrawal" countered that constructive approaches would generate greater support for the military withdrawal that everyone agreed was necessary. To build public support, movements must have credibility. For peace movements, this means addressing legitimate concerns for justice and human rights. In the age of terrorism, it means proposing policies that alter the underlying conditions that cause political extremism, while also advocating protection for innocent populations threatened by indiscriminate violence. Movements have a political and moral responsibility to devise constructive alternatives to the policies they oppose.

Nonviolence: The Constructive Alternative to Terrorism

In the months after 9/11, Jim Wallis challenged peace advocates to address the threat of terrorism. "If nonviolence is to have any credibility," he wrote, "it must answer the questions violence purports to answer, but in a better way."[34] Few activists have taken up Wallis's challenge. Many antiwar groups rightly condemn U.S. foreign policy, but they have little to say about the jihadist militants who kill innocent civilians. They have no solution for countering Al Qaeda–related threats and lack a non-violent strategy for preventing terrorism. The absence of concrete alternatives has left the field open to the Bush administration and its so-called global war on terror. Through the manipulation of fear and constant references to 9/11, leaders in Washington have maintained public support for their war policies even in the face of widespread skepticism about the military mission in Iraq. Until this "war" paradigm is challenged, the peace movement will be unable to make progress. Ours is a double challenge: countering the threat of mass murder by jihadist networks, and countering militarized U.S. policies that exacerbate this terrorist danger. Developing a constructive response to this twin danger is vitally important to the prospects for global peace.

The theories of nonviolence provide ample foundation for crafting an effective strategy against terrorism. The first require-ment is to balance the demand for peace with the requirement for justice. It is not sufficient to critique American militarism or to address the root causes of terrorism. It is also necessary to apply pressure on the militants who commit mass murder and to protect innocent victims. The indiscriminate killing of civilians is never acceptable for any purpose. Those who explode bombs in mosques, subway cars, and cafés must be indicted and prosecuted to the full extent of the law. This involves action by courts and police forces and may require the limited use of force. The ambiguities of seeking justice in an imperfect world sometimes require coercive measures, especially when the chal-lenge is protecting innocent victims.

Some absolute pacifists will object even to limited forms of coercion, but most peace advocates accept the use of police force, provided it is constrained, narrowly targeted against known criminals, and conducted within the rule of law. John Howard Yoder emphasizes the distinction between policing and war. The former is subject to legal and moral constraints and is ethically superior to war.[35] Political scientist Robert Johansen has proposed ways to use international courts and multilat-eral policing to achieve justice and protect the innocent while strengthening the rule of law.[36] Theologian Gerald Schlabach has integrated these concepts into a theory of "just policing."[37] These approaches stretch but do not contradict the core philosophy of nonviolence, which seeks to preserve peace but also uphold justice. The presumption is always against the use of force, but extreme circumstances may arise—such as countering terrorist attacks—where the demands of justice require some limited use of police power.

Law enforcement must be combined with protective measures. The "responsibility to protect" is widely recognized internationally as a political and moral imperative for the defense of justice and human rights.[38] Protecting against terrorism requires cooperative law enforcement and intelligence sharing among governments. It also involves efforts to defund terrorist networks and deny safe haven, travel, and the arming and training of terrorist militants.

The UN Security Council mandated such protective measures globally when it adopted Resolution 1373 a few weeks after the 9/11 attacks. The resolution encouraged countries to coordinate more effectively with one another in protecting against terrorism. Through dozens of additional Security Council resolutions, the UN counterterrorism program has evolved into a significant international campaign to apply nonmilitary pressure against terrorist networks. My colleagues and I have published a number of reports recommending ways to improve the UN counterterrorism program.[39] The vigorous enforcement of these UN mandates can protect the innocent and reduce the operational capacity of terrorist networks. Such protective efforts meet the requirement for justice and are fully compatible with the theory of nonviolence.

The principles of conflict prevention and transformation are also highly relevant to the fight against terrorism. This is where the theories of nonviolence are especially valuable, in identifying and transforming the underlying dynamics that lead to violent conflict. The practices of conflict resolution have proven effective in countless settings, and they can contribute to the struggle against terrorism as well. To prevent armed violence, it is necessary to understand why communities are in conflict and to address the underlying grievances and conditions that fuel violence. Peacemakers seek to engage with those affected by conflict and to search for solutions that enhance justice. In addressing the terrorist threat, this approach means recognizing the injustices that motivate support for militant groups and enabling affected communities to resolve grievances through democratic political means rather than terrorist violence.

This approach should not be confused with appeasement or a defeatist justification of terrorist crimes. The point is not to excuse criminal acts but to learn why they occurred and to use this knowledge to prevent such attacks in the future. A non-violent strategy does not mean appeasing hard-core militants. Rather, it seeks to reduce the appeal of extremist methods by addressing legitimate grievances and providing channels of nonviolent political engagement for those who sympathize with terrorist aims. A two-level response is needed: determined pressure against terrorist criminals, and active engagement with affected communities to resolve underlying grievances. The goal is to separate hard-core militants from their social base by addressing the injustices that motivate support for militancy. Counterterrorism must not repeat the wrongs of terrorism, Michael Walzer writes. It "must be aimed systematically at the terrorists themselves, never at the people for whom the terrorists claim to be acting."[40]

Terrorism is fundamentally a political phenomenon, and the strategies against it must be political as well. In the struggle against Al Qaeda and the global jihadist threat, this means recognizing the pernicious effects of U.S. foreign policies in Arab and Muslim countries. The hatred that many people in the region feel toward the U.S. government is rooted in specific American policies—military encroachments into Muslim countries, support for Israeli oppression of the Palestinians, and U.S. backing for authoritarian regimes in Saudi Arabia and beyond. The Bush administration's unjust war and military occupation in Iraq have added immeasurably to worldwide anger and resentment against U.S. policy. These concerns are reflected in the central demands of Al Qaeda—to overthrow U.S. client regimes in the region, end the occupations of Iraq and the Palestinian territories, and remove U.S. troops from the Islamic world. These are demands that are widely shared in Arab and Muslim countries, even among those who condemn terrorism and Al Qaeda's brutal methods.

These demands also have wide resonance among progressives in the United States and around the world. Many of us who work for peace and human rights have supported similar demands for many years. We oppose U.S. military intervention and domination in other countries, we support the rights of the Palestinian people, and we urge consistent support for democracy and human rights in all countries. We vigorously oppose the U.S. war and occupation in Iraq and demand the removal of all American troops and bases. These are just demands. They deserve our support—even as we condemn those who employ terrorist means to achieve them. Creating a less militarized U.S. foreign policy is necessary to undercut support for jihadist extremism. It is also important to create a more just and peaceful world order.

Most Pentagon officials and many political leaders in Washington continue to view terrorism primarily through the prism of war. Kill enough militants, they believe, and the threat will go away. In fact, the opposite is true. The more the United States attempts to impose its will by military force, the greater the terrorist threat becomes. The number of major terrorist incidents in the world tripled after the invasion of Iraq.[41] War is itself a form of terrorism. Using military means to counter terror is like pouring gasoline on a fire. It ignites hatred and vengeance and creates a cycle of violence that can spiral out of control. Better to take away the fuel that sustains the fire. Only nonviolent methods can do that, by attempting to resolve the underlying political and social factors that give rise to armed conflict.

Nonviolence offers hope in place of fear. It rejects the cruel calculus of ends justifying means and insists on the primacy of just means. Nonviolence is the exact opposite of and the most effective antidote to terrorism. It offers targeted police pressure on militants, protection for the innocent, and the prevention of extremist violence through conflict transformation. It is a strategy we must continually advocate to uphold justice and peace. Wallis calls us to "reject war, but unite to defeat terrorism."[42] This is the challenge of our age and an essential requirement for the credibility of nonviolent social change.

Means of Change

Nonviolent activists are often confused and uncertain when asked the simple question, How do you expect to win? Few have considered exactly how they anticipate achieving their objectives.

Will the adversary simply give up and concede to our demands, or will a compromise and negotiated settlement be necessary? Sharp addresses these issues in *The Politics of Nonviolent Action* and subsequent works.[43] He identifies four mechanisms of social change: conversion, disintegration, accommodation, and nonviolent coercion. These are the end points toward which the strategy of social change is directed. Anticipating which process is most likely to succeed in a particular setting is a crucial element of strategic analysis.

Conversion means convincing the opponent to change completely, to accept the movement's point of view. Gandhi considered this the primary mechanism of social change, as evidenced by his constant emphasis on religious teaching and moral persuasion. But Gandhi learned, as most activists do, that genuine conversion is a rare occurrence. Few British officials agreed with Gandhi that their colonial system was unjust. Civil rights activists also found few converts. Some southern whites genuinely repented of their racist past (the most prominent example being former Alabama governor George Wallace), but most simply adjusted to the demands of desegregation. A strategy that depends solely or primarily on the conversion of its adversaries will take a long time if ever to achieve success.

When Sharp published *The Politics of Nonviolent Action* in 1973, he listed only three mechanisms of social change. The concept of disintegration, of the complete collapse of political power, never occurred to him. It had not been observed in the history of nonviolent action. But then came the "velvet revolutions" of Central and Eastern Europe in 1989. The public yearning for freedom in the Soviet empire was so pervasive that the entire rotten edifice of communist power collapsed once people took to the streets in mass numbers. When Gorbachev signaled that the Soviet army would no longer intervene to prop up the corrupt regimes of Eastern Europe, the floodgates were opened to a vast outpouring of popular resistance. Lech Walesa, Vaclav Havel, and other resistance leaders went from being outcasts and dissidents to presidents and prime ministers in the twinkling of an eye.

Most of us have to settle for slower, more partial progress. Accommodation is the most common mechanism of change. This occurs when the adversary decides to grant some but not all of the movement's demands. The adversary could continue to stonewall, but the costs of doing so have increased. Concessions are offered not because the adversary has been persuaded but because the pressures of the campaign have convinced the opponent to make a change. Nonviolent coercion is similar. It occurs when the adversary is no longer able to resist and has no choice but to make concessions. Sharp attempts to draw a clear distinction between accommodation and nonviolent coercion, but in practice the two are quite similar. The difference depends on whether the adversary is acting willingly (accommodation) or not (coercion). There is no need to make so fine a distinction. Change occurs, whether through accommodation or coercion, when the pressure of nonviolent action brings concessions. This is evidence of a movement's effectiveness and should be acknowledged and celebrated as such.

The process of accommodation is essentially one of negotiation and compromise. Many activists dislike the idea of compromise. They consider it a form of betrayal or a surrender of ideals. But to the organizer, said Alinsky, "compromise is a key and beautiful word."[44] It is the means to achieving concrete change. Gandhi, King, and other nonviolent leaders considered negotiation an essential part of the process of social change. They understood that some degree of compromise is usually necessary to achieve progress. This can pose a dilemma for social movements. Activists are motivated to sacrifice for social change by visionary ideals: peace, freedom, and justice. Yet the realities of political struggle seldom produce great breakthroughs. Instead, activists may have to settle for negotiated agreements and compromises that yield only modest gains. Social movement leaders face the challenge of inspiring people on the basis of giant ideals, while mobilizing them in practical action to achieve small steps.

What Is Success?

Success is sometimes hard to recognize. In October 1987, I traveled to Bonn at the invitation of the Green Party to help evaluate the recently signed INF treaty banning intermediate nuclear forces in Europe. The German Greens had battled these NATO and Warsaw Pact missiles for a decade, helping mount the largest demonstrations in postwar German history (similar rallies occurred in nearly every Western European country). Yet they were surprisingly diffident and even glum about the historic treaty banning the weapons. Because the movement had not succeeded in preventing NATO missile deployments in November 1983, activists had come to look on their struggle against INF weapons as a failure. But the peace movement's ultimate goal, the withdrawal of both Soviet and U.S. nuclear missiles, was realized. The movement lost a battle but won the war.[45]

I told the assembled Green Party officials that they should take pride in the signing of the INF treaty and claim it as their own. The European disarmament movement had first proposed the so-called zero solution—no NATO or Soviet intermediate missiles—in the late 1970s. U.S. officials appropriated the idea in 1981, as a means of co-opting the peace movement, and adopted it as NATO's negotiating position. Although Henry Kissinger, Brent Scowcroft, and other national security leaders expressed misgivings about the zero option, the Reagan administration convinced NATO officials to accept the proposal, in part as a political ploy to parry growing antinuclear sentiment. Brezhnev-era Soviet leaders initially rejected the zero option, as White House officials expected, but Gorbachev later said yes. With Gorbachev's unexpected support for the proposal, Western governments found themselves hoist on their own petard and had to accept the deal.[46] The original peace movement idea became policy.

Activism can be effective even when a campaign does not achieve the stated objectives. A nuclear freeze was not enacted during the 1980s, but the freeze movement nonetheless had a significant impact in shaping the political climate and generating pressure for arms control. Activists can never be certain how their efforts will affect policy. The law of unintended effect operates in social movements as it does elsewhere. Often the pressures generated in an action campaign lead to compromises or policy initiatives that are quite unexpected. The Stop MX campaign of the 1980s led Congress to force the Reagan administration to moderate its arms control policies. This was not what MX opponents intended, but it was a beneficial side effect. When movements apply pressure, they can never be sure how political establishments will respond. The most important thing is to keep up the pressure and to understand that results may emerge in unexpected and even unrecognized ways.

Change often comes slowly, almost imperceptibly, after long years of difficult struggle. The movement for the women's vote in the United States began at Seneca Falls, New York, in 1848 but did not achieve final victory until the eighteenth amendment to the U.S. Constitution was ratified in 1920, more than seventy years later. Elizabeth Cady Stanton helped found the movement, but it was her daughter, Harriet Stanton Blatch, who carried the struggle through to the final triumph. Movements may experience failure and defeat even as they steadily build toward long-term achievement. Dorothy Day paid tribute to the labor movement by emphasizing "the slow and steady gains, wrung reluctantly from the employers," as the rights of workers steadily advanced. "In the labor movement every strike is considered a failure ... and yet in the long history of labor, certainly there has been a slow and steady bettering of conditions."[47] Social movements may achieve influence even when they appear to be unsuccessful. We can never know when, how, or even whether our efforts will be successful, so it is important not to give up. Success depends on persistence, on maintaining constant pressure for change.

The Long Haul

Working for justice is an arduous enterprise. Like the mythic Sisyphus, we push our boulder up the mountain, only to have it roll back down again. We labor mightily against the powers of privilege, inching our way toward a better world, only to face new injustices or have old ones reappear. Existentialism is a good philosophy for social activists, especially those who attempt to prevent war. A bit of the absurd is built into the very situation—small citizen groups fighting against giant political and military institutions, often on an international scale. The very idea seems ludicrous, the ultimate example of unequal odds.

What can motivate us to keep struggling for justice? Many find their inspiration in religious belief. Reason alone is not enough to explain our willingness to give time, money, and energy to causes that bring little or no material benefit and that may take years to achieve. It often takes the "sublime madness" of religion, as Reinhold Niebuhr puts it, to motivate the commitment to social activism.[48] When we volunteer, donate money, or go to demonstrations, we are practicing a theology of action. Our marching feet are an expression of faith, as Heschel and King would say. Working for justice gives spiritual meaning and purpose to life.

Others are motivated by solidarity with other human beings. We feel community with the human family and a responsibility to protect life. This feeling is especially strong in relation to environmental and nuclear threats, which put the entire human species, and perhaps all life, at risk. Solidarity means "standing with" victims of poverty and injustice. Many activists in the United States and Europe feel strong kinship with people in the developing world. We want to lift the burdens of violence and oppression that afflict hundreds of millions in the global South and that often result from the policies of our countries in the North. We believe that lives are in the balance, as the song by Jackson Browne says, and that we can make a difference in bettering the condition of those who are less fortunate.

The motivation to act is also an assertion of our identity. Our commitment to action defines the very essence of our being. It expresses our most deeply held beliefs. We resist the powers that be to avoid being defined by them. We assert our own values so as not to succumb to theirs. As activist preacher William Sloane Coffin put it, "If we don't stand for something, we'll fall for something." If we don't act on our beliefs, we will lose them. Not to rage against the machine is to give in to it, to become an efficient cog in the wheel of conformity. Better to remain a wrench in the works, to stand up for principle regardless of cost, to work for justice and peace despite the odds.

A commitment to the long haul can help resolve the dilemma of motivation. If we dedicate our entire lives to the struggle for justice and peace, the doubts and ambiguities about the present become less important. The issue of effectiveness becomes a question not for today but for a lifetime, and perhaps beyond. Martin Luther King Jr. was expressing the long-term faith of social activism when he said, "I may not get [to the mountaintop] with you." Even if the struggle goes beyond my own life, others will come forward to carry on the fight for justice. As King so often noted, "The arc of the moral universe is long, but it bends toward justice."

We can never be sure when or how our efforts will succeed. We plan and work for success, but our commitment does not depend on immediate gratification. We continue rolling that boulder up the hill, even when the chances of victory seem distant, believing that the cause of justice and peace ultimately will prevail. Movements for social justice need long-distance runners. To sprint and burn out after a few years is of little benefit. Better to be a long-distance runner—or walker, like Gandhi—to take the long march with him to the sea.

Notes

Introduction

1. This statement later appeared in the *New York Times* on 19 November 2001 as an appeal by religious leaders organized by Reverend Jim Wallis of *Sojourners* and Reverend Bob Edgar of the National Council of Churches.

2. United Nations General Assembly, Security Council, *Report of the Policy Working Group on the United Nations and Terrorism*, A/57/273–S/2002/875, New York, 6 August 2002, para. 13.

3. United Nations General Assembly, *A More Secure World: Our Shared Responsibility, Report of the High-level Panel on Threats, Challenges and Change*, A/59/565, New York, 29 November 2004, para. 148.

Chapter 1

1. Erik H. Erikson, *Gandhi's Truth: On the Origins of Militant Nonviolence* (New York: Norton, 1969), 234.

2. K. M. Sen, *Hinduism* (Baltimore, Md.: Penguin, 1961), 64.

3. Although the words Attenborough puts in Gandhi's mouth are generally authentic, my researcher, Linda Gerber, and I did not find this particular quote in Gandhi's collected works. Nor did the great scholar of religion and conflict Marc Gopin. See his *Between Eden and Armageddon: The Future of World Religions, Violence, and Peacemaking* (Oxford: Oxford University Press, 2000). But the general meaning of the quote is correct and reflects Gandhi's embrace of the

fundamental truths in all great religions of the world. See Mohandas Gandhi, *All Men Are Brothers*, ed. Krishna Kripalani (New York: Continuum, 1980), 55.

4. Quoted in Judith M. Brown, *Gandhi: Prisoner of Hope* (New Haven, Conn.: Yale University Press, 1989), 81.

5. Louis Fischer, *The Life of Mahatma Gandhi* (New York: Harper & Row, 1950), 30.

6. Fischer, *Life of Mahatma Gandhi*, 30–31.

7. As quoted in K. M. Sen, *Hinduism* (Baltimore, Md.: Penguin, 1961), 24.

8. Sen, *Hinduism*, 45.

9. Joan V. Bondurant, *Conquest of Violence: The Gandhian Philosophy of Conflict*, rev. ed. (Princeton, N.J.: Princeton University Press, 1988), 23.

10. Mohandas K. Gandhi, *An Autobiography, or the Story of My Experiments with Truth*, trans. Mahadev Desai (Ahmedabad: Navajivan: Beacon, 1927), 230. Quoted in Robert J. Burrowes, *The Strategy of Nonviolent Defense: A Gandhian Approach* (Albany: State University of New York Press, 1996), 107.

11. Fischer, *Life of Mahatma Gandhi*, 334.

12. Fischer, *Life of Mahatma Gandhi*, 84, 333.

13. Walter Wink, *Engaging the Powers: Discernment and Resistance in a World of Domination* (Minneapolis, Minn.: Fortress, 1992), 217.

14. Wink, *Engaging the Powers*, 185.

15. Wink, *Engaging the Powers*, 176.

16. Wink, *Engaging the Powers*, 185.

17. Leo Tolstoy, *Writings on Civil Disobedience and Nonviolence* (Philadelphia: New Society Publishers, 1987), 46.

18. The rate of desertion and unauthorized absence reached record levels during the Vietnam War, rising to 17 percent in 1971. See David Cortright, *Soldiers in Revolt: GI Resistance during the Vietnam War*, 2d ed. (Chicago: Haymarket Books, 2005), 10–14.

19. M. K. Gandhi, "Why Was India Lost?" *Hind Swaraj or Indian Home Rule*, 22 November 1909, from *The Life and Works of Mahatma Gandhi* 10, no. 160 (Patiala House, Tilak Marg, New Delhi: Publications Division, Ministry of Information and Broadcasting, Government of India, 1999). 262. CD-ROM, dynamic collection. Quoted in Stanley Wolpert, *Gandhi's Passion: The Life and Legacy of Mahatma Gandhi* (New York: Oxford University Press, 2001), 77. Also available at *Hind Swaraj or Indian Home Rule* (chapter VII),www.mkgandhi.org/swarajya/coverpage.htm (accessed 14 August 2002).

20. Leo Tolstoy, preface, "Letter to a Hindoo," 18 November 1909, from *The Life and Works of Mahatma* Gandhi 10, no. 158, 240. Quoted

in Raghavan Iyer, ed., *The Essential Writings of Mahatma Gandhi* (New Delhi: Oxford University Press, 1990), 74.

21. I Cor. 13:12; I am grateful to Patrick Mason, theology student at the University of Notre Dame, for this reference and insight.

22. M. K. Gandhi, *Speeches and Writings of Mahatma Gandhi*, 4th ed. (Madras: Nateson, [n.d.]), 506. Quoted in Bondurant, *Conquest of Violence*, 16.

23. M. K. Gandhi, *From Yeravda Mandir: Ashram Observances*, trans. Valji Govindji Desai (Ahmedabad: Navajivan, 1945), 8. Quoted in Bondurant, *Conquest of Violence*, 24. Also available at Mahatma Gandhi Archives, www.mahatma.org.in/books/showbook.jsp?id=13 &link=bg&book=bg0010&lang=en&cat=books (accessed 14 August 2002), 7.

24. Bondurant, *Conquest of Violence*, 25.

25. Gandhi, "History of the Satyagraha Ashram," II Prayer (iv), 11 July 1932, from *The Life and Works of Mahatma Gandhi* 56, no. 157, 158.

26. Gandhi, letter to P. G. Matthew, 9 July 1932, from *The Life and Works of Mahatma Gandhi* 56, no. 157, 128. Quoted in Bondurant, *Conquest of Violence*, 19.

27. Quoted in Brown, *Gandhi: Prisoner of Hope*, 190.

28. Jim Wallis, *Faith Works: Lessons from the Life of an Activist Preacher* (New York: Random House, 2000), 71–72.

29. Wolpert, *Gandhi's Passion*, 151.

30. Bondurant, *Conquest of Violence*, 189.

31. Bondurant, *Conquest of Violence*, 193.

32. Bondurant, *Conquest of Violence*, 20.

33. Hannah Arendt, *On Violence* (New York: Harcourt Brace, 1970), 4.

34. Gandhi, "Working of Nonviolence," 6 February 1939, from *The Life and Works of Mahatma Gandhi* 75, no. 47, 48. Quoted in Burrowes, *Nonviolent Defense*, 110.

35. Bondurant, *Conquest of Violence*, 14.

36. Burrowes, *Nonviolent Defense*, 108.

37. Bondurant, *Conquest of Violence*, 189–96.

38. Burrowes, *Nonviolent Defense*, 108.

39. Brown, *Gandhi: Prisoner of Hope*, 392.

40. Quoted in Johan Galtung, *The Way Is the Goal: Gandhi Today* (Ahmedabad, India: Gujurat Vidyapith, 1992), 42.

41. M. K. Gandhi, "On Satyagraha," 25 February 1919, from *The Life and Works of Mahatma Gandhi* 17, no. 29, 299.

42. George Orwell, "Reflections on Gandhi," in *A Collection of Essays* (Garden City, N.Y.: Doubleday Anchor Books, 1954), 183.

43. Bondurant, *Conquest of Violence*, 111.

44. Bondurant, *Conquest of Violence*, 234.

45. Eleanor Flexner and Ellen Fitzpatrick, *Century of Struggle: The Women's Rights Movement in the United States*, enlarged ed. (Cambridge, Mass.: Belknap Press of Harvard University Press, 1996), 244.

46. Wolpert, *Gandhi's Passion*, 63.

47. Brown, *Gandhi: Prisoner of Hope*, 55.

48. Gandhi, "When Women Are Manly, Will Men Be Effeminate?" *Indian Opinion* [from Gujarati], 23 February 1907, from *The Collected Works of Mahatma Gandhi* 6, no. 263 (Patiala House, Tilak Marg, New Delhi: Publications Division, Ministry of Information and Broadcasting, Government of India, 1999): 288. Also on CD-ROM, continuous collection. Quoted in Wolpert, *Gandhi's Passion*, 63.

49. Gandhi, "Indian National Congress," *Indian Opinion*, 5 January 1907, from *The Collected Works of Mahatma Gandhi* 6, no. 201, 208. Quoted in Wolpert, *Gandhi's Passion*, 63.

50. Stanley Wolpert, telephone interview by author, 1 February 2002.

51. Wolpert, *Gandhi's Passion*, 63.

52. Jim Wallis, *The Soul of Politics: A Practical and Prophetic Vision for Change* (New York: Orbis Books, 1994).

53. Burrowes, *Nonviolent Defense*, 108.

54. Fischer, *Life of Mahatma Gandhi*, 103.

55. Dave Dellinger, "Gandhi's Heirs," in *Revolutionary Nonviolence: Essays by Dave Dellinger* (New York: Anchor Books, 1971), 251.

56. Quoted in Brown, *Gandhi: Prisoner of Hope*, 190.

57. Wallis, *Soul of Politics*, 33.

58. Orwell, "Reflections on Gandhi," 178.

59. Brown, *Gandhi: Prisoner of Hope*, 113.

60. M. K. Gandhi, "The Crime of Chauri Chaura," *Young Indian*, 16 February 1922, from *The Life and Works of Mahatma Gandhi* 26, no. 82, 178. Quoted in Fischer, *Life of Mahatma Gandhi*, 198.

61. B. R. Nanda, *Mahatma Gandhi: A Biography*, unabridged (New Delhi: Oxford University Press, 1958, 1996), 232.

62. Nanda, *Mahatma Gandhi: A Biography*, 304–9.

63. Nanda, *Mahatma Gandhi: A Biography*, 304–9.

64. Wolpert, *Gandhi's Passion*, 38.

65. Peter Ackerman and Christopher Kruegler, *Strategic Nonviolent Conflict: The Dynamics of People Power in the Twentieth Century* (Westport, Conn.: Praeger, 1994), 158.

66. Wolpert, *Gandhi's Passion*, 4.

67. Ackerman and Kruegler, *Strategic Nonviolent Conflict*, 201.

68. Brown, *Gandhi: Prisoner of Hope*, 80–81.

69. Reinhold Niebuhr, *Moral Man and Immoral Society: A Study in Ethics and Politics* (New York: Scribner's, 1932, 1960), 243.

70. Niebuhr, *Moral Man and Immoral Society*, 272.

71. Walter Wink, *The Powers That Be: Theology for a New Millennium* (New York: Galilee/Doubleday, 1998), 159.

72. Niebuhr, *Moral Man and Immoral Society*, 243–44.

73. M. K. Gandhi, "The Law of Suffering," *Young Indian*, 16 July 1920, from *The Life and Works of Mahatma Gandhi* 20, no. 156, 367; Fischer, *Life of Mahatma Gandhi*, 341–48; and Nanda, *Mahatma Gandhi*, 460–61.

74. Quoted in Wolpert, *Gandhi's Passion*, 5.

75. Wolpert, *Gandhi's Passion*, 3.

76. Gandhi, *All Men Are Brothers*, 118; *Collected Works* 54, no. 48.

77. Kurt Schock, *Unarmed Insurrections: People Power Movements in Nondemocracies* (Minneapolis: University of Minnesota Press, 2005), 8.

78. Michael N. Nagler, *Is There No Better Way? The Search for a Nonviolent Future* (Berkeley, Calif.: Berkeley Hills Books, 2001), 125.

79. Gene Sharp, *Waging Nonviolent Struggle: 20th Century Practice and 21st Century Potential* (Boston: Porter Sargent, 2005), 383–84.

80. Sharp, *Waging Nonviolent Struggle*, 416.

81. Sharp, *Waging Nonviolent Struggle*, 410–12.

82. John Lewis, with Michael D'Orso, *Walking with the Wind: A Memoir of the Movement* (New York: Simon & Schuster, 1998), 85.

83. Brown, *Gandhi: Prisoner of Hope*, 35.

84. Dave Dellinger, "The Future of Nonviolence," in *Revolutionary Nonviolence*, 377.

85. Mohandas K. Gandhi, "From Passive Resistance to Direct Action," in *Nonviolence in Theory and Practice*, 2d. ed., ed. Robert L. Holmes and Barry L. Gan (Long Grove, Ill.: Waveland, 2005), 82.

86. Thomas Merton, *The Nonviolent Alternative* (New York: Farrar, Straus & Giroux, 1990), 217.

87. Fischer, *Life of Mahatma Gandhi*, 194.

88. Fischer, *Life of Mahatma Gandhi*, 28.

89. Bondurant, *Conquest of Violence*, 171.

90. M. K. Gandhi, "Cobblers v. Lawyers" *Young Indian*, 29 September, from *The Life and Works of Mahatma Gandhi*, 24, no. 175, 339. Quoted in Wink, *Engaging the Powers*, 187.

91. M. K. Gandhi, "Satyagraha in South Africa" (Madras: Ganesan, 1928), from *The Life and Works of Mahatma Gandhi* 5, no. 309, 336. Quoted in Barbara Deming, "On Anger," *Liberation*, November 1971.

92. Quoted in Fischer, *Life of Mahatma Gandhi*, 76.

93. Wink, *Engaging the Powers*, 207.
94. Galtung, *The Way Is the Goal*, 96.
95. Brown, *Gandhi: Prisoner of Hope*, 394.
96. Wolpert, *Gandhi's Passion*, 263.
97. Galtung, *The Way Is the Goal*, 12.

Chapter 2

1. Bob Woodward and Carl Bernstein, *The Final Days* (New York: Avon Books, 1976), 483, 501.
2. Staughton Lynd and Alice Lynd, eds., *Nonviolence in America: A Documentary History*, rev. ed. (Maryknoll, N.Y.: Orbis Books, 1995), xi.
3. Raghavan Iyer, ed., *The Essential Writings of Mahatma Gandhi* (New Delhi: Oxford University Press, 1994), 71.
4. Robert Cooney and Helen Michalowksi, eds., *The Power of the People: Active Nonviolence in the United States* (Philadelphia: New Society Publishers, 1987), 80.
5. Sudarshan Kapur, *Raising Up a Prophet: The African-American Encounter with Gandhi* (New Delhi: Oxford University Press, 1993), 37.
6. Sudarshan Kapur, "Prelude to Martin Luther King, Jr.: The Images of Gandhi and the Indian Independence Movement, 1921–1934," *Gandhi Marg* 14, no. 3 (October–December 1992): 427–29.
7. Kapur, "Prelude," 427.
8. Kapur, *Raising Up a Prophet*, 29.
9. John J. Ansbro, *Martin Luther King, Jr.: The Making of a Mind* (Maryknoll, N.Y.: Orbis Books, 1982, 1994), 204.
10. Kapur, *Raising Up a Prophet*, 17.
11. Kapur, "Prelude," 429.
12. Quoted in Kapur, "Prelude," 429–30.
13. Reinhold Niebuhr, *Moral Man and Immoral Society: A Study in Ethics and Politics* (New York: Scribner's, 1932, 1960), 252.
14. Niebuhr, *Moral Man and Immoral Society*, 254.
15. Harold Josephson, ed., "Richard Gregg," *Biographical Dictionary of Modern Peace Leaders* (Westport, Conn.: Greenwood, 1985), 354.
16. Kapur, *Raising Up a Prophet*, 73.
17. Quoted in Kapur, "Prelude," 423.
18. Quoted in Kapur, *Raising Up a Prophet*, 146.
19. Quoted in Kapur, *Raising Up a Prophet*, 86.
20. Kapur, *Raising Up a Prophet*, 134.
21. Cooney and Michalowski, *The Power of the People*, 151–52.
22. Quoted in Kapur, *Raising Up a Prophet*, 119.

23. Lynd and Lynd, *Nonviolence in America*, xxxiii.

24. David Dellinger, *From Yale to Jail: The Life Story of a Moral Dissenter* (New York: Pantheon Books, 1993), 66.

25. Nat Hentoff, *Peace Agitator: The Story of A. J. Muste* (New York: Macmillan, 1963; A. J. Muste Institute, 1982), 191.

26. Hentoff, *Peace Agitator*, 191.

27. Hentoff, *Peace Agitator*, 191.

28. Cooney and Michalowski, *Power of the People*, 139.

29. Hentoff, *Peace Agitator*, 133.

30. Kapur, *Raising Up a Prophet*, 118.

31. Kapur, *Raising Up a Prophet*, 114.

32. For the former, see Milton Katz, *Ban the Bomb: A History of SANE, The Committee for a SANE Nuclear Policy* (Westport, Conn.: Greenwood, 1986); for the latter, see Pam Solo, *From Protest to Policy: Beyond the Freeze to Common Security* (Cambridge, Mass.: Ballinger, 1988).

33. Horace Alexander, *Gandhi through Western Eyes* (London: Asia Publishing House, 1969).

34. S. Radhakrishnan, ed., *Mahatma Gandhi: Essays and Reflections on His Life and Work* (Bombay: Jaico, 1956), 125.

35. Radhakrishnan, *Mahatma Gandhi: Essays and Reflections*, 126.

36. Quoted in Marjorie Sykes, *Quakers in India: A Forgotten Century* (London: Allen & Unwin, 1980), 106.

37. Hugh Barbour and J. William Frost, *The Quakers* (Westport, Conn.: Greenwood, 1988), 255.

38. Margaret H. Bacon, *The Quiet Rebels: The Story of the Quakers in America* (New York: Basic Books, 1969), 197.

39. Guy F. Hershberger, *War, Peace, and Nonresistance* (Scottdale, Pa.: Herald, 1944), 53, 56, 191.

40. Mel Piehl, "The Catholic Worker and Peace in the Early Cold War Era," in *American Catholic Pacifism: The Influence of Dorothy Day and the Catholic Worker Movement*, ed. Anne Klejmont and Nancy L. Roberts (Westport, Conn.: Praeger, 1996), 83.

41. Charles Chatfield, "The Catholic Worker in the United States Peace Tradition," in *American Catholic Pacifism*, 6.

42. See John Dear, *The God of Peace: Toward a Theology of Nonviolence* (Maryknoll, N.Y.: Orbis Books, 1994), 12.

43. Homer Jack, the first director of SANE, was a Gandhi scholar who edited *The Gandhi Reader: A Sourcebook of His Life and Writings* (New York: Grove Weidenfeld, 1955).

44. Daniel Berrigan, *To Dwell in Peace: An Autobiography* (San Francisco: Harper & Row, 1987), 335.

45. See David Cortright, *Peace Works: The Citizen's Role in Ending the Cold War* (Boulder, Colo.: Westview, 1993), especially chap. 4, 40–60.

46. National Conference of Catholic Bishops, *The Challenge of Peace: God's Promise and Our Response* (Washington, D.C.: U.S. Catholic Conference, 3 May 1983), 50.

47. National Conference of Catholic Bishops, *The Challenge of Peace,* 136.

Chapter 3

1. Taylor Branch, *Parting the Waters: America in the King Years, 1954–63* (New York: Touchstone/Simon & Schuster, 1988), 74.

2. Andrew Young, *An Easy Burden: The Civil Rights Movement and the Transformation of America* (New York: HarperCollins, 1996), 128.

3. Martin Luther King Jr., *Stride toward Freedom: The Montgomery Story* (New York: Harper & Row, 1958), 96.

4. King, *Stride toward Freedom,* 96.

5. John J. Ansbro, *Martin Luther King, Jr.: The Making of a Mind* (Maryknoll, N.Y.: Orbis Books, 1994), 3.

6. King, *Stride toward Freedom,* 97.

7. King, *Stride toward Freedom,* 97.

8. Martin Luther King Jr., *Strength to Love* (New York: Harper & Row, 1963), 138.

9. Ansbro, *Making of a Mind,* 6.

10. Quoted in David J. Garrow, *Bearing the Cross: Martin Luther King Jr. and the Southern Christian Leadership Conference* (New York: Vintage Books, 1988), 75.

11. King, *Stride toward Freedom,* 100.

12. Carl Friedrich, ed. *The Philosophy of Kant, Immanuel Kant's Moral and Political Writings* (New York: Modern Library, 1977), 178.

13. Stewart Burns, *To the Mountaintop: Martin Luther King's Sacred Mission to Save America: 1955–1968* (New York: HarperSanFrancisco, 2004), 110.

14. George Kelsey, one of King's professors at Morehouse College, used the categories of Buber to explain the ideology of racism. See Ansbro, *Making of a Mind,* 108.

15. Martin Buber, *I and Thou,* trans. Walter Kaufmann (New York: Scribner's, 1970), 54–55.

16. Marc Gopin, *Between Eden and Armageddon: The Future of World Religions, Violence, and Peacemaking* (Oxford: Oxford University Press, 2000), 157.

17. Kenneth L. Smith and Ira G. Zepp, *Search for the Beloved Community: The Thinking of Martin Luther King Jr.* (Valley Forge, Pa.: Judson, 1974, 1998), 106–111.

18. Smith and Zepp, *Search for the Beloved Community*, 28–29.

19. King, *Stride toward Freedom*, 91.

20. Jim Wallis, *The Soul of Politics: A Practical and Prophetic Vision for Change* (New York: Orbis Books, 1994), 149–51.

21. Ansbro, *Making of a Mind*, 168–69.

22. Walter Rauschenbusch, *Christianity and the Social Crisis*, ed. Robert D. Cross (New York: Harper & Row, 1964), 287.

23. King, *Stride toward Freedom*, 91.

24. Martin Luther King Jr., "Letter from a Birmingham Jail," in *A Testament of Hope: The Essential Writings and Speeches of Martin Luther King, Jr.*, ed. James M. Washington (San Francisco: Harper-SanFrancisco, 1991), 299.

25. King, "Letter from a Birmingham Jail," 300.

26. King, *Stride toward Freedom*, 91.

27. Branch, *Parting the Waters*, 87.

28. Branch, *Parting the Waters*, 81.

29. Branch, *Parting the Waters*, 87.

30. King, *Strength to Love*, 58.

31. King, *Stride toward Freedom*, 99.

32. Reinhold Niebuhr, *Moral Man and Immoral Society: A Study in Ethics and Politics* (New York: Scribner's, 1960), 44.

33. Niebuhr, *Moral Man and Immoral Society*, 84.

34. Martin Luther King Jr., *Where Do We Go from Here: Chaos or Community?* (New York: Harper & Row, 1967), 128–29.

35. Quoted in Ansbro, *Making of a Mind*, 137–38.

36. King, *Stride toward Freedom*, 104.

37. Martin Luther King Jr., *Loving Your Enemies* (New York: A. J. Muste Institute, Essay Series, [n.d.]), 6.

38. King, *Stride toward Freedom*, 106; Ansbro, *Making of a Mind*, 6.

39. King, *Stride toward Freedom*, 98.

40. King, *Stride toward Freedom*, 102.

41. King, "Letter from a Birmingham Jail," 301.

42. Quoted in Ansbro, *Making of a Mind*, 185.

43. King, *Stride toward Freedom*, 102.

44. Dave Dellinger, "The Future of Nonviolence," in *Revolutionary Nonviolence: Essays by Dave Dellinger* (New York: Anchor Books, 1971), 372–73.

45. Ansbro, *Making of a Mind*, 59.

46. Stewart Burns, *To the Mountaintop: Martin Luther King's Sacred Mission to Save America: 1955–1968* (New York: HarperSanFrancisco, 2004), 92–93.

47. John Lewis, with Michael D'Orso, *Walking with the Wind: A Memoir of the Movement* (New York: Simon & Schuster, 1998), 73.

48. Smith and Zepp, *Search for the Beloved Community*, 130.

49. Lewis, *Walking with the Wind*, 87.

50. Lewis, *Walking with the Wind*, 129.

51. Quoted in Lewis, *Walking with the Wind*, 142.

52. Lewis, *Walking with the Wind*, 87.

53. Susannah Heschel, "God and Society in Heschel and King," 8, personal account, the Shalom Center, Philadelphia, www.shalomctr.org/html/hesch07.html (accessed 10 January 2002).

54. Heschel, "God and Society," 5.

55. King, *Strength to Love*, 64.

56. King, "Letter from a Birmingham Jail," 292–93.

57. Smith and Zepp, *Search for the Beloved Community*, 155.

58. King, "Letter from a Birmingham Jail," 296.

59. Quoted in Ansbro, *Making of a Mind*, 162.

60. King, *Stride toward Freedom*, 103.

61. Lewis, *Walking with the Wind*, 85.

62. Ansbro, *Making of a Mind*, 140.

63. Quoted in Ansbro, *Making of a Mind*, 140.

64. King, *Loving Your Enemies*, 11.

65. Young, *An Easy Burden*, 156.

66. King, "An Experiment in Love," in *A Testament of Hope*, 16.

67. Garrow, *Bearing the Cross*, 66.

68. King, "An Experiment in Love," 17.

69. Garrow, *Bearing the Cross*, 68.

70. Quoted in Stanley Wolpert, *Gandhi's Passion: The Life and Legacy of Mahatma Gandhi* (New York: Oxford University Press, 2001), 264.

71. King, "My Trip to the Land of Gandhi," in *A Testament of Hope*, 24.

72. Branch, *Parting the Waters*, 250–53.

73. King, "My Trip to the Land of Gandhi," 25.

74. Garrow, *Bearing the Cross*, 114.

75. Burns, *To the Mountaintop*, 331.

76. Branch, *Parting the Waters*, 259.

77. Peter Ackerman and Jack DuVall, *A Force More Powerful: A Century of Nonviolent Conflict* (New York: St. Martin's, 2000), 308.

78. Lewis, *Walking with the Wind*, 85.

79. *A Time for Justice*, VHS, directed by Charles Guggenheim (Montgomery, Ala.: Southern Poverty Law Center, 1992).

80. Lewis, *Walking with the Wind*, 85.

81. Young, *An Easy Burden*, 127.

82. Young, *An Easy Burden*, 189–90.

Chapter 4

1. Quoted in Robert Lindsey, "Cesar Chavez, Founder of Union for Farm Workers, Is Dead at 66," *New York Times*, 25 April 1993, 1.

2. Quoted in Lindsey, "Cesar Chavez," 1.

3. See Susan Ferris and Ricardo Sandoval, *The Fight in the Fields: Cesar Chavez and the Farmworkers Movement*, ed. Diana Hembree (New York: Harcourt Brace, 1997), 67, 98.

4. Joan London and Henry Anderson, *So Shall Ye Reap* (New York: Cromwell, 1970), 183.

5. Ferris and Sandoval, *The Fight in the Fields*, 13.

6. Quoted in London and Anderson, *So Shall Ye Reap*, 185.

7. Ferris and Sandoval, *The Fight in the Fields*, 46.

8. Interview with Cesar Chavez, in Catherine Ingram, *In the Footsteps of Gandhi: Conversations with Spiritual Social Activists* (Berkeley, Calif.: Parallax, 1990), 119.

9. Richard Griswold del Castillo and Richard A. Garcia, *Cesar Chavez: A Triumph of Spirit* (Norman: University of Oklahoma Press, 1995), 105.

10. Ferris and Sandoval, *The Fight in the Fields*, 47.

11. Quoted in John C. Hammerback and Richard J. Jensen, *The Rhetorical Career of Cesar Chavez* (College Station: Texas A&M University Press, 1998), 18.

12. Kurt Schock, *Unarmed Insurrections: People Power Movements in Nondemocracies* (Minneapolis: University of Minnesota Press, 2005), xvii.

13. See, for example, Gene Sharp, *Waging Nonviolent Struggle: 20th Century Practice and 21st Century Potential* (Boston: Porter Sargent, 2005), 19 and 344–45.

14. London and Anderson, *So Shall Ye Reap*, 182.

15. Quoted in Ferris and Sandoval, *The Fight in the Fields*, 89.

16. Jim Forest, *Love Is the Measure: A Biography of Dorothy Day* (New York: Paulist, 1986), 169–70.

17. Quoted in London and Anderson, *So Shall Ye Reap*, 183.

18. Hammerback and Jensen, *Rhetorical Career*, 37.

19. Hammerback and Jensen, *Rhetorical Career*, 36.

20. Quoted in Ferris and Sandoval, *The Fight in the Fields*, 97.

21. Hammerback and Jensen, *Rhetorical Career*, 36.

22. Quoted in Ferris and Sandoval, *The Fight in the Fields*, 97.

23. Ferris and Sandoval, *The Fight in the Fields*, 87.

24. Quoted in Ferris and Sandoval, *The Fight in the Fields*, 114.

25. Quoted in Ferris and Sandoval, *The Fight in the Fields*, 116.

26. Quoted in Ferris and Sandoval, *The Fight in the Fields*, 117.

27. Hardy Merriman, "California Grape Workers' Strike and Boycott—1965–1970," in Sharp, *Waging Nonviolent Struggle*, 178.

28. Ferris and Sandoval, *The Fight in the Fields*, 139.

29. Merriman, "California Grape Workers' Strike and Boycott," in Sharp, *Waging Nonviolent Struggle*, 185.

30. Lindsey, "Cesar Chavez," 11.

31. Merriman, "California Grape Workers' Strike and Boycott," in Sharp, *Waging Nonviolent Struggle*, 184–85.

32. Ferris and Sandoval, *The Fight in the Fields*, 160.

33. Ferris and Sandoval, *The Fight in the Fields*, 170.

34. Ferris and Sandoval, *The Fight in the Fields*, 221.

35. Gene Sharp, *The Politics of Nonviolent Action* (Boston: Porter Sargent, 1973), 229.

36. Judith M. Brown, *Gandhi: Prisoner of Hope* (New Haven, Conn.: Yale University Press, 1989), 241.

37. Peter Ackerman and Christopher Kruegler, *Strategic Nonviolent Conflict: The Dynamics of People Power in the Twentieth Century* (Westport, Conn.: Praeger, 1994), 190–91.

38. Ackerman and Kruegler, *Strategic Nonviolent Conflict*, 203.

39. Peter Ackerman and Jack DuVall, *A Force More Powerful: A Century of Nonviolence* (New York: St. Martin's, 2000), 310.

40. Sharp, *Politics of Nonviolent Action*, 249, n. 18.

41. Ackerman and DuVall, *A Force More Powerful*, 324.

42. John Lewis, with Michael D'Orso, *Walking with the Wind: A Memoir of the Movement* (New York: Simon & Schuster, 1998), 113.

43. Andrew Young, *An Easy Burden: The Civil Rights Movement and the Transformation of America* (New York: HarperCollins, 1996), 226–28.

44. Schock, *Unarmed Insurrections*, 60.

45. Schock, *Unarmed Insurrections*, 60.

46. Robert M. Price, *The Apartheid State in Crisis: Political Transformation in South Africa, 1975–1990* (Oxford: Oxford University Press, 1991), 196, 267.

47. Jeremy Seekings, *The UDF: A History of the United Democratic Front in South Africa, 1983–1991* (Athens: Ohio University Press, 2000), 207.

48. Schock, *Unarmed Insurrections*, 63.

49. Schock, *Unarmed Insurrections*, 62–63.

50. Paul S. Kaku, Aigbe Akhigbe, and Thomas M. Springer, "The Financial Impact of Boycotts and Threats of Boycotts," *Journal of Business Research* (September 1997): 1, 15, 40.

51. I am indebted to my former student, Ismael Muvingi, for information and insight on the Nestlé boycott.

52. Marshall Glickman, "Pocketbook Power," *The Environmental Magazine* (May–June 1998) 3, 9, 44.

53. Eric Schlosser, "A Side Order of Human Rights," *New York Times*, 6 April 2005, A23.

54. Evelyn Nieves, "Accord with Tomato Pickers Ends Boycott of Taco Bell," *Washington Post*, 9 March 2005, A6.

55. See the interpretation of Robert Payne, *The Life and Death of Mahatma Gandhi* (New York: Dutton, 1969; Calcutta: Rupa, 1997), 557–58.

56. Interview in Ingram, *Footsteps of Gandhi*, 110.

57. Ferris and Sandoval, *The Fight in the Fields*, 143.

58. Brad Bennett, "Fasting," in *Protest, Power, and Change: An Encyclopedia of Nonviolent Action from ACT-UP to Women's Suffrage*, ed. Roger S. Powers and William B. Vogele (New York: Garland, 1997), 177.

59. Seekings, *The UDF,* 240–41.

60. Quoted in Emily Taft Douglas, *Margaret Sanger: Pioneer of the Future* (New York: Holt, Rinehart & Winston, 1970), 118.

61. Brown, *Gandhi: Prisoner of Hope*, 266.

62. Brown, *Gandhi: Prisoner of Hope*, 393.

Chapter 5

1. Jim Forest, *Love Is the Measure: A Biography of Dorothy Day* (New York: Paulist, 1986), 36.

2. Dorothy Day, *The Long Loneliness: The Autobiography of Dorothy Day* (New York: HarperSanFrancisco, 1980), 76.

3. Day, *Long Loneliness*, 77–79.

4. Day, *Long Loneliness*, 81.

5. Quoted from her obituary in *Commonweal* in Robert Ellsberg, ed., *Dorothy Day: Selected Writings* (Maryknoll, N.Y.: Orbis Books, 1992), xvii.

6. Forest, *Love Is the Measure*, 41–42.

7. Day, *Long Loneliness*, 38.

8. Tom Cornell, telephone interview by author, 17 May 2002.

9. Robert Coles, *Dorothy Day: A Radical Devotion* (Reading, Mass.: Addison-Wesley, 1987), 23.

10. Quoted in Ellsberg, ed., "Introduction," in *Dorothy Day: Selected Writings*, xxii.

11. Quoted in Forest, *Love Is the Measure*, 63.

12. Ellsberg, "Introduction," xvii.

13. Ellsberg, "Introduction," xvii.

14. Day, *Long Loneliness*, 149.

15. Forest, *Love Is the Measure*, 17.

16. Quoted in Coles, *Dorothy Day*, 58.

17. Day, *Long Loneliness*, 150.

18. Quoted in Coles, *Dorothy Day*, 51.

19. For a scathing critique of the church's relationship to fascism, see John Cornwell, *Hitler's Pope: The Secret History of Pius XII* (New York: Viking Penguin, 2000).

20. Coles, *Dorothy Day*, 4.

21. Coles, *Dorothy Day*, 4.

22. Forest, *Love Is the Measure*, 77–78.

23. Quoted in Day, *Long Loneliness*, 170.

24. Forest, *Love Is the Measure*, 76.

25. Day, *Long Loneliness*, 182.

26. In the 1960s, a movement for dialogue between Marxism and Christianity identified important philosophical and theological principles in common. See Alasdair MacIntyre, *Marxism and Christianity*, 2d ed. (Notre Dame, Ind.: University of Notre Dame Press, 1984).

27. Day, *Long Loneliness*, 166.

28. Ellsberg, "Introduction," xviii.

29. Quoted in Forest, *Love Is the Measure*, 128.

30. Dorothy Day, "On Pilgrimage—September 1950," *Catholic Worker* (September 1950), www.catholicworker.org/dorothyday/reprint.cfm?texlID=64 (accessed 29 May 2002).

31. Tom Cornell, telephone interview by author, 17 May 2002.

32. Dorothy Day, "We Mourn Death of Gandhi Nonviolent Revolutionary," *Catholic Worker* (February 1948): 1.

33. Coles, *Dorothy Day*, 54.

34. Tom Cornell, telephone interview by author, 17 May 2002.

35. Quoted in Coles, *Dorothy Day*, 24.

36. Dorothy Day, "On Pilgrimage—September 1963," *Catholic Worker* (September 1963), www.catholicworker.org/dorothyday/reprint.cfm?TextID=806 (accessed 29 May 2002).

37. Coles, *Dorothy Day*, 34–35.

38. Tom Cornell, telephone interview by author, 17 May 2002.

39. Day, "We Mourn Death of Gandhi."

40. Mel Piehl, *Breaking Bread: The Catholic Worker and the Origin of Catholic Radicalism in America* (Philadelphia: Temple University Press, 1982), 206–7.

41. Ellsberg, *Dorothy Day: Selected Writings*, 328.

42. Day, *Long Loneliness*, 231.

43. Quoted in Ellsberg, "Introduction," xxxi.

44. Hanna Rosin, "Vatican to Weigh Sainthood for Reformer Dorothy Day," *Washington Post*, 17 March 2000, A3.

45. Forest, *Love Is the Measure*, 113.

46. Stephen T. Krupa, "Dorothy Day and the Spirituality of Non-violence" (Ph.D. diss., Graduate Theological Union, Berkeley, Calif., December 1997), 239.

47. Day, *Long Loneliness*, 248.

48. Ellsberg, "Introduction," xxxiii.

49. Forest, *Love Is the Measure*, 135.

50. Forest, *Love Is the Measure*, 137.

51. Forest, *Love Is the Measure*, 138–39.

52. For an account of the role of citizens in halting nuclear testing in the 1960s, see Lawrence S. Wittner, *Resisting the Bomb: A History of the World Disarmament Movement, 1954–1970* (Stanford, Calif.: Stanford University Press, 1997).

53. Forest, *Love Is the Measure*, 159–61.

54. Coles, *Dorothy Day*, 96.

Chapter 6

1. Malcolm X, *By Any Means Necessary*, ed. George Breitman (New York: Pathfinder, 1970), 42.

2. Andrew Young, *An Easy Burden: The Civil Rights Movement and the Transformation of America* (New York: HarperCollins, 1996), 120.

3. Young, *An Easy Burden*, 120.

4. M. K. Gandhi, "The Jews," *Harijan*, 26 November 1938, from *The Life and Works of Mahatma Gandhi* 74, no. 319 (Patiala House, Tilak Marg, New Delhi: Publications Division, Ministry of Information and Broadcasting, Government of India, 1999), 241; Available on CD-ROM, dynamic collection. Quoted in Blair B. Kling, "Gandhi, Nonviolence, and the Holocaust," *Peace and Change* 16, no. 2 (April 1991): 177.

5. Quoted in Maurice Friedman, *Encounter on the Narrow Ridge: A Life of Martin Buber* (New York: Paragon House, 1993), 214.

6. Murray Polner and Naomi Goodman, eds., *The Challenge of Shalom: The Jewish Tradition of Peace and Justice* (Philadelphia: New Society, 1994), 55–58.

7. Gandhi, "Some Questions Answered," *Harijan* (17 December 1938), from *The Life and Works of Mahatma Gandhi* 74, no. 399, 298.

8. George Orwell, "Reflections on Gandhi," in *A Collection of Essays* (Garden City, N.Y.: Doubleday Anchor Books, 1954), 184.

9. Orwell, "Reflections on Gandhi," 184–85.

10. Gene Sharp, *The Politics of Nonviolent Action* (Boston: Porter Sargent, 1973), part 1: 87–90.

11. This account is drawn from Nathan Stoltzfus, "Saving Jewish Husbands in Berlin—1943," in Gene Sharp, *Waging Nonviolent Struggle: 20th Century Practice and 21st Century Potential* (Boston: Porter Sargent, 2005), 143–47; see also Nathan Stoltzfus, *Resistance of the Heart: Intermarriage and the Rosenstrasse Protest in Nazi Germany* (New York: Norton, 1996).

12. Examples include workers struggles in Poland in 1956, 1970–1971, and 1980–1981; the resistance movement in East Germany in 1953; and the uprisings against Communist rule in Hungary in 1956 and Czechoslovakia in 1968. See Adam Roberts, *Civil Resistance in the East European and Soviet Revolutions*, Monograph Series Number 4 (Cambridge, Mass.: Albert Einstein Institution, 1991).

13. Martin Luther King Jr., "A Time to Break Silence," in *A Testament of Hope: The Essential Writings and Speeches of Martin Luther King, Jr.*, ed. James Washington (San Francisco: HarperSanFrancisco, 1991), 233.

14. Stewart Burns, *To the Mountaintop: Martin Luther King's Sacred Mission to Save America: 1955–1968* (New York: HarperSanFrancisco, 2004), 398.

15. Barbara Deming, "Preface," in *Revolution and Equilibrium* (New York: Grossman, 1971), xiv.

16. Quoted in Jane Meyerding, ed., "Introduction," in *We Are All Part of One Another: A Barbara Deming Reader* (Philadelphia: New Society, 1984), 3.

17. Quoted in Meyerding, "Introduction," 3.

18. Judith McDaniel, "Biographical Essay," in *Prisons That Could Not Hold* (Athens: University of Georgia Press, 1995), xi.

19. McDaniel, "Biographical Essay," ix.

20. Judith McDaniel, telephone interview by author, February 2002.

21. Deming, "Nonviolence and Radical Social Change," in *Revolution and Equilibrium*, 223.

22. Deming, "Nonviolence and Radical Social Change," 223.

23. Deming, "On Revolution and Equilibrium," in *Revolution and Equilibrium*, 203–4.

24. Peter Ackerman and Jack DuVall, *A Force More Powerful: A Century of Nonviolent Conflict* (New York: St. Martin's, 2000), 7.

25. Deming, "On Revolution and Equilibrium," 195.

26. Dave Dellinger, "Gandhi's Heirs," in *Revolutionary Nonviolence: Essays by Dave Dellinger* (New York: Anchor Books, 1971), 249.

27. Deming, "On Revolution and Equilibrium," 199.

28. Quoted in Judith M. Brown, *Gandhi: Prisoner of Hope* (New Haven, Conn.: Yale University Press, 1989), 375.

29. Dellinger, "The Future of Nonviolence," in *Revolutionary Nonviolence*, 368.

30. Sharp, *Politics of Nonviolent Action*, part 1: 75–78.

31. Walter Wink, *Engaging the Powers: Discernment and Resistance in a World of Domination* (Minneapolis, Minn.: Fortress, 1962), 252.

32. Michael McFaul, "Transitions from Postcommunism," *Journal of Democracy* 16, no. 3 (July 2005): 6.

33. Deming, "On Revolution and Equilibrium," 198.

34. "On Respecting Others and Preventing Hate: A Conversation with Elie Wiesel," in *Cultural Variation in Conflict Resolution: Alternatives to Violence*, ed. Douglas P. Fry and Kaj Björkqvist (Mahwah, N.J.: Erlbaum, 1997), 239.

35. See especially Sharp's analyses of social, economic, and political noncooperation and the methods of nonviolent intervention, in *Politics of Nonviolent Action*, part 2: 183–435.

36. Reinhold Niebuhr, *Moral Man and Immoral Society: A Study in Ethics and Politics* (New York: Scribner's, 1960), 241.

37. See *Political Gain and Civilian Pain: Humanitarian Impacts of Economic Sanctions*, ed. Thomas G. Weiss, David Cortright, George A. Lopez, and Larry Minear (Boulder, Colo.: Rowman & Littlefield, 1997).

38. See David Cortright and George A. Lopez, "Sanctions against Iraq," in *The Sanctions Decade: Assessing UN Strategies in the 1990s* (Boulder, Colo.: Rienner, 2000), 37–61; see also Richard Garfield, *Morbidity and Mortality among Iraqi Children from 1990 to 1998: Assessing the Impact of Economic Sanctions*, Occasional Paper Series 16:OP:3 (Goshen, Ind.: Joan B. Kroc Institute for International Peace Studies at the University of Notre Dame and the Fourth Freedom Forum, March 1999),www.fourthfreedom.org/php/t-si-index.php?hinc=garf.hinc (accessed 10 February 2004).

39. See David Cortright and George A. Lopez, eds., *Smart Sanctions: Targeting Economic Statecraft* (Lanham, Md.: Rowman & Littlefield, 2002).

40. Barbara Deming, "Interfering with the Smooth Functioning of the Warfare State," in *Revolution and Equilibrium*, 252–53.

41. Barbara Deming, "On the Necessity to Liberate Minds," in *We Are All Part of One Another*, 202.

42. Deming, "On the Necessity to Liberate Minds," 199.

43. See David Cortright, *Soldiers in Revolt: GI Resistance during the Vietnam War*, 2d ed. (Chicago: Haymarket Books, 2005), 123–24.

44. For two critical perspectives, see Stacia M. Brown, "Swinging Back," *Sojourners* 31, no. 4 (July–August 2002): 37–41; and David Cortright, "The Power of Nonviolence," *The Nation* (18 February 2002): 13–14.

45. See, for example, Kadd Stephens, "Breaking a Store Window Violent? Nonsense!" *Nonviolent Activist* (July–August 2001): 4–5.

46. Lelia Spears, "Stopping the Runaway Train," and David McReynolds, "Rules? Which Rules? And Whose?" *Nonviolent Activist* (July–August 2001): 8–9.

47. Deming, "Interfering with the Smooth Functioning of the Warfare State," 253.

48. See the participant accounts in the *Nonviolent Activist* (July–August 2001).

49. Both ELF and ALF refer to themselves as nonviolent movements, but they encourage property damage and other forms of financial sabotage. By operating in cells (small groups that consist of one to several people without knowledge of the identity of other groups), the security of group members is maintained.

Members of ELF cells inflict economic damage on those profiting from the destruction and exploitation of the natural environment. The organization also seeks to publicize these atrocities and educate the public on the harm inflicted on the Earth and all species that populate it. Since 1997, ELF has caused more than $30 million in property damage. See www.earthliberationfront.com/about/ (accessed 19 August 2002).

ALF carries out direct action against perceived animal abuse by rescuing animals and causing financial loss to animal exploiters. The front seeks to reveal the horror and atrocities committed against animals behind locked doors by performing nonviolent direct actions and liberations, while taking all necessary precautions against harming any animal, human and nonhuman. In 2001, ALF cell members liberated almost five thousand animals, many from facilities of major corporations, and set fires and destroyed property in these facilities. See www.animalliberationfront.com/ALFront/WhatisALF.htm (accessed 19 August 2002).

50. Deming, "On the Necessity to Liberate Minds," 266.

51. Deming, "On Revolution and Equilibrium," 207–8.

52. Niebuhr, *Moral Man and Immoral Society,* 248.

53. Sharp, *Waging Nonviolent Struggle,* 405–6.

54. See the discussion on these points in Sharp, *Politics of Nonviolent Action,* 110–13.

55. Deming, "On Revolution and Equilibrium," 211.

56. Richard Gregg, *The Power of Nonviolence* (New York: Schocken Books, 1966), 53.

57. Gregg, *Power of Nonviolence,* 63.

58. Niebuhr, *Moral Man and Immoral Society,* 248.

59. Niebuhr, *Moral Man and Immoral Society,* 248.

60. Deming, "On Revolution and Equilibrium," 214.

61. Sharp, *Politics of Nonviolent Action,* pt. 3: 657–58.

62. Deming, "On Revolution and Equilibrium," 209, 211.

63. Deming, "On Revolution and Equilibrium," 211.

64. Sharp, *Politics of Nonviolent Action,* pt. 3: 658.

65. Dellinger, "The Future of Nonviolence," 376.

66. Louis Fischer, *The Life of Mahatma Gandhi* (New York: Harper & Row, 1950), 275.

67. Niebuhr, *Moral Man and Immoral Society,* 250.

68. William Gamson, *The Strategy of Social Protest,* 2d ed. (Belmont, Calif.: Wadsworth, 1990), 147.

69. Gregg, *Power of Nonviolence,* 48.

70. "India: Defying the Crown," *A Force More Powerful,* VHS, produced by Steve York (Lawrenceville, N.J.: Films for the Humanities and Sciences, 2000).

71. Quoted in Fischer, *The Life of Mahatma Gandhi,* 273.

72. Ackerman and DuVall, *A Force More Powerful,* 332.

73. Young, *An Easy Burden,* 358.

74. John Lewis, with Michael D'Orso, *Walking with the Wind: A Memoir of the Movement* (New York: Simon & Schuster, 1998), 331.

75. Lewis, *Walking with the Wind,* 335.

76. President Lyndon B. Johnson, "Special Message to Congress: The American Promise," 15 March 1965, www.lbjlib.utexas.edu/johnson/archives.hom/speeches.hom/650315.asp (accessed 30 September 2005).

77. David Garrow, *Bearing the Cross: Martin Luther King, Jr., and the Southern Christian Leadership Conference* (New York: Vintage Books, 1986), 409.

78. Johan Galtung, "Principles of Nonviolence: The Great Chain of Nonviolence Hypothesis," in *Nonviolence and Israel/Palestine* (Honolulu: University of Hawaii Press, 1989), 13–33.

79. Galtung, "Principles of Nonviolence," 25.

80. Galtung, "Principles of Nonviolence," 20.

81. Ackerman and DuVall, *A Force More Powerful,* 332.

Chapter 7

1. David J. Garrow, *Bearing the Cross: Martin Luther King, Jr. and the Southern Christian Leadership Conference* (New York: Vintage Books, 1988), 173–75.

2. Garrow, *Bearing the Cross,* 187.

3. Garrow, *Bearing the Cross,* 226.

4. Garrow, *Bearing the Cross*, 226.

5. Garrow, *Bearing the Cross*, 226.

6. Saul D. Alinsky, *Rules for Radicals: A Practical Primer for Realistic Radicals* (New York: Vintage Books, 1989), 98–101.

7. John Lewis, with Michael D'Orso, *Walking with the Wind: A Memoir of the Movement* (New York: Simon & Schuster, 1998), 186.

8. Andrew Young, *An Easy Burden: The Civil Rights Movement and the Transformation of America* (New York: HarperCollins, 1996), 186.

9. Garrow, *Bearing the Cross*, 227.

10. Stewart Burns, *To the Mountaintop: Martin Luther King's Sacred Mission to Save America: 1955–1968* (New York: HarperSanFrancisco, 2004), 40.

11. Garrow, *Bearing the Cross*, 239.

12. Quoted in Garrow, *Bearing the Cross*, 251.

13. Martin Luther King Jr., "Letter from a Birmingham Jail," in *A Testament of Hope: The Essential Writings and Speeches of Martin Luther King, Jr.*, ed. James M. Washington (San Francisco: HarperSanFrancisco, 1986, 1991), 290.

14. Young, *An Easy Burden*, 207.

15. Quoted in Garrow, *Bearing the Cross*, 264.

16. Stewart Burns, *To the Mountaintop: Martin Luther King's Sacred Mission to Save America: 1955–1968* (New York: Harper San Francisco, 2004), 205.

17. King, "Letter from a Birmingham Jail," 291.

18. William Gamson, *The Strategy of Social Protest*, 2d ed. (Belmont, Calif.: Wadsworth Publishing, 1990), 156.

19. Frances Fox Piven and Richard A. Cloward, *Poor People's Movements: Why They Succeed, How They Fail* (New York: Vintage Books, 1977, 1979), 24.

20. Gamson, *Strategy of Social Protest*, 156.

21. Much of the street violence associated with antiwar protest was initiated by police forces. The most important incident was the "police riot" in Chicago against the Students for a Democratic Society (SDS) during the Democratic National Convention in August 1968.

22. Andrew E. Hunt, *The Turning: A History of Vietnam Veterans against the War* (New York: New York University Press, 1999), 2, 118.

23. Richard Stacewicz, *Winter Soldiers: An Oral History of the Vietnam Veterans against the War* (New York: Twayne, 1997), 250.

24. Hunt, *The Turning*, 117.

25. I consider the term *antiglobalization* a confused and ill-defined term (are we opposed to the Internet and world travel?) and have chosen instead *global justice* to describe the movement.

26. For an eyewitness account from Seattle, see Alexander Cockburn and Jeffrey St. Clair, *Five Days That Shook the World: Seattle and Beyond* (London: Verso, 2000), 21–22.

27. Ewen MacAskill, John Vidal, and Rory O'Carroll, "Riots Force Review of Summits: Violence Overshadows Minor Achievements: Surprise Pact by Putin and Bush on Missiles," *The Guardian* (London), 23 July 2001, 1.

28. According to published accounts, the trashing of McDonald's on 29 November 1999 preceded the police attack on 30 November. See Janet Thomas, *The Battle in Seattle: The Story Behind and Beyond the WTO Demonstrations* (Golden, Colo.: Fulcrum, 2000), 28–29.

29. Ted Glick, "On Winning Hearts and Minds," e-mail communication with author, May 2001.

30. "Genoa: Letter from a U.S. Black Blocer," 29 July 2001, A-Infos, www.ainfos.ca/01/aug/ainfos00151.html (accessed 11 August 2001).

31. It should be noted that media coverage of destructive action can at times draw attention to a movement's grievances, and in some cases, it may even result in ameliorative action. The African American urban riots of the late 1960s increased public awareness of oppressive conditions in the ghettoes, which was one of the goals of those who participated in these actions. As white Americans became more aware, government officials responded with urban development and social welfare programs. See Joseph R. Feagin and Harlan Hahn, *Ghetto Revolts: The Politics of Violence in American Cities* (New York: Macmillan, 1973), and National Advisory Commission on Civil Disorders, *Report of the National Advisory Commission on Civil Disorders* (New York: Bantam Books, 1968). See also N. Eugene Walls, "The Impact of Public Perception of Social Actors on Perception of Violent Social Action: Government, Police Treatment, and Civil Rights Leadership as Predictors of Riot Legitimacy" (master's thesis, Department of Sociology, University of Notre Dame, Notre Dame, Ind., 2001); and Daniel J. Myers, N. Eugene Walls, Keely Jones, and Matthew Baggetta, "Violence in the Movement: Rioting and Public Opinion in Four Cities, 1967–1968" (paper presented at the 2001 Annual Meeting of the Midwest Sociological Society, St. Louis, Mo., 5–8 April 2001).

32. Cockburn and St. Clair, *Five Days That Shook the World*, 47–48.

33. See Yaroslav Trofimov and Helene Cooper, "Antiglobalization Activists Are Shifting Focus to Multinational Corporations," *Wall Street Journal*, 21 July 2001; and "Stars Condemn G8 Violence," *BBC News*, 22 July 2001, www.news.bbc.co.uk (accessed 7 December 2005).

34. Joe Garofoli and Jim Herron Zamora, "S. F. Police Play Catch Up; Protestors Roam in Small, Swift Groups to Stall City Traffic," *San Francisco Chronicle*, 21 March 2003.

35. Martha Mendoza, "Antiwar Demonstrations Continue," *San Francisco Chronicle,* 21 March 2003.

36. George Lakey, "Mass Action since Seattle: Seven Ways to Make Our Protests More Powerful," 2001, www.trainingforchange.org/reports_0010_massactionR.html (accessed 30 August 2001).

37. Lakey, "Mass Action since Seattle."

38. John Lofland, *Polite Protesters: The American Peace Movement of the 1980s* (Syracuse, N.Y.: Syracuse University Press, 1993).

39. David Cortright, *Peace Works: The Citizen's Role in Ending the Cold War* (Boulder, Colo.: Westview, 1993), 21–22.

40. Cortright, *Peace Works.*

41. Immanuel Wallerstein, "U.S. Weakness and the Struggle for Hegemony," *Monthly Review* 55, no. 3 (July–August 2003): 28.

42. For crowd number estimates, see Petula Dvorak, "Antiwar Fervor Fills the Streets; Demonstration Is Largest in Capital since U.S. Military Invaded Iraq," *Washington Post,* 25 September 2005; and Duane Shank, "When the People Lead the Leaders Will Follow," *Sojomail,* 28 September 2005,www.sojo.net (accessed 13 October 2005).

43. Rebecca Solnit, "Acts of Hope: Challenging Empire on the World Stage," *Orion* (20 May 2003), www.oriononline.org/pages/oo/sidebars/Patriotism/index_SolnitPR.html (accessed 24 November 2003).

Chapter 8

1. Quoted in Gloria Steinem, "The 100 Most Important People of the 20th Century: Margaret Sanger," *Time,* 13 April 1998, www.time.com/time/time100/leaders/profile/sanger.html (accessed 12 August 2002).

2. Ellen Chesler, *Woman of Valor: Margaret Sanger and the Birth Control Movement in America* (New York: Simon & Schuster, 1992), 80.

3. Chesler, *Woman of Valor,* 163.

4. M. K. Gandhi, "Influences of Attitudes," 2 September 1926, in *The Life and Works of Mahatma Gandhi* 36, no. 356 (Patiala House, Tilak Marg, New Delhi: Publications Division, Ministry of Information and Broadcasting, Government of India, 1999): 315; Available on CD-ROM, continuous collection. Quoted in Louis Fischer, *The Life of Mahatma Gandhi* (New York: Harper & Row, 1950), 240.

5. M. K. Gandhi, "Birth Control," *Young Indian,* 12 March 1925, in *The Life and Works of Mahatma Gandhi* 30, no. 236, 390–91.

6. M. K. Gandhi, "Interview with Margaret Sanger," 3–4 December 1935, in *The Life and Works of Mahatma Gandhi* 68, no. 238, 190. Quoted in Chesler, *Woman of Valor,* 356.

7. Chesler, *Woman of Valor*, 353.

8. Margaret Sanger, *An Autobiography* (New York: Dover, 1971), 70.

9. Chesler, *Woman of Valor*, 80.

10. Chesler, *Woman of Valor*, 87.

11. Chesler, *Woman of Valor*, 59.

12. Chesler, *Woman of Valor*, 231.

13. Day's articles for the *New York Call* of February 1917 are available at the Memorial Library archives, Marquette University, Milwaukee, Wisc.

14. Chesler, *Woman of Valor*, 131.

15. "Gandhi and Mrs. Sanger," *Asia* (New York) 36 (November 1936): 699.

16. "Gandhi and Mrs. Sanger," 699.

17. "Gandhi and Mrs. Sanger," 700.

18. "Gandhi and Mrs. Sanger," 702.

19. "Gandhi and Mrs. Sanger," 700.

20. Margaret Sanger, "Gandhi and Sanger Debate Love, Lust, and Birth Control," *Margaret Sanger Papers Project Newsletter* 23 (Winter 1999/2000): 5. Quoted from the transcript of the Gandhi-Sanger conversations from the Margaret Sanger Papers Project, www.nyu.edu/projects/sanger/gandhi.htm (accessed 12 August 2002).

21. "Gandhi and Mrs. Sanger," 701.

22. "Gandhi and Mrs. Sanger," 700.

23. Chesler, *Woman of Valor*, 364.

24. Steinem, "Margaret Sanger."

25. Stanley Wolpert, *Gandhi's Passion: The Life and Legacy of Mahatma Gandhi* (New York: Oxford University Press, 2001), 148.

26. Judith M. Brown, *Gandhi: Prisoner of Hope* (New Haven, Conn.: Yale University Press, 1989), 209.

27. M. K. Gandhi, "Speech at a Women's Meeting, Dohad," 31 August 1919, in *The Life and Works of Mahatma Gandhi* 18, no. 253, 331. Quoted in Pushpa Joshi, comp., *Gandhi on Women (Collection of Mahatma Gandhi's Writings and Speeches on Women)* (Ahmedabad: Navajivan Publishing House, 1988), 31.

28. M. K. Gandhi, "Position of Women," 21 July 1921, in *The Life and Works of Mahatma Gandhi* 23, no. 226. Quoted in Joshi, *Gandhi on Women*, 78.

29. Venkatapathy Arunachalam Vidya, "The Gandhian Fabric of Religion, Politics, and Gender" (manuscript, Joan B. Kroc Institute for International Peace Studies, University of Notre Dame: Notre Dame, Ind., November 2000), 13.

30. Vidya, "The Gandhian Fabric," 17.

31. M.K. Gandhi, "Speech at Delhi," 13 December 1931, from *The Hindustan Times*, 22 February 1931, in *The Life and Works*

of Mahatma Gandhi 51, no. 226, 163. Quoted in Joshi, *Gandhi on Women*, 246.

32. M. K. Gandhi, "Speech at a Women's Meeting, Rome," *Young India*, 14 January 1932, 22 February 1931, in *The Life and Works of Mahatma Gandhi* 54, no. 162, 289. Quoted in Joshi, *Gandhi on Women*, 259.

33. Wolpert, *Gandhi's Passion*, 148.

34. Vidya, "The Gandhian Fabric," 21.

35. M. K. Gandhi, "Talks to Ashram Women," [1926] Bapuna Patro—Ashramni Behnone, in *The Life and Works of Mahatma Gandhi* 37, no. 208, 468. Quoted in Joshi, *Gandhi on Women*, 142.

36. Sudhir Kakar, *Intimate Relations: Exploring Indian Sexuality* (Chicago: University of Chicago Press, 1990), 127.

37. Kakar, *Intimate Relations*, 127.

38. M. K. Gandhi, "Speech at Second Gujarat Educational Conference," 20 October 1917, in *The Life and Works of Mahatma Gandhi* 16, no. 37, 94. Quoted in Joshi, *Gandhi on Women*, 15.

39. N. B. Sen, comp., *The Wit and Wisdom of Mahatma Gandhi* (New Delhi: New Book Society of India, 1960), 206.

40. Sen, *Wit and Wisdom*, 242.

41. M. K. Gandhi, "Speech at Meeting of Mill-Hands, Ahmedabad," 25 February 1920, Navajivan, in *The Life and Works of Mahatma Gandhi* 19, no. 260, 422. Quoted in Joshi, *Gandhi on Women*, 43.

42. M. K. Gandhi, "Speech at Meeting of Mill-Hands, Ahmedabad," 43.

43. Vidya, "The Gandhian Fabric," 9.

44. Vidya, "The Gandhian Fabric," 23.

45. Mohandas K. Gandhi, *An Autobiography: The Story of My Experiments with Truth* (Boston: Beacon, 1993), 91.

46. Gandhi, *Autobiography*, 12.

47. Gandhi, *Autobiography*, 277–78

48. Quoted in Brown, *Gandhi: Prisoner of Hope*, 393.

49. B. R. Nanda, *Mahatma Gandhi: A Biography*, unabridged (New Delhi: Oxford University Press, 1958, 1966), 474.

50. Quoted in Brown, *Gandhi: Prisoner of Hope*, 40–41.

51. Dave Dellinger, "Not Enough Love," in *Revolutionary Nonviolence: Essays by Dave Dellinger* (New York: Anchor Books, 1971), 335.

52. George Orwell, "Reflections on Gandhi," in *A Collection of Essays* (Garden City, N.Y.: Doubleday Anchor Books, 1954), 182.

53. 1 John 4:20.

54. M. K. Gandhi, "To the Women of India," 10 March 1930, *Young India*, in *The Life and Works of Mahatma Gandhi* 49, no. 51, 57. Quoted in Joshi, *Gandhi on Women*, 222.

55. Joshi, *Gandhi on Women*, 258, 316.

56. Sen, *Wit and Wisdom*, 243.

57. Sen, *Wit and Wisdom*, 244.

58. M. K. Gandhi, "A Letter," 30 May 1932, *Mahadevbhaini Dairy*, in *The Life and Works of Mahatma Gandhi* 55, no. 536, 445. Quoted in Joshi, *Gandhi on Women*, 268.

59. M. K. Gandhi, "A Letter."

60. Sen, *Wit and Wisdom*, 151.

61. M. K. Gandhi, *The Last Phase*, vol. 1, book 2, 219, in *The Life and Works of Mahatma Gandhi* 55, no. 536, 445; Quoted in Joshi, *Gandhi on Women*, 381.

62. Quoted in Fischer, *The Life of Mahatma Gandhi*, 240.

63. Wolpert, *Gandhi's Passion*, 238.

64. Joshi, *Gandhi on Women*, 375.

65. Vidya, "The Gandhian Fabric," 8.

66. Vidya, "The Gandhian Fabric," 8.

67. Erik H. Erikson, *Gandhi's Truth: On the Origins of Militant Nonviolence* (New York: Norton, 1969), 234.

68. Kakar, *Intimate Relations*, 125.

69. Kakar, *Intimate Relations*, 96.

70. Vidya, "The Gandhian Fabric," 10, 19; Sanger, "Gandhi and Sanger Debate Love, Lust, and Birth Control," 5.

71. Joseph S. Alter, *Gandhi's Body: Sex, Diet, and the Politics of Nationalism* (Philadelphia: University of Pennsylvania Press, 2000), 32.

72. Brown, *Gandhi: Prisoner of Hope*, 83.

73. Kakar, *Intimate Relations*, 99.

74. Quoted in Vidya, "The Gandhian Fabric," 29.

75. Kakar, *Intimate Relations*, 107.

76. Quoted in Ved Mehta, *Mahatma Gandhi and His Apostles* (New York: Viking, 1977), 203.

77. Mehta, *Gandhi and His Apostles*.

78. Rajmohan Gandhi, *The Good Boatman: A Portrait of Gandhi* (New Delhi: Viking, 1995), 195.

79. M. K. Gandhi, "Letter to Satis Chandra Mukerji," 1 February 1947; in *The Life and Works of Mahatma Gandhi* 93, no. 489, 350. Quoted in Wolpert, *Gandhi's Passion*, 229.

80. M. K. Gandhi, "Letter to Nirmal Kumar Bose," 17 March 1947, in *The Life and Works of Mahatma Gandhi* 94, no. 149, 133. Quoted in Joshi, *Gandhi on Women*, 350.

81. Wolpert, *Gandhi's Passion*, 227.

82. Wolpert, *Gandhi's Passion*, 227.

83. Kakar, *Intimate Relations*, 108.

84. Brown, *Gandhi: Prisoner of Hope*, 378.

85. Joshi, *Gandhi on Women*, 379.

86. Kakar, *Intimate Relations,* 108.

87. Wolpert, *Gandhi's Passion,* 186.

88. R. Gandhi, *Good Boatman,* 194.

89. Kakar, *Intimate Relations,* 108.

90. M. K. Gandhi, "Discussion with A. V. Thakkar," 24 February 1947, in *The Life and Works of Mahatma Gandhi* 94, no. 41, 37 n. 1. Quoted in Wolpert, *Gandhi's Passion,* 231.

91. Wolpert, *Gandhi's Passion,* 75

92. David J. Garrow, *Bearing the Cross: Martin Luther King Jr. and the Southern Christian Leadership Conference* (New York: Vintage Books, 1988), 375.

93. Both quotes from Michael Eric Dyson, *I May Not Get There with You: The True Martin Luther King, Jr.* (New York: Free Press, 2000), 211, 217.

94. Dyson, *I May Not Get There with You,* 157, 162, 163.

95. John Lewis, with Michael D'Orso, *Walking with the Wind: A Memoir of the Movement* (New York: Simon & Schuster, 1998), 70.

96. Lewis, *Walking with the Wind,* 217.

97. Lewis, *Walking with the Wind,* 162.

98. Quoted in Garrow, *Bearing the Cross,* 375.

99. Dyson, *I May Not Get There with You,* 194.

100. Garrow, *Bearing the Cross,* 360.

101. Andrew Young, *An Easy Burden: The Civil Rights Movement and the Transformation of America* (New York: HarperCollins, 1996), 28–29.

102. Young, *An Easy Burden,* 331–32.

103. Quoted in Dyson, *I May Not Get There with You,* 211.

104. Quoted in Dyson, *I May Not Get There with You,* 213.

105. Michael Eric Dyson, "Moral Leaders Need Not Be Perfect," *New York Times,* 22 January 2002, A23.

106. Lewis, *Walking with the Wind,* 212.

107. Dyson, *I May Not Get There with You,* 194, 204–5.

108. Taylor Branch, *Parting the Waters: America in the King Years, 1954–63* (New York: Touchstone/Simon & Schuster, 1988), 880.

109. Lewis, *Walking with the Wind,* 92.

110. Lewis, *Walking with the Wind,* 298.

111. Lewis, *Walking with the Wind,* 92.

112. Quoted in Dyson, *I May Not Get There with You,* 207.

113. Harriet Hyman Alonso, *Peace as a Women's Issue: A History of the U.S. Movement for World Peace and Women's Rights* (Syracuse, N.Y.: Syracuse University Press, 1993), 226.

114. Rosemary Reuther, "Feminism and Peace," in *Christian Century* 100 (31 August–7 September 1983): 771–76, www.religion-online.org/ (accessed 13 August 2002).

115. Virginia Woolf, *Three Guineas* (New York: Harcourt, Brace & World, 1938), 6.

116. See Mary Caprioli and Mark A. Boyer, "Gender, Violence, and International Crisis," *Journal of Conflict Resolution* 45, no. 4 (August 2001): 503–18; and Monty G. Marshall and Donna Ramsey Marshall, "Gender Empowerment and the Willingness of States to Use Force" (paper presented at the annual meeting of the International Studies Association, Washington, D.C., 19 February 1999), 1–43.

117. Amartya Sen, *Freedom as Development* (New York: Anchor Books, 1999), 191.

118. James Gilligan, *Preventing Violence* (New York: Thames & Hudson, 2001), 56.

119. Sen, *Freedom as Development*, 200.

120. Quoted in Jim Forest, *Love Is the Measure: A Biography of Dorothy Day* (New York: Paulist, 1986), 85.

121. For a detailed social science analysis of this phenomenon, see Richard C. Eichenberg, "Gender Differences in Public Attitudes toward the Use of Force by the United States, 1990–2003," *International Security* 28, no. 1 (Summer 2003): 110–41.

122. Jean Bethke Elshtain, *Women and War*, 2d ed. (Chicago: University of Chicago Press, 1993).

123. Sara Ruddick, *Maternal Thinking: Toward a Politics of Peace* (Boston: Beacon, 1989), 221.

124. Ruddick, *Maternal Thinking*, 154.

125. bell hooks, *Feminist Theory: From Margin to Center*, 2d ed. (Cambridge, Mass.: South End Press, 2000), 129.

126. Berenice A. Carroll, "Feminism and Pacifism: Historical and Theoretical Connections," in *Women and Peace: Theoretical, Historical and Practical Perspectives*, ed. Ruth Roach Pierson (London: Croom Helm, 1987), 15.

127. Betty Friedan, *The Feminine Mystique* (New York: Norton, 1972), 391–92.

128. Ruddick, *Maternal Thinking*, 243.

129. Carroll, "Feminism and Pacifism," 19.

130. Pamela Johnson Conover and Virginia Sapiro, "Gender, Feminist Consciousness, and War," *American Journal of Political Science* 37, no. 4 (November 1993), 1082.

131. *Reuther*, "Feminism and Peace."

Chapter 9

1. Saul D. Alinsky, *Rules for Radicals: A Practical Primer for Realistic Radicals* (New York: Vintage Books, 1971), 52–53.

2. Martin Luther King Jr., "Where Do We Go from Here?" in *A Testament of Hope: The Essential Writings and Speeches of Martin*

Luther King, Jr., ed. James M. Washington (San Francisco: Harper-SanFrancisco, 1991), 577–78.

3. King, "Where Do We Go from Here?" 577–78.

4. Gene Sharp, *Waging Nonviolent Struggle: 20th Century Practice and 21st Century Potential* (Boston: Porter Sargent, 2005), 27–28.

5. Gene Sharp, *The Politics of Nonviolent Action* (Boston: Porter Sargent, 1973), 25.

6. Alinsky, *Rules for Radicals,* 113.

7. Alinsky, *Rules for Radicals,* 113.

8. Peter Ackerman and Christopher Kruegler, *Strategic Nonviolent Conflict: The Dynamics of People Power in the 20th Century* (Westport, Conn.: Praeger, 1994), 26.

9. Johan Galtung, *The Way Is the Goal: Gandhi Today* (Ahmedabad, India: Gujarat Vidyapith, 1992), 34.

10. Judith M. Brown, *Gandhi: Prisoner of Hope* (New Haven, Conn.: Yale University Press, 1989), 163, 226.

11. Frances Fox Piven and Richard A. Cloward, *Poor People's Movements: Why They Succeed, How They Fail* (New York: Vintage Books, 1977, 1979), 77, 309.

12. George Packer, "Smart-Mobbing the War," *New York Times Magazine,* 9 March 2003.

13. Jim Wallis, *Faith Works: Lessons from the Life of an Activist Preacher* (New York: Random House, 2000), 314.

14. Ackerman and Kruegler, *Strategic Nonviolent Conflict,* 25.

15. Alinsky, *Rules for Radicals,* 106–7.

16. See my discussion of these issues in David Cortright, *Peace Works: The Citizen's Role in Ending the Cold War* (Boulder, Colo.: Westview, 1993), especially chaps. 7, "Accommodation: The Reagan Administration's Response to the Freeze," and 14, "Who Won the Cold War?"

17. Brown, *Gandhi: Prisoner of Hope,* 54.

18. William Gamson, *The Strategy of Social Protest,* 2d ed. (Belmont, Calif.: Wadsworth, 1990), 147.

19. George Lakoff, *Don't Think of an Elephant: Know Your Values and Frame the Debate* (White River Junction, Vt.: Chelsea Green, 2004).

20. Gamson, *Strategy of Social Protest,* 147.

21. Brian Martin, *Social Defense, Social Change* (London: Freedom Press, 1993), 47.

22. Rebecca Solnit, "Acts of Hope: Challenging Empire on the World Stage," *Orion,* 20 May 2003,www.oriononline.org/pages/oo/sidebars/Patriotism/index_SolnitPR.html (accessed 24 November 2003).

23. "India: Defying the Crown," *A Force More Powerful,* VHS, produced by Steve York (Lawrenceville, N.J.: Films for the Humanities and Sciences, 2000).

24. Ackerman and Kruegler, *Strategic Nonviolent Conflict*, 34–35.

25. Brown, *Gandhi: Prisoner of Hope*, 236.

26. Sharp, *The Politics of Nonviolent Action*, pt. 2: 117–445.

27. Sharp, *The Politics of Nonviolent Action*, pt. 2: 117–445.

28. Barbara Deming, *Revolution & Equilibrium* (New York: Grossman, 1971), 206.

29. Alinsky, *Rules for Radicals*, 127–28.

30. The student of Alinsky will note that I do not include in my listing Alinsky's advice to personalize a dispute. This tactic can be counterproductive and is contrary to basic Gandhian principles, to focus on the sin, not the sinner.

31. Brown, *Gandhi: Prisoner of Hope*, 241.

32. Ultimately the demonstrations and the countless other acts of antiwar opposition helped bring an end to the war. The best account of the antiwar movement and its impact is Tom Wells, *The War Within: America's Battle over Vietnam* (Berkeley: University of California Press, 1994).

33. Teresa Wiltz, "Give Peace Another Chance," *Washington Post*, 25 September 2005, D1.

34. Jim Wallis, *God's Politics: How the Right Gets It Wrong and the Left Doesn't Get It* (New York: HarperSanFrancisco, 2005),160.

35. John Howard Yoder, *The Politics of Jesus*, 2d ed. (Grand Rapids, Mich.: Eerdmans, 1994), 204.

36. Robert C. Johansen, "Enforcement without Military Combat: Toward an International Civilian Police," in *Globalization and Global Governance*, ed. Raimo Vayrynen, 173–98 (New York: Rowman & Littlefield, 1999); and "Reviving Peacebuilding Tools Ravished by Terrorism, Unilateralism, and Weapons of Mass Destruction," *International Journal of Peace Studies* 9, no. 2 (Autumn/Winter 2004): 31–55.

37. Gerald Schlabach, "Just Policing, Not War," *America* 189, no. 1 (7–14 July 2003): 19–21.

38. Gareth Evans et al., *The Responsibility to Project: Report of the International Commission on Intervention and State Sovereignty* (Ottawa: International Development Research Centre, 2001).

39. See the following two reports of the Counter-Terrorism Evaluation Project of the Fourth Freedom Forum and the Joan B. Kroc Institute for International Peace Studies at the University of Notre Dame: *Toward a More Secure America: Grounding U.S. Policy in Global Realities* (Goshen, Ind.: Fourth Freedom Forum, November 2003), www.secureamerica.us/index.shtml (accessed 10 October 2005); and *Recommendations for Improving the United Nations Counter-Terrorism Committee's Assessment and Assistance Coordination Function* (Goshen, Ind.: Fourth Freedom Forum, October 2005).

40. Michael Walzer, *Arguing about War* (New Haven, Conn.: Yale University Press, 2004), 60–61.

41. Susan Glasser, "U.S. Figures Show Sharp Global Rise in Terrorism," *Washington Post*, 27 April 2005.

42. Wallis, *God's Politics*, 171.

43. Sharp, *The Politics of Nonviolent Action*, 705–76; see also Sharp, *Waging Nonviolent Struggle*, 415–21.

44. Alinsky, *Rules for Radicals*, 59.

45. For a full account of the peace movement struggle against the INF missiles, see Thomas Rochon, *Mobilizing for Peace: The Antinuclear Movements in Western Europe* (Princeton, N.J.: Princeton University Press, 1988); see also Cortright, "The Zero Solution and the European Peace Movement," in *Peace Works*.

46. See Richard Nixon and Henry Kissinger, "A Real Peace," *National Review* 39 (22 May 1987): 32; and John Deutsch, Brent Scowcroft, and R. James Woolsey, "The Danger of Zero Option," *Washington Post*, 31 March 1987, 21. The prime ministers of Germany and the United Kingdom, Helmut Kohl and Margaret Thatcher, expressed public support for the zero option but were privately skeptical, according to Eugene Rostow, former head of the U.S. Arms Control and Disarmament Agency, interview by the author, 15 October, 1991.

47. Dorothy Day, *The Long Loneliness: The Autobiography of Dorothy Day* (San Francisco: HarperSanFrancisco, 1952), 100, 216–17.

48. Reinhold Niebuhr, *Moral Man and Immoral Society* (New York: Scribner's, 1932), 255.

Index

9-11peace.org, 195

Abernathy, Ralph, 64
abolitionists, 38
accommodation, 216–17
accountability, 125
Ackerman, Peter, 25, 86, 191, 193,
    205
action: descriptive, 20–21; for truth,
    18–20. *See also* principles of
    action
Addams, Jane, 186
adversary: cognitive processes
    disrupted, 128–29; control of,
    126–28
advertising, 201
AFL-CIO, 80, 146
African Americans: challenges to
    nonviolence, 115–16; influence
    of Gandhi on, 37–44, 46–47
agape, 60–61
Agricultural Workers Organizing
    Committee, 80
ahimsa (nonharm), 12, 15, 61, 122,
    178
AIDS quilt, 210
air raid shelter protests, 107–8
Alabama Christian Movement for
    Human Rights (ACMHR), 141
Albany, Georgia, 137–40

Alexander, Horace, 47
Alinsky, Saul, 73, 75, 251n30;
    on power tactics, 192–93;
    principles of action, 191–95,
    198, 207–11, 217
Allen, Woody, 16–17
All-India Women's Conference, 163
alternatives, constructive, 210–11
American Anti-enlistment League,
    38
American Birth Control League, 165
American Friends Service
    Committee (AFSC), 42, 47–48,
    68
American Workers Party, 45
anarchists, 149; black bloc, 147–48
Andrews, C. F., 41
Andrews, Tom, 155
anger, 32
Animal Liberation Front (ALF),
    125–26, 240n49
antiapartheid movement, 87
Anti-Election Campaign (South
    Africa), 87
Anti-Imperialist League, 100
anti-Semitism, 107
Arendt, Hannah, 18
arms control experts, 185
army of nonviolence (shanti sena),
    69

asceticism, 104–5
atomic bomb, 107–8
Attenborough, Richard, 171
Aung San Suu Kyi, 3, 33

Baker, Ella, 183
Barth, Karl, 114
Batterham, Forster, 100
Beloved Community, 62–64
Berlin protest, 114
Berrigan, Daniel, 50, 108
Berrigan, Phillip, 108
Bevel, James, 69–70
Bhagavad Gita, 11–12
bin Laden, Osama, 4
biological determinism, 187–88
Birmingham campaign, 86, 88,
    137–38, 140–44; media
    attention, 143–44
birth control rights movement, 94,
    163–66, 204
black bloc, 147–48
black power movement, 116, 119
Blades, Joan, 195
Blatch, Harriet Stanton, 219
Bloody Sunday incident, 133
Bondurant, Joan, 15, 18
Bonhoeffer, Dietrich, 113–14
Bono, 149
Bose, N. K., 179
Bowles, Chester, 68
boycotts, 206; civil rights
    movement, 86, 88, 123;
    consumer, 87–88; detrimental
    effects of, 122; electoral, 87;
    grapes and lettuce, 81–85;
    India, 27, 85–86, 169;
    limitations, 90–91; media
    communications, 88–89;
    Montgomery bus boycott,
    44, 55, 67–69, 86, 197, 208;
    political, 87; power of, 85–91;
    South Africa, 87–88; targeted,
    88, 123
Boyd, Wes, 195
Branch, Taylor, 59
Brethren, 47, 49
Brightman, Edgar S., 56

Bristol, James, 48
Britain: Iraq war and, 157; third-
    party effect and, 131, 132
Brotherhood of Sleeping Car
    Porters, 46
Brown, Judith, 22, 26, 33, 94, 168,
    171, 178, 200, 205
Browne, Jackson, 220
Brown v. Board of Education, 208
Buber, Martin, 56, 113
Bud Antle, 84
Bulletin of the Atomic Scientists,
    210
Bunche, Ralph, 64
Burma, 3, 115
Burns, Stewart, 116–17
Burrowes, Robert, 18
Bush, George W., approval ratings,
    161
Bush administration, 3, 5, 156. *See
    also* Iraq war
Byrne, Ethel, 93, 166

California Agricultural Labor
    Relations Act, 91
California Peace Action, 209
campaigns, limited objectives,
    197–98. *See also individual
    campaigns*
Camus, Albert, 119
Caochella Valley, 80
Carmichael, Stokely, 115, 184
Castro, Fidel, 118
Catholic Church, 33, 50, 75,
    100–102, 164
Catholic Peace Fellowship, 108
Catholics to Fight Anti-Semitism,
    107
Catholic Worker, 103, 106, 107
Catholic Worker movement, 49–50,
    77, 103–4, 108
causa, la, 73
celebrities, 203
celibacy, 105, 175–79
Central America solidarity
    movement, 45
Central and Eastern Europe, 3, 115,
    121, 216, 238n12

Challenge of Peace, The (U.S. Catholic bishops), 50–51
charity, 101
Chauri-Chaura noncooperation campaign, 23
Chavez, Cesar, 73–74; early influences on, 74–76; fasting, 91–95, 93, 95; influence of Gandhi on, 76–79. *See also* farmworker movement
Chavez, Helena Fabela, 91
Chesler, Ellen, 166
Chiapas, 74–75
Chicago Defender, 39, 40, 47
Chicago Eight defendants, 45
Children, The (Halberstam), 69
China, 3, 115
Chomsky, Noam, 148–49
Christianity: personalism, 56–57; social gospel movement, 57; teachings of Jesus, 54, 55, 57, 60, 63. *See also* Catholic Church; Jesus
Christian passivism, 40
Churchill, Winston, 9, 132
citizen lobbying effort, 153
citizenship schools, 70
civil disobedience, 44, 88
Civil Rights Act of 1964, 71
civil rights movement, 27; boycotts, 123; casualties, 130; influence on Chavez, 77; limited goals, 197; media attention, 204; moral power of, 65, 70–71, 208; sacrifice and, 29; third-party effect, 131–32, 133–34. *See also* Albany, Georgia; Birmingham campaign; March on Washington; Montgomery bus boycott
Clark, Jim, 131
Clinton, Bill, 195
Cloward, Richard A., 144–45, 194
Coalition of Immokalee Workers, 89–90
Coates, Michael, 48
coercion, 49, 121–23, 216; fasting and, 93–95; satyagraha and, 25–27; terrorism and, 212

Coffin, William Sloane, 220
cognitive processes, disruption of, 128–29
cold war, 115
Coles, Robert, 102, 105
Committee for a SANE Nuclear Policy (SANE), 1, 47, 50, 193, 194, 197
Committee on Nonviolent Action, 117
communism, 44–45, 61, 104, 197
Communist Party, 104
Community for Creative Nonviolence, 93
Community Service Organization (CSO), 75, 80
Comstock laws, 166
Confessing Church, 114
conflict resolution, 213–14
confrontation, 141
Congress, 195
Congress of Race Equality (CORE), 41, 43
Congress of South African Trade Unions, 87
Connor, Bull, 131, 141
conscience, crisis of, 1
conscientious objectors, 49
constructive program, 169
consumer boycott, 87–88
control, maintenance of, 126–28
conversion, 216
cooperative law enforcement, 4–5
Cornell, Tom, 105, 108
Cost of Discipleship (Bonhoeffer), 113–14
Coughlin, Charles, 107
Council for a Livable World, 50
courage, 30–34; Chavez on, 78–79; King's view, 65–66; sacrifice and, 30–34, 65–66
Courage to Be, The (Tillich), 65
creative energy, 128–30
creative tension, 144
credibility, 160–61
Crisis, The, 39
Crusader without Violence (Reddick), 68

Cuba, 118
cynicism, 2

daisy ad, 201
Davis, George W., 53
Day, Dorothy, 49–50, 166, 219; early
    influences on, 98–102; fasting,
    97–98; influence of Gandhi on,
    104–7; influence on Chavez,
    77–78; as pacifist, 107–9; on
    women, 187
Day, Tamar, 100
death, in nonviolent struggle, 32–33
Deaver, Michael, 202
decision-making structure, 155
dehumanization of victims, 135,
    188
Dellinger, David (Dave), 22, 29–30,
    45, 61–62, 120
Deming, Barbara, 32, 116–21, 129,
    136, 151; coercion, view of, 121–
    22; influence of Gandhi on, 118–
    21; property damage, view of,
    123–24, 126; reconciliation, view
    of, 130; two hands phenomenon,
    127–28; visit to India, 118
Democratic Party, 129
demonstrations, 86, 88
Department of Defense, 82–83
Depression, 103
descriptive action, 20–21
DeWolf, L. Harold, 56
dialectic, 18
disintegration, 216
disruptive methods, 144–45,
    150–51
divine pathos, 63
dominant symbolism, 121
doomsday clock, 210
doubt, 2–3
Douglass, Frederick, 65
Du Bois, W. E. B., 38–39, 41
Dunlap, Marion Wallace, 94
Dyson, Michael Eric, 180–81, 183

Earth Liberation Front (ELF),
    125–26, 240n49
Easter season boycotts, 86, 140–41

Eastman, Max, 100
economic nonviolence, 122–23, 206
economic power, 139
ecoterrorism, 125–26
Eichmann, Adolf, 114
electoral boycott, 87
Ellsberg, Robert, 100
Elshtain, Jean Bethke, 187
empowerment, 198
entertainment, use of, 208–9
environmentalists against the war
    event, 208–9
Erikson, Erik, 10, 175
Esquivel, Laura, 176
European Social Forum, 209
evil, reality of, 59
experience, 207

failures, impact of, 3, 157–59
Fanon, Frantz, 119
Farmer, James, 43
farmworker movement: allegations
    of violence, 91–92; boycotts,
    81–85; media attention, 73–74,
    204. See also Chavez, Cesar;
    United Farmworkers of America
fascism, 102
fasting, 91–95, 166; coercive
    element, 93–95; forced feeding,
    94, 98
Federal Bureau of Investigation
    (FBI), 146, 181–82
Fellowship of Reconciliation, 38,
    40–41, 45–46, 50, 67
feminism, nonviolence and, 186–
    89. See also women's rights
    movement
Fenton Communications, 203
Filipino grape workers, 80
Fischer, Louis, 27, 104, 113, 131
force, violence vs., 26
Forrestal, U.S.S., 124
Fourth Freedom Forum, 1
Franceschato, Maria Grazia, 149
Francis of Assisi, 48
freedom rides, 43, 69, 131
Free Hindustan, 14
Free India Committee, 43

Friedan, Betty, 188
fund-raising, 199–201

Gallo, 84
Galtung, Johan, 33, 134–35
Gamson, William, 144, 145, 202–3
Gandhi, Abha (Chatterji), 176–77
Gandhi, Harilal, 171–72
Gandhi, Kasturba, 171–73, 175–76
Gandhi, Manu, 176–78, 179
Gandhi, Mohandas, 1, 3, 5, 131, 136; action for truth, 18–20; as agitator-negotiator, 24–25; assassination of, 54, 104, 177; aversion to coercion, 25–27; celibacy, vow of, 175–79; Chavez, influence on, 76–79; Christian influences on, 12–14; courage, view of, 30–34; Day, influence on, 104–7; Deming, influence on, 118–21; family life, 171–73; fasting, 91, 92, 94; fund-raising, 200; gender roles and, 168–70; highlights of life, 35; Hindu influence on, 11–12; human failings, 176–80; individual Americans, influence on, 38–41; influence of women's movement on, 20–21; on Jews, 112–13; means and ends, view of, 17–18; paradoxes of, 9–10, 34; political inadequacies, 23–25; principles of action and, 194; record of success, 53–54, 76–77; sacrifice and strength, view of, 28–30; Sanger's visit to, 163–68; sense of guilt and shame, 175–76; sexuality and women, view of, 10, 163–64, 166–68, 173–76; social reforms and, 23; spiritual form of politics and, 21–25; truth, search for, 14–17; violence, view of, 112–13; visits from Americans, 40–41, 42; women, limits on support for, 170–73; women, relationships with,
176–80; women, support for, 168, 185–86
Gandhi, Mohandas, influence on America, 37; African American community, 37–44, 46–47; early impressions, 37–41; peace movement and, 43–44; religious pacifist community, 47–51; social justice and, 44–47
Gandhi, Rajmohan, 178–79
Gandhi (movie), 11, 171
Gandhi's Ideas (Andrews), 41
Gandhi through Western Eyes (Alexander), 47
Garrison, William Lloyd, 38, 44
Garrow, David, 134, 180, 181
Garvey, Marcus, 39
Genoa protest, 124, 147, 149
Georgia, 121
Gestapo, 114
GI peace movement, 1, 14, 30–31, 82–83, 124, 208, 224n18. See also Vietnam antiwar movement
GIs for Peace (Fort Bliss), 84
Giumarra, 82, 83
global justice, as term, 242n25
global justice movement, 111, 146–52; violence and, 124, 131, 147, 243n28
goals: clarifying, 196–99; focused, 139, 140, 155
God, truth as, 14–17
God in Search of Man (Heschel), 63
Goebbels, Joseph, 114
Goldman, Emma, 164–65
Gold Star Mothers for Peace, 160
Gorbachev, Mikhail, 216, 218
Goshen College, 4
grape strike (la huelga), 79–81
great chain of nonviolence, 134–36
great salt satyagraha, 23, 25, 39, 81, 85, 169; evaluation of, 204–5; tactics, 207–8; third-party effect, 131, 132–33
Green Party (Germany), 217–18
Green Party (Italy), 149
Greenpeace, 126

Gregg, Richard, 40–41, 69, 128
Guadalupe, virgin of, 75

Halberstam, David, 69
Haldeman, H. R., 146
Havel, Vaclav, 216
Hayden, Casey, 184
Haywood, Bill, 99, 164
Hegel, Georg, 18
Hell's Kitchen (New York), 57
Herman, Edward, 148–49
Hershberger, Guy F., 49
Heschel, Abraham Joshua, 63, 64
Hinduism, 11–12
Holmes, John Haynes, 38
Holocaust, 112–14
homeless, 93
hooks, bell, 187
Hoover, J. Edgar, 181–82
houses of hospitality, 103–4
Howard University, 42–43
Huerta, Dolores, 80
hunger strikes. See fasting
Hussein, Saddam, 5, 154, 155

image problems, 153–54
I May Not Get There With You
    (Dyson), 180–81, 183
immanence, theology of, 100
India: boycotts, 27, 85–86, 169;
    constructive program, 169;
    noncooperation campaign,
    19–20, 39; partition of, 23,
    178; spinning movement, 85,
    169; success of independence
    movement, 53–54, 76–77;
    women and boycotts, 169. See
    also great salt satyagraha
Indian Congress, 170, 194, 204
Indian Opinion, 14, 21, 38
indirect effects of nonviolence, 122–23
Industrial Workers of the World, 99
infant formula boycott, 88–89
INF treaty, 217–18
Institute for Nonviolent Resistance
    to Segregation, 69, 70
InterHarvest, 84
International Criminal Court, 4

Internet, 155, 156, 159, 194–96
intervention, 205, 206
Iran, boycotts, 87
Iraq, economic sanctions on, 123
Iraq antiwar movement, 150,
    154–56; continuing challenges,
    159–61; Internet organizing
    and, 195; vigils, 156, 157, 159
Iraq Veterans against the War, 160
Iraq war, 3, 5, 101; constructive
    alternatives, 211; lack of
    legitimacy, 156, 157–58
I-Thou relationship, 56–57

Jainism, 11
Jesus: message of, 12–13; Sermon
    on the Mount, 12, 48, 55, 67,
    114; suffering of, 65; teachings
    of, 54, 55, 60, 63. See also
    Catholic Church; Christianity
Jews, Gandhi on, 112–13
Johansen, Robert, 212
John Paul II, 51
Johnson, Lyndon, 133–34, 201
Johnson, Mordecai, 42, 54
Johnson administration, 129
Jones, Rufus, 47–48
Journey of Reconciliation, 43
Judgment at Nuremberg (movie),
    133
justice, 101

Kakar, Sudhir, 170, 175, 179
Kant, Immanuel, 56
Kelly Ingram Park, 143, 144
Kennedy, Edward, 89
Kennedy, Ethel, 81
Kennedy, John F., 143–44
Kennedy, Kerry, 90
Kennedy, Robert F., 80–81, 90
Kennedy administration, 129, 137,
    142
Kierkegaard, Søren, 2
King, Coretta Scott, 68, 180, 182–83
King, Martin Luther, Jr., 1, 22, 80,
    134, 220; address at Riverside
    Church, 116; Albany and, 138–
    39; application of Gandhianism,

69–71; Birmingham campaign and, 140–44; Christian roots, 55–58; courage of, 65–66; divine inspiration, view of, 62–65; experience in civil rights movement, 66–69; fund-raising, 200–201; Gandhi's influence on, 3, 53–55; human failings, 180–83; "I Have a Dream" speech, 44; influence of Gandhi on, 38, 41; "I've been to the mountain top" speech, 66; "Letter from a Birmingham Jail," 58, 66, 141–42; on means and ends, 61; national holiday, 121; on power, 192; realistic pacifism of, 59–60, 61; on reconciliation, 130; sacrifice and, 29, 65–66; skepticism of, 59; violence, view of, 112; visit to India, 48, 67–68

King, Mary, 184
Kosovo, 115
Krishna, 12
Kruegler, Christopher, 25, 86, 191, 193, 205
Ku Klux Klan, 112, 141

Lafayette, Bernard, 86
Lakey, George, 151
Lakoff, George, 202
Lawson, James, 69
Lee, Bernard, 182
Lee, Spike, 191–92
leftists, 104
legitimacy, 192–93
"Letter from a Birmingham Jail" (King), 58, 66, 141–42
"Letter to a Hindu" (Tolstoy), 14
Lewis, John, 62, 65, 69–70, 86, 133, 181
Liberation, 45, 116–17
Like Water for Chocolate (Esquivel), 176
lobbying, 195
Long Loneliness, The (Day), 98
longshoremen, 81–82
love, 54–55, 79, 192; agape, 60–62; Beloved Community,

62–64; disruption of cognitive processes, 128–29
Ludlow, Robert, 106
Lynd, Alice, 38
Lynd, Staughton, 38

McDonnell, Donald, 75
machismo, 74–75
Magnes, Judah, 113
Mahatma versus Gandhi (play), 172
mainstream, 153–56
Malcolm X, 1–2, 111, 112, 136
male values, 74–75, 182, 188
Mandela, Nelson, 112
Manufacturing Consent (Chomsky and Herman), 148–49
March on Washington, 1963, 44, 46–47, 183–84
Marcos, Ferdinand, 3
Marcos, Subcomandante, 112
martyrdom, 32
Marxism, 18, 45, 61, 104
Masses, The, 100
Maurin, Peter, 102–3
Mays, Benjamin, 42
means and ends, 17–18, 61, 77
media, 125; Birmingham campaign, 143–44; birth control rights movement, 166; boycotts and, 88–89; power of, 201–4; third-party effect and, 132–33, 136; violence and, 148–49
Mennonites, 47, 48–49
Merton, Thomas, 30
messages, framing of, 202–3
Mexican American culture, 74–75
military draft records, destruction of, 124–25
Military Families Speak Out, 160
Miller, Webb, 133
Milošević regime, 3
ministers, 181, 182
mobile civil disobedience tactics, 150
Mobilization for Global Justice, 150
Mobilization for Survival, 45
money, 194

Montgomery bus boycott, 44, 55, 67–69, 86, 197, 208
moral dilemmas, 122–23
moral ideals, 196
moral power, 26, 79, 91; of civil rights movement, 65, 70–71, 208. *See also* power
moratoriums, 208
Morehouse College, 42
MoveOn, 155, 159, 195
Muslim countries, 214
Muslim-Hindu conflict, 42, 91, 92
Muste, A. J., 18, 45–46
MX basing system, 153
MX missile, 197, 218
My Experiments in Truth (Gandhi), 9–10, 38
myth of time, 64–65

Nagler, Michael, 28
Nanda, B. R., 23
Nash, Diane Bevel, 69, 184
Nashville protests, 86, 140, 148
Nashville Workshops on Nonviolence, 69, 70
National Association for the Advancement of Colored People (NAACP), 38, 39, 139, 155, 194
National Council of Churches, 89, 155
National Farmworkers Association, 79, 80. *See also* United Farmworkers of America
National Organization for Women, 155, 194
Nayar, Pyarelal, 176
Nayar, Sushila, 176, 177
Nazis, 112–14
Negro World, The, 39
Nehru, Jawaharlal, 24, 67–68
Nelson, William Stuart, 42–43
Nestlé Corporation boycott, 88–89
Nevada test site civil disobedience, 152–53
Newark Commune, 45
New England Non-Resistance Society, 38
New England transcendentalists, 38
new Gandhians, 69–70

New York Call, 99
Niebuhr, Reinhold, 26–27, 40, 59, 122, 219; on immorality, 129; on moral power, 132; on objectivity, 128; on spiritual discipline, 127
Niemöller, Martin, 114
Nietzsche, Friedrich, 54, 55
Nixon, Richard, 37, 82, 145
nonattachment, 60
noncooperation, 22, 27, 43–44, 192–93, 205–6; mass, 19–20, 39, 44, 120–21
nonharm principle (ahimsa), 12, 15, 61, 122, 178
nonretaliation, 4
nonviolence: ambiguity of, 27; challenges to, 115–16, 136; courage and, 30–34; duality of, 126–28; economic, 122–23, 206; effectiveness of questioned, 2, 111–12; failures, 3, 157–59; feminism and, 186–89; four steps of, 141–42; great chain of, 134–36; importance of love in, 79; indirect effects of, 122–23; individual approaches, 120; limitations of, 113–15; list of methods, 205–6; mass social action, 44, 120–21; means and ends, 17–18; political power of, 77, 122; principled, 77, 136; stages of, 22; successes, 2, 53–54, 76–77, 144–46; tradition in America, 38; as undeveloped method, 120–21
nonviolent intervention, 205, 206
Norfolk Journal and Guide, 42
Norway, 114
"Notes for Soliders" (Tolstoy), 14
nuclear freeze movement, 47, 74, 152–54, 193–94; European, 217–18, 252n46; limited objectives, 198–99; media attention, 204
nuclear weapons peace movement, 1950s, 50–51, 107–8

obedience, 192
O'Connor, John, 106

On Civil Disobedience (Thoreau), 38
O'Neill, Eugene, 99
"On Revolution and Equilibrium" (Deming), 116–17, 119–20
Operation Ceasefire festival, 210
Oppenheimer, Robert, 11
oppressed populations, 134–35
Orange Revolution (Ukraine), 3
organizational strength, 193–95
organizational unity, 139
organizing methods, 75–76
Orwell, George, 19, 22, 113, 115, 173
other, 135

pacifism, realistic, 59–60, 61
Pakistan, 23
Pariser, Eli, 195
Parks, Rosa, 184
passive resistance, 19, 40
Paul, St., 14–15
Pax Christi, 50–51
Peace Works (Cortright), 153
Penn, William, 48
peregrinación, 81
person, social role vs., 5
personalism, 56–57
"Personal Word" (Erickson), 10
persuasion, 22, 29–30, 205, 206
petitions, 195
Pettus Bridge incident, 131, 133
Philippines, 3, 121
Pickett, Clarence, 47
Piven, Frances Fox, 144–45, 194
Planned Parenthood Federation, 165
Pledge of Non-participation, 153
Plowshares actions, 125
Poland, 75, 197
policing, just, 212–13
politeness, 152–53
political boycotts, 87
political force, 77, 122
political ju-jitsu, 127
political nonviolence, 206
politics: power as determinant of, 59–60; spiritual, 21–25
Politics of Nonviolent Action (Sharp), 191, 205–6, 216, 217

Poor People's Movements (Piven and Cloward), 144–45
Pope, Carl, 149
popular culture, 121
Porter, Cole, 40
poverty, challenging, 101
power: of boycotts, 85–91; as determinant of politics, 59–60; empowerment, 198; of love, 60–62, 192; of media, 201–4; negative connotation, 191–92; speaking truth to, 48, 192; understanding, 191–93. *See also* moral power
Power of Nonviolence, The (Gregg), 40–41
pragmatic nonviolence, 77, 122, 125, 136
Prague protest, 146, 147
principled nonviolence, 77, 136
principles of action, 191, 195; Alinsky's rules, 207–11; clarifying goals, 196–99; constructive alternatives, 210–11; evaluating tactics, 204–7; financing changes, 199–201; long-term outlook, 219–21; means of change, 215–17; organizational strength, 193–95; success, 217–19; understanding power, 191–93
Pritchett, Laurie, 139–40
Progressive, The, 154
Project "C," 141
property damage, 91, 92, 108, 111, 123–26; global justice movement and, 147–50
Provance, Terry, 47
purification, 79, 91–92

al Qaeda, 212
Quakers, 38, 47–48
Quebec protest, 146, 148

Rally to Halt the Arms Race, 152, 199, 201
Randolph, A. Philip, 46
Ranger, U.S.S., 124
rape, Gandhi's view of, 174
Rauschenbush, Walter, 57, 64
Reagan, Ronald, 193, 202

Reagan administration, 153, 218
Reagan-Gorbachev Summit, 202
Reagon, Cordell, 138
reconciliation, 130. *See also*
    Fellowship of Reconciliation
Reddick, Lawrence, 68
Reed, John, 100
religious pacifist community, 47–51
Religious Society of Friends
    (Quakers), 38, 47–48
rent boycotts, 87
repression, sympathetic response
    to, 28–29
resentment, resistance to, 127
Resolution 1373 (UN Security
    Council), 213
responsibility to protect, 213
Reuther, Walter, 80
revolutionary romanticism, 112
Roosevelt administrations, 107
Ross, Frederick, 75
Ruddick, Sara, 187, 188
Rules for Radicals (Alinsky), 191,
    207–11
Rustin, Bayard, 43–44, 67, 69

sabotage, 123–24
sacrifice, 22, 28–30; courage and,
    30–34, 65–66; Day on, 106;
    Gandhi's view of women's,
    173–74; King and, 29, 65–66
salt satyagraha. *See* great salt
    satyagraha
Sanger, Margaret, 93, 163–68, 204
satya, 15
satyagraha, 19–20; coercion and,
    25–27; courage and, 31;
    sacrifice and, 28–30; as social
    method, 106; as spiritual
    discipline, 106
Satyagraha in South Africa
    (Gandhi), 174
Schlabach, Gerald, 212–13
Schwartz, Tony, 201
Scowcroft, Brent, 218
Seattle protest, 124, 146–48
self, 135
self-interest, 55

Selma campaign, 63, 81, 131, 133–34
Sen, Amartya, 186
September 11, 2001, terrorist
    attacks, 4, 195, 211–12
Serbia, 3, 121
Sermon on the Mount, 12, 48, 55,
    67, 114
sexism, overcoming, 183–86
sexuality: celibacy, 105, 175–79;
    Day on, 105; Gandhi's view, 10,
    163–64, 166–68, 173–76
shanti sena (army of nonviolence), 69
Sharp, Gene, 130, 191, 205–6, 216–
    17; documentation of successes,
    114, 120, 122; power, view of,
    192; pragmatic focus of, 77;
    sacrifice, view of, 28
Sharpeville killings, 87
Sheehan, Casey, 160
Sheehan, Cindy, 160–61
Sheen, Martin, 90
Sherrod, Charles, 138
Shock, Kurt, 28
Shridharani, Krishnalal, 41, 46
Shuttlesworth, Fred, 141
Sierra Club, 149, 155, 194, 209
Sinclair, Upton, 99
sit-down strikes, 27
sit-in movement, 43, 69, 86
Slade, Madeline, 41
Sleeper (movie), 16–17
smart sanctions, 123
Smiley, Glen, 67
Smith, Kenneth, 62
Smuts, Jan, 24
Snyder, Mitch, 93
social force, 122
social gospel movement, 57
Socialist Party, 50, 99, 165
socialists, 164
social justice, as divinely inspired,
    62–65
social nonviolence, 206
social role, person vs., 5
Sojourners, 155
Solidarity, 75, 197
solidarity with others, 220
Solnit, Rebecca, 161, 203

Solo, Pam, 47
South Africa, 33, 93, 112, 120;
    boycott, 87–88
Southern Christian Leadership
    Conference (SCLC), 44, 70,
    139; Birmingham campaign
    and, 140–41
Soviet Union, 153
Soweto uprising and massacre, 87
speaking truth to power, 48, 192
spinning movement, 85, 169
spirit of history, 62
spiritual discipline, 106, 127
spiritual politics, 21–25
spiritual rebirth, 79
Stalinism, 115
Stanton, Elizabeth Cady, 219
Star Wars program, 153
stayaways, 87
Steinem, Gloria, 168
Stone, Oliver, 112
Stop MX campaign, 153, 218
"Stop the War before It Starts"
    (Cortright), 154
Strategic Nonviolence Conflict
    (Ackerman and Kruegler), 191,
    193
"Strategy and Tactics of Nonviolent
    Social Change, The" (course), 43
Strategy of Social Protest, The
    (Gamson), 144, 145
Stride Toward Freedom (King), 61,
    65, 140
strikes, 206
structural violence, 101
Student Nonviolent Coordinating
    Committee (SNCC), 138, 139, 184
success, 217–19; of nonviolent
    movements, 2, 53–54, 76–77,
    144–46
suffrage movement, 20–21, 165,
    219; fasting, 94, 97–98
Sweeney, John, 146

Taco Bell boycott, 89–90
Teamsters, 83–84
terrorism, 211–15; ecoterrorism,
    125–26; strategies against, 4–5

third-party effect, 28–29, 60,
    65, 79, 130–34; civil rights
    movement, 70–71; great chain
    of nonviolence, 134–36; media
    and, 132–33, 136
Thoreau, Henry David, 38
Three Guineas (Woolf), 186
Thurman, Howard, 42, 43
Thurman, Suu Bailey, 42
Tiananmen Square, 3, 33
Tillich, Paul, 65
Tobey, Barkeley, 100
Tobias, Channing, 42
Tolstoy, Leo, 13–14
totalitarianism, 113, 192
tree spiking, 125
Trotskyism, 45
True Majority, 155, 196, 203
truth: action for, 18–20; search for,
    14–17
two hands phenomenon, 126–28

Ukraine, 3, 121
UN High-level Panel, 5
unions, 45, 75–76, 194
Unitarians, 38
United Auto Workers, 80
United Democratic Front (South
    Africa), 87–88, 93
United Farmworkers of America
    (UFWA), 79; allegations of
    violence by, 91, 92; membership,
    85. See also Chavez, Cesar;
    farmworker movement
United for Peace and Justice,
    154–56
United Methodist Church, 89
United Nations, 123
Unity, 38
Universal Negro Improvement
    Association (UNIA), 39
UN Security Council, 156–58, 213
untouchability, 39, 92
UN Working Group on Terrorism, 5
urban riots, 243–31
U.S. foreign policy: terrorism and,
    214–15. See also Vietnam
    antiwar movement

Vatican, 101
velvet revolutions, 3, 115, 216
Vietnam antiwar movement,
    30–31, 63, 101, 116, 251n32;
    alienation of supporters, 131;
    Day and, 108; medal-throwing
    ceremonies, 145–46; sabotage
    attempts, 124; violence, 131,
    145, 242n21. See also GI peace
    movement
Vietnam Mobilization Committee, 45
Vietnam moratorium, 208–9
Vietnam Veterans against the War
    (VVAW), 145–46, 160
vigils, 195; Iraq antiwar movement,
    156, 157, 159
violence, 112–13; culture of, 116;
    farmworker movement and,
    91–92; force vs., 26; at global
    justice protests, 124, 131, 147,
    243n28; loss of supporters and,
    131, 145–46; media attention
    and, 148–49; as sexual
    conquest, 188; structural, 101;
    Vietnam antiwar movement and,
    131, 145, 242n21
"Virtual March on Washington," 156
voter registration campaigns, 70
Voting Rights Act of 1965, 71, 134

Walesa, Lech, 216
Walker, Wyatt T., 141, 144
Wallace, George, 216
Wallerstein, Immanuel, 156
Wallis, Jim, 21, 57, 196, 211–12, 215
Walzer, Michael, 214
war, sexism, link with, 188
war on terror, 212, 214
War, Peace, and Nonresistance
    (Hershberger), 49
War Resisters League, 38, 43, 117
War without Violence: A Study
    of Gandhi's Method and
    Its Accomplishments
    (Shridharani), 41, 46

Washington, Booker T., 41
Wells, H. G., 163
"When Women Are Manly, Will Men
    Be Effeminate?" (Gandhi), 21
Wiesel, Elie, 121
Wink, Walter, 13, 31–32, 120–21
Win Without War, 1, 155–56, 159,
    195, 199; media attention and,
    203–4
Wofford, Harris, 68
Wolpert, Stanley, 17, 21, 24–25,
    33–34, 168–69, 178, 179
women: biological determinism
    and, 187–88; Gandhi on nature
    of, 173–74; Gandhi's view of,
    10, 163–64, 166–76, 185–86;
    political empowerment, 186–87;
    sexism and, 183–86
Women's Peace Camp, 117
women's rights movement, 163,
    184–85; India, 168–70;
    influence on Gandhi, 20–21.
    See also birth control rights
    movement; suffrage movement
Women's Strike for Peace, 50
Woolf, Virginia, 186
Woolman, John, 48
Working Assets, 155, 196, 209
World Health Organization, 89
World Social Forum, 209
World War II, 107
Wretched of the Earth, The (Fanon),
    119

yagna, 178
Yoder, John Howard, 1, 212
Young, Andrew, 54, 66–67, 70,
    86, 112, 133; on Birmingham
    campaign, 140; on King's
    private behavior, 182
Yum! Brands, 90

Zapata, Emilio, 74–75
Zapatistas, 74–75, 112
Zepp, Ira, 62

About the Author

David Cortright, a research fellow at the Joan B. Kroc Institute for International Peace Studies at the University of Notre Dame, is president of the Fourth Freedom Forum in Goshen, Indiana, and a cofounder of the Win Without War coalition. He has also taught in the Peace, Justice, and Conflict Studies Department at Goshen College, Goshen, Indiana.

Cortright has served as consultant or adviser to various agencies of the United Nations, the Carnegie Commission on Preventing Deadly Conflict, the International Peace Academy, and the John D. and Catherine T. MacArthur Foundation. The author or editor of fourteen books and numerous articles and reports, he has written widely on nuclear disarmament, nonviolent social change, and the use of incentives and sanctions as tools of international peacemaking.

While serving in the U.S. Army during the Vietnam War, Cortright experienced a crisis of conscience and began to speak out against what he considered an evil and unjust war. His army experience set him on a lifelong course of advocacy and research for peace. He served for ten years as director of the disarmament organization SANE. Over the past decade he has become a leading authority on the use of incentives and sanctions as tools of international peacemaking.